MW00809980

"*God's Image and Global Cultures* is a well-written and insightful exploration of the multiplicity of issues related to changing cultures in the globalized world. Drawing upon anthropology, theology, and biblical studies, Kenneth Nehrbass opens up the world of culture to discover both the diversities and the universalities of human life and experience. Written from an evangelical perspective, the book presents a 'high' view of culture-making as part of what it means to be made in God's image. It concludes with evaluative tools and practical advice, making it essential reading for students of missiology, and for other Christian practitioners."

—ELOISE MENESES, Professor of Anthropology, Eastern University

"Anthropologists and missiologists have always taught that global cultures were dynamic; however, the 21st century realities of globalization, urbanization, and migration have increasingly complicated cultures and how one perceives and responds to them. For this reason, Kenneth Nehrbass's book is a timely and needed work as it aims to assist the evangelical Christian in appropriately relating to global cultures while in the work of mission. Nehrbass combines evangelical convictions (a high view of Scripture) with training in cultural anthropology for a useful 21st century text on an evangelical theology of culture."

—EDWARD L. SMITHER, Associate Professor of Intercultural Studies, Columbia International University

"I starting reading (couldn't stop) and quickly realized that Kenneth Nehrbass has written a book we need. *God's Image and Global Cultures* is well-written, well-researched, and is a very readable introduction to a missiological theology for understanding the meaning of culture. He combines a solid multidisciplinary perspective with sound biblical thinking to focus on culture in relation to God's Kingdom. His focus on the image of God as the center of culture not only avoids pitfalls of other perspectives—and sets his arguments in current thought—but also establishes a solid foundation for intercultural ministry from a multicultural perspective with global engagement as the end goal. He convincingly points the reader to cultural pluralism as a Christian balance between ethnocentrism and philosophical relativism. This book will be on my students' textbook list."

—MARCUS DEAN, Associate Professor of Intercultural Studies and Missions, Houghton College

"*God's Image and Global Cultures* will take the reader down roads that all have traveled, but few have sufficiently thought through the specifics. What is your theology of culture? How extensive and pervasive is it? Kenneth Nehrbass will guide you through this foundational life-maze with clarity and comprehensiveness."

—Tom Steffen, Emeritus Professor of Intercultural Studies, Cook School of Intercultural Studies, Biola University

"Globalization does not leave us in our comfort zone. In fact, there is no comfort zone anymore. God tells you to go to a place that you have never been to and your zeal for God and theological training may only prove that you will be obedient and that you will have a steep cultural learning curve. To be a good Christian and cross-cultural worker today, one needs to study culture. Every year when I teach Cross-cultural Communication and Anthropology for Cross-cultural Ministry, I look for good textbooks for my students. While there are many good books on Christianity and culture, today's context cries for new books with new perspectives and approaches. Nehrbass's willingness to engage in the subject from today's perspective makes this book very interesting. His cross-cultural experience and knowledge of anthropological theory help him to do this well. Nehrbass poses questions and answers as if readers are in a conversation with him and the flow of the content is natural. This book is comprehensive and contemporary while not compromising theoretical and practical issues. I can't wait until I see a copy of this book on my desk and use it in my class."

—Hansung Kim, Assistant Professor, Asian Center for Theological Studies and Mission, South Korea

"As a professor of intercultural studies I believe this book would be one that anyone who studies the theology of culture and globalization and the gospel would be interested in. Nehrbass identifies and explains emerging divergent sociological attitudes among Evangelical Christians (and others) in America and discusses important contemporary issues such as immigration, diversity, multiculturalism, Western exceptionalism, and stereotyping. His main focus is culture and missions—where the two connect and where they disconnect. The book addresses many important questions facing us in the 21st century (e.g. multiculturalism and diversity, globalism), and suggests a systematic approach to the study of culture. Although likely to be considered controversial at points, the book would be of interest for many involved in intercultural studies."

—Dave Beine, Professor of Intercultural Studies, Moody Bible Institute

God's Image and Global Cultures

God's Image and Global Cultures

Integrating faith and culture in the twenty-first century

KENNETH NEHRBASS

CASCADE *Books* · Eugene, Oregon

GOD'S IMAGE AND GLOBAL CULTURES
Integrating Faith and Culture in the Twenty-First Century

Cascade Books
An Imprint of Wipf and Stock Publishers
199 W. 8th Ave., Suite 3
Eugene, OR 97401

www.wipfandstock.com

Paperback ISBN 13: 978-1-4982-3909-7
Hardcover ISBN 13: 978-1-4982-3911-0
Ebook ISBN 13: 978-1-4982-3910-3

Cataloging-in-Publication data:

Names: Nehrbass, Kenneth.

Title: God's Image and Global Culture: integrating faith and culture in the twenty-first century / Kenneth Nehrbass.

Description: Eugene, OR: Cascade Books, 2016 | Includes bibliographical references and index.

Identifiers: ISBN 978-1-4982-3909-7 (paperback) | ISBN 978-1-4982-3911-0 (hardcover) | ISBN 978-1-4982-3910-3 (ebook)

Subjects: 1. Christianity and culture. 2. Multiculturalism religious aspects Christianity. 3. Culture. I. Title.

Classification: BR115.A35 N50 2016 | BR115.A35 (ebook)

Manufactured in the USA.

For my wife and partner in life and ministry, Mendy.

"Glorify the LORD with me; let us exalt his name together."
(Ps 34:3 NIV)

Contents

List of Tables

List of figures

Acknowledgements

DR. DANIEL FREDERICKS, THE provost and vice president of Belhaven University, is the one who is most responsible for awakening in me the theology of work—and more broadly, the conviction that God's kingdom extends to all aspects of our cultural lives here on earth. Some of the ideas about the impact of globalization come from a course that I taught at Belhaven University called "Globalization and Culture." I inherited much of that course content from Dr. Sara Kimmel, and her contributions have certainly influenced chapter 1. Chapter 4 was part of an unpublished presentation that I co-presented with Doug Hayward at the On Knowing Humanity Conference at Eastern University in May 2015. Thanks to my father Dr. Richard Nehrbass, my mother Marilynn Nehrbass, and brother Dr. Daniel Nehrbass for proofreading the manuscript. Dr. Tom Steffen, Dr. Ed Smither, Dr. Marcus Dean, Dr. Eloise Meneses, Dr. David Beine, and Dr. Hansung Kim all reviewed the manuscript and gave helpful editorial or substantive comments. Students at Biola University, especially in my theology of culture class, have asked numerous questions about the content of this book, which have helped me to make the material more clear.

Introduction

IN THE TWENTIETH CENTURY Christians recognized the value of studying culture—and *cultures*—so that they could go "out there" and be effective witnesses overseas. Increasingly, though, we are recognizing that a good grasp of how culture influences our thoughts, behavior, and faith is essential for understanding ourselves and others, and for developing effective practices in business, education, and just about every other social endeavor. In the past few decades, the phenomenon of globalization—rapidly increasing cultural diversity—has moved the study of culture from an exotic subject to a core competency in any discipline. This urgency for cultural competence is felt even more strongly by evangelical Christians, who are serious about Jesus' imperative to change the world (whether *here* or *there*). In the world of the twenty-first century, our posture toward culture must be deliberate, rather than subconscious or haphazard. We must think about culture the way God does, and possess a comprehensive *theology* of culture that is practical, and is relevant for this generation. Such a theology would then inform us about our global social responsibilities and our role as the church in the world. Those who attain these perspectives and competencies would indeed be well-positioned to be world changers.

Globalization has raised numerous questions at the nexus of our faith and culture. Does God approve of some cultures more than others? How should Western Christians respond to multiculturalism at home and the exporting of their national culture (as well as their jobs) overseas? Should Christians embrace their culture, or is it better to be countercultural? Is it even possible to be countercultural? Should we be engaged in culture at all? Is there any eternal value of culture—and why did God even create us to need culture? Why are cultures so different, and are there universals? Is it appropriate to change cultures?

As a professor of intercultural studies at a Christian university, I have wanted to direct my students to a book that examines God's eternal plan for culture and then proceeds to develop a systematic approach toward diversity, cultural accommodation, the evaluation of other cultures, and the Christian's role in various subsystems of culture. However, I have been surprised to discover that there is no suitable book from the evangelical perspective that develops such a theology of culture *for the twenty-first century*. I began mapping out how such a text would need to be organized. I asked, what central questions would the text seek to address (see Figure 1)?

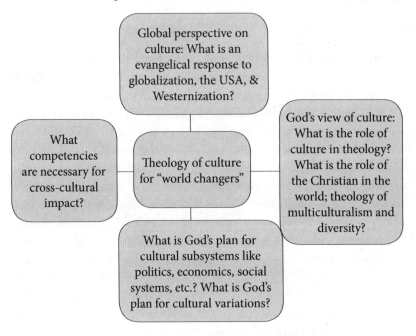

Figure 1: Mapping a theology of culture for world changers

As I laid down what "seeing culture God's way" would entail, I discerned that such a perspective must be global, since God cares for every corner of this world. It must be up to date on the role of Western Christians in the wider international setting. It must cover Christian responses to contemporary issues like globalization, migration, homogenization (sometimes considered Americanization), and anti-Western (or anti-American) sentiment.

Integrating theology and culture in this century also requires us to respond to the realities of multiculturalism and diversity. It is a central tenet of this book that while the cross-cultural process can be confusing and frustrating, the end results of working cross-culturally will be the development of better products, better policies and strategies, and increased mutual understanding. Working cross-culturally creates a synergy which we fail to leverage when our work is carried out in a homogenous cultural context. It is not difficult to find voices encouraging diversity; but the basis for multiculturalism is often grounded in an empty philosophical relativism. An evangelical approach must integrate biblical views of diversity ever since the time God confused the languages at the Tower of Babel, and must evaluate cultural values in light of biblical standards. It must empower Christians to explain and even evaluate cultural systems without veering into the traps of ethnocentrism, on the one hand, or philosophical relativism on the other.

An evangelical theology of culture must revisit how we theorize about the fundamental purpose that culture serves for human beings. Often, Christian thought concerning the cross-cultural process has mimicked prevailing anthropological theories of the day (though perhaps ten or fifteen years behind the times). For example, missiologists have adopted a version of the biological or social-functionalist views of culture, concluding that kinship and ritual exist only to serve some primordial biological function (e.g., safety), or social functions (e.g., division of labor), or perhaps a hidden psychological function (e.g., the mitigation of desires). This book argues that while functionalist, idealist, structuralist, and particularist theories certainly provide some explanatory scope for the existence of culture, the most satisfying etiology for human culture is that we are made in the image of God. We reflect God's character to be creative, to live in society, to speak, and even to rule. These components of God's image and the corruption of his image are the foundational aspects of human culture.

Once a theology of culture situates our cultural nature in the image of God, it must lay out a plan for global engagement. It must demonstrate how all of our cultural lives—social organization, politics, economics, aesthetics, and so on—are interconnected and grounded in the cultural mandate of Genesis 1:28 and 2:15. Francis Schaeffer began to lay such a foundation by connecting worldview to culture.[1] Unfortunately, Schaeffer's project, while groundbreaking and commendable, was largely limited to visual arts and music—erroneously giving the impression that one must be familiar with the paintings of Monet and Cézanne to be theologically

---

1. Schaeffer, *How Should We Then Live?*

sound—and even to avoid inadvertently wandering into heresy. We must move beyond Schaeffer's limited view of culture, and address the variegated systems within *any* culture (not just "high culture" in the West), so that our twenty-first-century theology of culture may be relevant as we encounter people from all over the globe.

A robust and relevant integration of theology and culture must discuss the competencies necessary for engaging actual human cultures, rather than speaking only of culture in general. Cultural specifics have been dealt with most commonly though the nearly ubiquitous model of value orientations, which was proposed by Hall[2] and Hofstede,[3] and was adapted for missions by Lingenfelter and Mayers.[4] The aim of these theorists has been to understand differing value orientations, but they often postponed critical examination of those value orientations, for fear of encouraging ethnocentrism. Moreau, et al.,[5] give a Christian perspective on several value orientations related to intercultural communication. A theology of culture would continue that project to systematically examine the cultural value orientations that communication theorists have discovered, from uncertainty avoidance, to fate and meritocracy, to crisis and non-crisis orientation, and so on.

However, the "cultural difference paradigm" of Hall and Hofstede— which was so prevalent in cross-cultural theory in the 1990s—has come under severe scrutiny lately for reinforcing stereotypes (or "identity freezing") and for utilizing a reductionist approach.[6] For example, a (perhaps unfair) characterization of value-orientation theorists would give the impression that *all* Japanese are collectivists who *always* speak with an indirect and highly formal style, possessing little capacity for individual agency or direct speech. Hall, Hofstede, Benedict, Lingenfelter, and Mayers gave only cursory recognition that cultural values are *modal preferences*, and are not deterministic or universal within a society. Now that we have begun the third millennium, there is so much crossing of borders (both geographic and cultural) that we must find a way to reify cultural value orientations while also recognizing that humans are creative enough to break out of

---

2. Hall, *The Silent Language.*

3. Hofstede, *Culture's Consequences.*

4. Lingenfelter and Mayers, *Ministering Cross-Culturally.*

5. Moreau, *Effective Intercultural Communication.*

6. Holliday, "Small Cultures."

these cultural bonds. We know more than ever now that ethnic and national cultures are heterogeneous and fluid rather than impermeable and static.

Since we are crossing cultures more than ever, an *evangelical* theology of culture for the twenty-first century must address the models of cross-cultural engagement that have become widely used in evangelical churches. Livermore's implementation of cultural intelligence (CQ),[7] Bennett's model of intercultural sensitivity,[8] and Storti's *Art of Crossing Cultures*[9] are decent models for acquiring cross-cultural competence. However, these materials tend to omit the study of how cultures are organized in terms of kinship, politics, ritual, and economics, and can even fail to address God's plan for culture in the first place. Approaching the theory of culture from a different angle, introductory anthropological textbooks from Christian anthropologists like Howell and Paris[10] and Grunlan and Mayers[11] cover these cultural subsystems of kinship, economics, power, etc., but are not heavily focused on the role of the cross-cultural worker in resolving conflict, or engaging in leadership roles. A practical theology of culture should begin with an understanding of God's nature as a cultural being, and can then focus on God's plan in each of the cultural subsystems. Practical applications for crossing cultures would be developed out of that theological understanding. Christian workers must know how to conduct meaningful research on the subsystems that comprise the various societies they encounter. After students of culture have done diligent inquiry, they are positioned to impact the world.

In other words, a *theology of culture* must be highly practical even as it delves deeply into theory. Tillich,[12] Jenson,[13] and Tanner[14] attempted theologies of culture, but their low view of Scripture caused them to narrow their focus only to the role that culture plays in shaping theological inquiry. They each concluded that since all theology is done in human cultural contexts, there can be no theological propositions which are transcultural or

---

7. Livermore, *Cultural Intelligence*.

8. Bennett, "Towards Ethnorelativism."

9. Storti, *The Art of Crossing Cultures*.

10. Howell and Paris, *Introducing Cultural Anthropology*.

11. Grunlan and Mayers, *Cultural Anthropology*.

12. Tillich, *Theology of Culture*.

13. Jenson, *Essays in Theology of Culture*.

14. Tanner, *Theories of Culture*.

super-cultural (that is, true for all times and places). Flett's[15] study of T. F. Torrance's theology of culture gives us a much higher view of culture: humans, as bearers of the image of the triune God, are stewards of the order of creation, and social activity is the way we maintain this order. However, each of these highly theoretical monographs misses practical application, as they rarely relate theory to actual cultures, or consider how our cross-cultural work would be shaped by our theology of culture.

On the other hand, Niebuhr's innovative essay[16] was far more practical in the way it connected the theology of culture to the role of Christians in the world. However, the past several decades' worth of scholarship has shown numerous deficiencies in Niebuhr's taxonomy, including his lack of a consistent definition of culture, and his assumption of the hegemony of Western Christendom.[17] Certainly, an evangelical theology of culture for the twenty-first century would interact with the seminal works of Tillich and Niebuhr and others, but would need to begin with the presupposition that God as a triune being is cultural (God speaks, is highly social, and is creative) and works through culture, not despite it.[18] As T. M. Moore put it, "We may not treat culture with *indifference*, because God does not."[19]

It is a central tenet of this book that Christians will be more effective if they embrace their cultural activity, rather than feel ambivalent about their place in this world. Christians are called to glorify God and enjoy him forever, and it turns out that we can only achieve this end through cultural activity.[20] We are indeed called to be world changers, and we will be best prepared for this task if we possess a biblical theology of culture for our time.

15. Flett, *Persons, Powers and Pluralities.*

16. Niebuhr, *Christ and Culture.*

17. See Carson, *Christ and Culture Revisited,* and Carter, *Rethinking Christ and Culture.*

18. Tennent, *Invitation to World Missions.*

19. T. M. Moore, *Culture Matters,* 103

20. Van Til, *The Calvinistic Concept of Culture,* 37.

PART I: The gospel and global trends

CHAPTER 1

Why globalization matters for Christians

A THEOLOGY OF CULTURE for the twenty-first century requires interacting with the realities of globalization, which has been described as the "dominant feature of modern society."[1] In this chapter I focus on why the phenomenon of globalization matters to the "average person" and especially to the Christian. I have tried to resolve the predominant competing attitudes towards globalization, which range from vehemently negative to naively optimistic. I specifically consider an evangelical response to five trends that are a result of globalization: 1) the homogenization of a "global culture;" 2) outsourcing; 3) the ways in which increased immigration flows are changing our cultural landscapes; 4) the exporting of Western culture and 5) the way globalization is affecting the poor.

IS THE WORLD REALLY "FLAT"?

A few years ago, my family and I moved to Jackson, Mississippi so I could teach international studies at Belhaven University. Several of my acquaintances responded with surprise, "You teach about *culture* in *Jackson*? I bet your students haven't traveled out of the South, let alone outside of the USA!" This turned out to be far from the truth. I surveyed each class about their travel experiences, and discovered that in classes with an average of forty, the students would collectively list twenty or more other countries that they had visited, on all six of Earth's inhabited continents. Some of these globe-trotters are international students; others have gone on mission

1. Anderson et al., *International Studies*, 1.

elled overseas for sports, music, or dance competitions.
arochial towns like Jackson, Mississippi are globalizing.
Hindu temple each day on my way home from the uni-
se-Thai fusion restaurant where the waiters were from
suppose I could continue describing the forces of globaliza-
at this one restaurant by listing the countries where the menus were
printed, the furniture was manufactured, the rice was grown, and so on.

By relating anecdotes of globalization in small-town USA, I don't
mean to paint a naively optimistic picture of a "flat" world as Thomas Friedman did,[2] promising that global shifts like the opening of international
borders, more competitive prices, and falling trade barriers would level the
playing field between superpowers and economic newcomers. Friedman
argued that this new flat world of a global economy would be like a rising
tide that lifts all ships, resulting in strong economies overseas and more
fulfilling jobs for everyone[3] including US-Americans.[4] A more balanced
view argues that globalization is not a panacea for world peace, nor will
it inevitably forge a path toward free markets throughout the world. The
phenomenon of globalization faces, and presents, many challenges (as we
will see throughout this chapter). But the international exposure of these
students who live in a modest-sized town in the Southern US can illustrate
that virtually everyone in the Western world is now regularly involved in
the cross-cultural process. True, US-Americans are still painfully monocultural in their outlook—we are even less culturally aware than many Aus-
tralians or Europeans—but we are not by any means isolated from other
cultures.

This rapidly increasing interconnectedness and interdependence of
peoples and countries is what we mean by "globalization."[5] The weakness of
the World Health Organization's rather "sterile" definition of globalization
is that it points to a phenomenon but does not evaluate the merits of whether this rapid increase in interconnectedness is desirable or deplorable. A
more significant weakness of this definition is that it does not describe the
standard by which the "rapid increase" is measured. How would we actually

2. Friedman, *The World is Flat*.

3. Ibid., 28–29.

4. The phrase "US-Americans" may seem unnecessary or cumbersome to some readers; however, it seems like the most pithy moniker for "North Americans who live in
the USA, not Canada or Mexico, and who may or may not be citizens." So I will use the
phrase US-Americans throughout.

5. http://www.who.int/trade/glossary/story043/en/index.html.

go about proving that we are more interconnected now than we were a decade or century ago? Can "interconnectedness" be measured—and if not, then why speak of "increased interconnectedness"?

It has become cliché to say "globalization is not new"[6] and is inevitable. If globalization is (misleadingly) defined as cultural sharing, diasporas, immigration, and urbanization, we can point to these movements of human societies since the early histories in the book of Genesis (see Gen 4, 10, 11, 12, and 15). However, globalization is rightly understood only as a phenomenon that started in the mid-twentieth century, where we observed a steady increase in international interdependence.

To "prove" that we are increasingly interconnected, enthusiasts of globalization usually use anecdotes that resound with us. The most common way we experience the interconnected world is when we call a company like Dell Computers for technical support, and we have a hunch that the call has been transferred to a customer care center in Mumbai, India. Others may tell their own experience of globalization while traveling: An American tourist recounts how she saw a man wearing Michael Jordan T-shirt in Tibet; or a tourist giddily posts on Facebook that he ate fries at a McDonald's in Thailand.

But we do not need to resort to anecdote; below we will see that there are scientific ways of measuring the increase in interconnectedness, and each of these measures present theological challenges for Christians who want to impact the world.

HOW SHOULD CHRISTIANS RESPOND TO INCREASED MULTICULTURAL CONNECTIVITY?

A significant measure of globalization is the increase in multicultural connectivity. In 1950 world exports totaled around $61 billion. By the late 1990s, exports exceeded $6 trillion annually.[7] We could also measure whether the number of multinational corporations (MNCs) is increasing. In 1970, there were only 7,000 MNCs.[8] By 2009, "The World Investment Report," published by the United Nations Conference on Trade and Development (UNCTAD), stated there were 889,416 multinational companies around

6. In fact, a Google search of "globalization is not new" turns up more than 35,000 results.

7. Anderson et al., *International Studies*, 2.

8. Warhurst, *Corporate Social Responsibility and the Mining Industry*, 1.

the world.[9] In fact, the number of MNCs quadrupled between 1995 and 2009.[10] In 1994, MNCs accounted for $5.5 trillion in sales,[11] but by 2008, the "100 largest MNCs' sales combined amounted to nearly $8.5 trillion."[12] We can say for certain that not only are our enterprises more connected, but this interconnectedness is now essential to life as we know it.

Another way to measure the increased multicultural connectivity is to track the creation of regional trade alliances. For instance, the fall of the Berlin Wall in 1989, the creation of the European Union (EU), in 1992 and the North American Free Trade Agreement (NAFTA) in 1994 were early harbingers of globalization. The numerous nation-states in Europe and North America are often at odds in ideology, but we agree on our need to share labor pools, markets, and products. Other regional trade alliances have been created in South America (e.g., Mercosur), Asia (e.g., ASEAN) as well as smaller agreements throughout the Caribbean, West Africa, etc. Christian entrepreneurs are increasingly seeing globalization as God's way of allowing Christians to gain access to formerly insular regions of the world.[13]

Unfortunately, many US-Americas have not kept up with the pace of multicultural connectivity. Instead, we are complaining of growing pains. Perhaps the most poignant indicator of our cross-cultural illiteracy is our attrition rate in foreign assignments. Four out of five mid- to large-sized companies send personnel overseas nowadays. An alarming 10 to 20 percent of these employees return early and another 30 to 35 percent operate below their organization's expectations while overseas.[14] Rundle and Steffen report that "as many as 40 percent of Western business professionals who are given foreign assignments return early."[15] The Business Council for International Understanding gathered statistics on expatriates who return to the US prematurely from specific foreign fields: from Saudi Arabia, 68 percent; Japan 36 percent, London 18 percent, Brussels 27 percent. Ferraro

9. http://www.numberof.net/number%C2%A0of%C2%A0mncs–in–the–world/.

10. Rundle & Steffen, *Great Commission Companies*, 54.

11. Harris et al., *Managing Cultural Differences*, 27.

12. http://www.numberof.net/number%C2%A0of%C2%A0mncs–in–the–world/.

13. Rundle and Steffen, *Great Commission Companies*, 29.

14. Kohls, *Survival Kit for Overseas Living*, 119–20.

15. Rundle and Steffen, *Great Commission Companies*, 61.

reported that US expatriates have failure rates of 10 percent in at least 75 percent of companies surveyed—higher than Asian or European rates.[16]

High attrition rates are a challenge for mission organizations as well. Missionaries often return to their home country for perfectly acceptable reasons: children need further education; there may be health problems or the missionaries' parents may be aging.[17] And teams also return because of job mismatch, problems working with their fellow expatriates, family problems, or personal struggles. However, a high attrition rate in foreign assignments is due, in part, to our cross-cultural illiteracy. About 26 percent of World Evangelical Fellowship (WEF) members who returned prematurely cited problems with the host society, culture, or team as the most important reason.[18] Adequate cross-cultural training (CCT) is an essential part (combined with institutional support and proper selection) of successful performance in cross-cultural work. In fact, only about one in seven employees sent abroad will succeed overseas if "left to chance."[19] Leaving the field before the project is completed is costly to companies, the expatriate workers, their indigenous counterparts, their families, and their sponsoring organizations. Organizations incur the initial cost of relocating the expatriate family, supporting them while in the field, plus the cost of repatriation. There are other less tangible (but very real) costs like damage to the organization's reputation when their expatriate worker cannot navigate the social setting in the host country, not to mention the stress that the expatriate, family, and national counterparts endure when the assignment turns sour.

The ways some MNCs and mission organizations have dealt with cross-cultural illiteracy reflect some trends related to globalization: They are reducing the expatriate presence overseas; or they send their workers on shorter (several weeks or months) tactical assignments, instead of the traditional three-to-four–year international term. Other MNCs and mission organizations are taking their expatriates out of host countries altogether.[20] As capacities are built among leaders in developing nations, host country nationals (HCNs) are increasingly filling managerial positions that parent companies used to assign to expatriates. In some regions, HCNs are

---

16. Ferraro, *The Cultural Dimension of International Business*, 176.

17. Taylor, "Introduction," 10.

18. Brierley, "Missionary Attrition," 91.

19. Kohls, *Survival Kit for Overseas Living*, 1.

20. Ferraro, *The Cultural Dimension of International Business*, 175.

well received by their compatriots (after all, they speak the language fluently and are experts on their own culture). Besides, HCNs are drastically less expensive to employ, and deal with fewer security issues. (Europeans and North Americans require extra security while living in many overseas environments than the indigenous counterparts).

Some interpret this reduction as a blessing of globalization. Taylor called this "desirable attrition."[21] Slimming Western presence abroad is considered a long overdue step in moving beyond colonialism. Mission organizations are also passing the baton to leaders in the host country. Mission leaders recognize that it is a biblical imperative to build capacity in indigenous leaders and transfer the ministry to them. Mission organizations and MNCs now recognize that HCNs are increasingly qualified to take the reins. A reduction in the expatriate missions force, then, may not indicate cross-cultural illiteracy; rather, it may signal that Westerners are finally putting a nail in the coffin of paternalism.

This transfer of leadership to the host countries (where it belongs) is encouraging; however, we cannot ignore the fact that there are many less flattering reasons for the diminishing presence of Western workers in international settings. Some Westerners see going overseas as a necessary evil, or as a stepping-stone for their career, rather than a great opportunity to develop their own skills while fostering cross-cultural partnerships. With these attitudes, they begin their cross-cultural work reluctantly. And people's attitudes about crossing cultures have a major impact on their adjustment and success.

While some strategists have encouraged MNCs and mission organizations to work toward the complete transfer of their leadership and labor to host country nationals, many missiologists contend that wholesale withdrawal from the cross-cultural process hurts everyone—especially in a world that is globalized. Instead, the current trend in missions is an emphasis on partnerships,[22] which are part of a continual crossing of cultures. There is an organizational synergy that is created by the sharing of ideas, language, and values from various cultures.[23] The cross-cultural process gives us more effective marketing strategies, better and safer products, and broader perspectives. It seems that God always intended for us to be

21. Taylor, "Introduction," 10.

22. See Chukueku, "Partnership in Mission"; Lee, "Beyond Partnership"; Morales and Eleazar, "North American Mission Agencies."

23. Ferraro, *The Cultural Dimension of International Business*, 49.

crossing cultures (Ps 2:8; Jer 1:5), rather than withdrawing. True, the time is overdue for host country nationals to take the reins in their contexts; but there will never be a time when sojourners and migrants (regardless of national origin) should be removed from any society's organizational structures.

In fact, a number of MNCs and mission organizations agree that there are benefits to ramping up cross-cultural engagement, rather than withdrawing. These organizations have observed the growth pains of globalization, and have implemented CCT programs to increase cross-cultural literacy. In 2001, 69 percent of companies surveyed offered CCT before sending their employees on foreign assignments. This was up from 50 percent in 1990.[24] Companies have reported a positive relationship between CCT and self-confidence, job performance, plus more accurate interpretations of cross-cultural interactions.

In summary, US-Americans are undoubtedly stunted in their cross-cultural literacy. But if they withdraw from the international scene (what we mean by attrition) they would be less likely to keep up with the global trends. However, as many MNCs and mission organizations have recognized the need to keep up with the pace, they have implemented better CCT, and have engaged in the global cultures in relevant and less paternalistic ways.

HOW SHOULD CHRISTIANS RESPOND TO ACCULTURATION?

Another way to actually measure globalization is to count the increase of migrants and refugees. The phenomenon of increased migration raises questions for world changers about how people should acculturate. That is, should they assimilate (become like the majority culture), integrate (coexist), or simply adjust (i.e., put up with the host culture without actually accommodating it)?

By 2009, 190 million people were living outside of their home nation-state—this is proportionally more than any other time in history.[25] Of those, 44 million have been forcibly displaced.[26] If all of these immigrants, migrant workers, foreign students, and refugees were placed into a single

24. Lang, "Cross-Cultural Training" para. 7.

25. Rowntree et al., *Diversity Amid Globalization*, 7.

26. Snarr, "Introducing Globalization," 2.

country, it would be the seventh largest country in the world. The phenomena of immigration and diasporas have taken place for thousands of years; but the rapid increase is both made possible by, and a cause of, our "flattening world."

Churches and mission organizations are capitalizing on these realities of globalization in two ways: as the world "flattens" it becomes easier to travel, and safer to cross borders. Churches are sending out half a million volunteers on short-term mission trips every year—this is increasing annually.[27] Second, Christians are now more aware than ever that the world is in diaspora, and while it may be difficult to reach people in "restricted access countries," those who have been displaced or have emigrated are now to be found in urban centers throughout the world. We can now reach Senegalese in Little Senegal (Manhattan), Kurds in Nashville, Afghans in Fremont, California, and so on. However, the degree to which these migrant communities acculturate to their new host cultures varies significantly.

Globalization requires some degree of acculturation for all of us. Should Christians who work cross-culturally change their behaviors to fit in? What is God's view of how immigrant communities acculturate to their new home? Should your country be a melting pot, or a salad bowl? On the one hand, Scripture has models of conforming and not conforming. Romans 12:2 (NIV) says "Do not conform to the pattern of this world, but be transformed by the renewing of your mind." Isaiah 52:11, Ezekiel 20:34, and 2 Corinthians 6:17 call for God's people to live separate lives. Today, there are some cross-cultural missionaries who interpret these passages as warnings to not look to the cultural cues around them to dictate their behavior. A missionary told me, "The way *they* do things is not in the Bible. If it is not in the Bible, I do not want anything to do with it." What is ironic about this polemic is that the New Testament actually builds a strong case for fitting in to the society where we find ourselves. Jesus came and lived among Jews. He spoke Aramaic, used illustrations that fishermen and farmers would understand, and addressed the political climate of his day. Paul was thoroughly grounded in the Old Testament but also studied contemporary Greek philosophy. In fact, Paul recorded his approach toward acculturation, which was nearer to accommodation than adaptation:

> Though I am free and belong to no man, I make myself a slave to
> everyone, to win as many as possible. To the Jews I became like
> a Jew, to win the Jews. To those under the law I became like one

27. Slimbauch, "First, Do No Harm."

under the law (though I myself am not under the law), so as to win those under the law. To those not having the law I became like one not having the law (though I am not free from God's law but am under Christ's law), so as to win those not having the law. To the weak I became weak, to win the weak. I have become all things to all men so that by all possible means I might save some. I do all this for the sake of the gospel, that I may share in its blessings (1 Cor 9:19–23, NIV).

We can observe a spectrum of biblical responses toward acculturation, from withdrawal, to coexistence (integration), to enthusiastic embracing of various cultures (assimilation). Which model to implement depends on context. And context involves a number of factors, including whether the Christian co-culture is a minority or majority voice, the degree of urbanization, solidarity of the in-group, etc. So a theology of acculturation must take into account these variables.

For example, in urban area with many immigrants, people adapt to the majority culture (but almost never fully *assimilate*) at different rates and to different degrees. Some have a penchant for learning new languages; some are more cross-culturally literate than others (so they pick up on the dominant culture quicker). Some may live in the US for a short time and draw no attention to themselves through their clothes, gait, or cars. Others may live in the US for decades and continue to appear quite foreign. Likewise, US expatriates exhibit the same phenomenon: Some can live overseas for years and continue to look, think, talk, walk, and shop like majority culture US-Americans. Others accommodate their host culture relatively quickly. The process toward accommodation varies from person to person—and it also varies depending on the openness of the host society.

Imagine that humans eventually developed colonies under the ocean. However we went about accomplishing this feat, we would need to change the environment around us in order to survive—but we would not change *our very nature*. We would retain everything about us that makes us human—even if those traits made it impossible to thrive under the ocean. We might adapt to the environment by changing some behaviors, expectations, or attitudes—but we would never be assimilated into marine life. That is what an adaptation model of acculturation looks like: We retain all of our Americanness (or Koreanness or Britishness) because we believe it would be impossible, undesirable, or unreasonable to change.

We see a version of this "adaptation" or coexistence approach in the ethnic enclaves that emerged in urban centers. There are large Chinatowns in San Francisco, Vancouver, and Lima. There is a Little Italy in New York and a Greektown in Toronto. These international districts allow (especially first generation immigrants) to maintain their native language, culture, social structures, and even political structures to some extent. But in this era of globalization, even ethnic enclaves are becoming heterogeneous as second generation immigrants attain the skills to be upwardly mobile, and as multiple other ethnic groups move in to the ethnic district.[28] So it seems that the acculturation model of withdrawal or the "enclave" is less viable than ever.

However, we often have a different expectation regarding people from other cultures when they live in "our territory." For example, when the British colonized Australia, their predominant plan for incorporating aborigines into the dominant British society was assimilation, not withdrawal or integration. Tribal children were taken from their parents and placed in foster homes so they would exclusively learn the King's English and a British worldview. The British colonizers (keenly) surmised that if native children remained in their traditional homes, they would grow up with competing ideologies about vernacular use, work ethic, religion, and family structure. Children would inevitably retain some of their aboriginal identity; and the colonizers (in their paternalism) decided such a retention would retard the "progress" of the natives.[29] Some US-Americans possess a similar attitude toward immigrants in their hometown: "Why don't they just learn English?" "Why do they import their neighborhood here?"

Many of us maintain, then, a double standard regarding acculturation. When it is *us* living among *them,* our acculturation is voluntary, measured, and temporary (i.e., adjustment). When *they* are living among *us,* we expect acculturation to be permanent and unfettered (i.e., assimilation). Consider how our twenty-sixth president, Theodore Roosevelt, conceptualized assimilation:

> In the first place we should insist that if the immigrant who comes here in good faith becomes an American and assimilates himself to us, he shall be treated on an exact equality with everyone else, for it is an outrage to discriminate against any such man because of creed, or birthplace, or origin. But this is predicated upon the man's becoming in very fact an American, and nothing but an American. . . . There can be no divided allegiance here. Any

28. Casey, "How Shall They Hear?"

29. Probyn-Rapsey, *Made to Matter.*

man who says he is an American, but something else also, isn't an American at all. We have room for but one flag, the American flag, and this excludes the red flag, which symbolizes all wars against liberty and civilization, just as much as it excludes any foreign flag of a nation to which we are hostile. . . . We have room for but one language here, and that is the English language . . . and we have room for but one sole loyalty and that is a loyalty to the American people.[30]

Roosevelt's plan for assimilation was only convenient for the ethnic majority. Researchers have discovered that the effects of the assimilation approach on immigrant communities (which make up roughly 15 percent of the population in the US) are quite negative. On the one hand, retaining one's home culture in a new environment results in marginalization. On the other hand, completely relinquishing one's home culture (assimilation) can be equally as demoralizing.[31]

With so much immigration today, attitudes about acculturation are changing. For instance, only 60 percent of Hispanics in the USA agreed that "immigrants have to speak English to say they are part of American society."[32] And certainly there are degrees of adjustment. Look at the behaviors below, and decide whether you think one would need to adopt this behavior to be an acculturated North American. (Note that part of the point here is to show that people will have different opinions on what it means to acculturate).

- Enjoy eating hot dogs
- Believe in Christ
- Doubt Christ
- Speak English
- Drive aggressively

Acculturation has always been intertwined with themes of dominance and social injustices. Migrants can retain their original culture when it is economically possible for them to do so. And they may be passively required to retain their culture, against their wishes, if they are denied access to the dominant culture. Or they may willingly relinquish their original culture

---

30. Roosevelt, "Letter to the President."
31. Ward, "Thinking Outside the Berry Boxes."
32. Rowntree et al., *Diversity Amid Globalization*, 104.

when they are ridiculed for retaining it. Cases where culture loss (sometimes called ethnocide) is demanded are not melting pots, but pressure cookers.[33] And the degree of acculturation is correlated with the amount of contact with the dominant culture. First-generation immigrants tend to have less contact (because of the ethnic enclave) than second-generation immigrants. So acculturation is about access—about opportunities that are given to sojourners to gain exposure to the dominant culture.

We see the theological side of acculturation when we begin thinking about power, prejudice, dominance, and injustice. God does not approve of the pressure cooker approach. In fact, this book builds a case that God's plan is multiculturalism. We need to keep in mind that there is no one-size-fits-all plan for acculturation. We need to be aware of specific intercultural pasts, where power has used unjustly to kill culture, or how prejudice plays a part in the acculturation process. There are many variables to acculturation, including how the sojourners arrived, at what age, their social standing in their new host culture, and their personal psychological makeup.

If we can understand how sojourners and immigrants respond to a new cultural environment, we can be more supportive during the process; and we can understand ourselves better as we move across cultural boundaries.

In previous decades, CCT offered through Christian organizations had several goals to facilitate cross-cultural adjustment of their workers. 1) Trainers taught that cultural differences were based on cultural values, so that cross-cultural workers would postpone judgment. If workers could see that the patterns of behavior and thoughts in the host culture made sense according to the emic logic, the workers would be less ethnocentric. 2) Trainers hoped that cross-cultural workers from Western nations could perhaps cast aside some of the rough edges—especially the blind acceptance of full-fledged individualism, direct speech, and distaste for formality. If cross-cultural workers could embrace some "Eastern" values like collectivism, formality, honorifics and tact, and lose time reckoning, they would fit in better. So cross-cultural adjustment would require giving up some—not all—of yourself, and taking on some of the host culture's values.

This cultural give-and-take is not a zero-sum game. Lingenfelter and Mayers[34] argued that well-adjusted individuals would perhaps give up 25 percent of their home culture (the roughest parts, of course) and would

---

33. Berry, "Conceptual Approaches to Acculturation," 25.

34. Lingenfelter and Mayers, *Ministering Cross-Culturally*, 117–24.

embrace as much as 75 percent of the host culture, thus becoming more like 150 percent individuals. That is, the cross-cultural process would be synergistic, helping the sojourner to grow in deeper ways than she or he imagined.

However, Lingenfelter and Mayers' model of 150 percent persons contains a limitation: Because the process of socialization is so efficient, many of us operate with the cultural "software" (to use Hofstede's term) that we need to be effective in our culture of origin. Wouldn't significant alterations in my cultural values of individualism, precise time reckoning, and task-orientation make me less effective in my home culture? Is it even possible to give up those deeply embedded orientations? If Mary, a US-American, spends twenty years in Korea, is she more or less culturally intelligent if she returns to the USA valuing highly contextual speech, hierarchy, and collective decision-making? Such new values would impede her when she retuned to the USA. The goal of acculturation is not simply a give-and-take of our cultural patterns. It is, instead, learning to be effective in every situation.

Livermore's[35] CQ model allows us to move beyond this limitation of Lingenfelter and Mayers' 150 percent persons. Instead, CQ measures our ability to move seamlessly between cultures. To be truly culturally competent is to have the software necessary for achieving your goals in your home culture, and in the host cultures where you work. It means making decisions collectively in collectivist cultures, and behaving like an individualist in individualist cultures. It means using highly contextual speech where that is appropriate, and speaking directly when that's appropriate. It means accepting the culturally determined degree of spontaneous hospitality and privacy or inclusion.

To summarize, a Christian response to acculturation—the approach which seems most viable in the globalized world of the twenty-first century—is one which dignifies both the home and the host culture. Full-fledged assimilation is demoralizing; ethnic enclaves are less viable than ever; integration does not facilitate flourishing cross-culturally. Instead, cross-cultural competence is really the key to successful acculturation in a new cultural environment.

---

35. Livermore, *Cultural Intelligence.*

HOW SHOULD CHRISTIANS RESPOND TO THE EXPORTING OF WESTERN CULTURE?

From the heyday of colonialism in the nineteenth century until about 1950, the exporting of culture was essentially a one-way street. European superpowers set up colonies across the globe which were governed according to Western political systems. They created cash-based markets, reorganized education according to European norms, and established virtually every Christian denomination and sect that had already been founded in the West. While colonizers were busy exporting Western culture, their home countries were importing very little from foreign countries. True, traders brought in foreign commodities like exotic spices, occasionally ancient artifacts, and for a period of time, they brought slaves; but the balance of cultural influence was heavily weighted on the European transfer to foreign settings. While many of these native cultures survived and even thrived (though certainly changed), native cultures suffered devastating losses (e.g., the loss of language or autonomy) due to the early form of globalization which we now recognize as imperialism.

Today, some people disparage globalization for its part in continuing the imperial past. Critics say that globalization is in effect *Westernization*. Or often, more specifically, *Americanization*. This has led to the pejorative label of ubiquitous Western fads—and yes, especially McDonald's—as "McWorld."[36] Veseth satirically reduces this criticism of globalization to a simple mantra: Western icons with global influence and vast resources like Michael Jordan, Nike, and ESPN + sweatshops, over-consumption, and inequality = Americanization.[37] If globalization means sweatshops, inequality, and the exporting of American consumerism, critics want nothing to do with it. Globalization, as the critics define it, is truly a bane.

But is globalization really Westernization as the critics say? Are global influences like Hollywood and Walmart really creating a McWorld? Since decolonization began in full force in the 1950s, the trend of exporting culture has become a two-way street. Non-European countries are now viable players in the marketplace and in the world of ideas. In 1950, Western nations were responsible for 64.1 percent of the world's gross economic product; this fell to 48.9 percent by 1992. Less developed countries (LDCs) are certainly catching up in the manufacturing sector. In 1928, Western

36. Barber, "Jihad vs. McWorld."
37. Veseth, *Globaloney 2.0*, 68.

countries produced 84.2 percent of manufactured goods compared to 57.8 percent by 1980. And the exporting of Western political power has all but ceased. In 1950, 48 percent of the world's population was under the political control of Western governments; in 2000, the number had dropped to 12.5 percent.[38] We could argue that globalization has not meant the continuation of imperialism at all; instead, it has dealt it a serious blow by empowering non-Western nations.

While travelers can see Michael Jordan on T-shirts, and can find fast food chains (especially Subways) all over the world, US-Americans are not securing an increasing monopoly on the exporting of culture. True, Walmart (born in the USA) is the world's largest employer, with over one million employees, but why not point to France's Carrefour as proof of the *Frenchification* of the world? Carrefour has 10,000 stores in twenty-nine countries compared to the 4,500 Walmarts in ten countries of Europe. And after all, isn't soccer, epitomized by the World Cup, the international sport franchise—and not the NBA?[39]

As Christians, we are rightfully concerned about the influence that US-American culture (especially Hollywood) has on people throughout the world. However, we would be wrong (and tacitly ethnocentric) to conclude that US-American culture will inexorably replace the many diverse cultures in the world. If anything, globalization has opened up opportunities for many other cultures in the world to export—as well as import—cultural influence.

HOW SHOULD CHRISTIANS RESPOND WHEN THEIR JOBS MOVE OVERSEAS?

One of the most obvious and measurable effects of globalization is outsourcing. Friedman has pointed the increase in India's purchasing power as hard data which proves the rate of globalization is increasing.[40] As India's economy has grown—partly due to outsourcing jobs that were created in the country, spending on US products increased in India from US \$2.5B to \$5B between 1990 and 2006. So as technical support jobs move overseas, the income in those countries increases, which enables the workers to buy

---

38. Pearse, *Why the Rest Hates the West*, 17.

39. Veseth, *Globaloney*, 224–25.

40. Friedman, *The World is Flat*, 28–29.

more products from the USA. That strengthens US businesses and adds jobs at home.

Westerners, including Christians, may also be concerned that globalization means that they are losing their competitive edge. Western nations no longer monopolize the exportation of culture. This reality adds to the concerns that some US-Americans have about globalization. They see economics as a zero-sum game, where new jobs in China or India mean fewer jobs in the USA. Your neighbors may have the fear summed up by economists Greenwald and Kahn: "a shrinkage of lower-skilled manufacturing jobs, an increase of higher-skilled and better-paid technical jobs, and an anxious concern that the two trends will still leave many workers out in the cold, or at best serving up unhealthful fast foods to an already-obese population."[41] If your neighbors wanted to keep their manufacturing jobs, yes, their fears about losing that particular job are well-founded. But if they are content to work in the service sector at a slightly higher wage, they will likely find such employment in this age of globalization.

However, it is erroneous to think of the economics of globalization as a zero-sum game where every job created overseas is one lost at home. Financial successes have largely to do with political decisions made *within* the borders of a nation-state, not the rise of foreign economies. China's rise as an economic giant, for instance, has to do with its pro-capitalist shift, incremental improvements in productivity and investment in human capital.[42] If countries that are experiencing outsourcing wished to experience the same growth, they need not worry as much about protecting jobs from going overseas; instead, they should invest in their own human capital (especially by improving education).

In fact, the forces of the balance of trade do not work like a zero-sum game at all. Countries that export more than they import, because they have low wages, end up with highly valued currencies, which in turn raises the prices, and eventually results in a slowing down of exports.[43] Eventually, jobs move to other foreign markets where production is even cheaper. Japan experienced this cycle during the 1970s and '80s. US-Americans used to worry that Japan would take their jobs, but this did not actually happen. The number of jobs in the US went from 78.5 million in 1970 to 142 million in 2005. This means that "during 35 years of increasing globalization,

41. Greenwald and Kahn, *Globalization*, 56.

42. Ibid., 33–38.

43. Ibid., 58.

employment in the United States actually increased by over 80 percent
. . . overall participation in the labor force rose steadily from 60.3 percent
of the adult population n 1970 to 63.8 percent in 1983 to 66.1 percent in
2005."[44] So if thirty-five years of globalization is any indication of the future,
jobs will continue to be created—not lost—even as manufacturing jobs are
exported. Wages have also increased in the past decade more than they did
from 1970 to 2000.[45] True, the nature of jobs is changing—many who had
low-paying manufacturing jobs are now in slightly better jobs in the service
industry. And the "quality of jobs improved, along with the total number of
jobs, throughout the recent era of globalization."[46]

While globalization has been good news for MNCs and for the global
missions effort, some majority-culture US-Americans are not as enthusiastic about this new reality. If they work in manufacturing, they are concerned
that they will lose their jobs to someone in Mexico, India, or China. What
they don't realize is that globalization itself is not a problem; in fact, the
problem is that we (especially North Americans) are often cross-culturally
illiterate. To help objectors to multiculturalism understand this, I would
use a metaphor: Imagine my daughter needed a new pair of shoes at seven,
and a year later needed a larger size. By age ten she had upsized three times.
I would not blame her for growing; I would see it as my own responsibility
to keep up with her needs. The leveling of the playing field on a global scale
is a sign of maturity—and we can keep up with it rather or gripe about it.
Cross-cultural interactions are part of our everyday lives. The solution is
not to close the borders, to buy only American products, and require everyone to learn English. We hear this sort of rhetoric—as if such a retreat from
the world were even possible—but such a withdrawal would quickly cause
the USA to fall behind in the global marketplace. We would miss out on
the world's tremendous pool of skilled workers, managers, and even global
customers who want to purchase our products, study in our schools, and
experience our films and music. And we would miss out on the opportunity
to transform, and be transformed, by the cultures around us.

Now, the shift of industries overseas does raise another legitimate
concern for socially conscious folks: are these employees who are newly
entering the workforce being treated fairly? Is globalization actually a boon
to their quality of life?

44. Ibid., 60.
45. Ibid., 76.
46. Ibid., 62.

HOW HAS GLOBALIZATION AFFECTED THE GLOBAL POOR?

Our sense of Christian responsibility tells us that with increased access to foreign borders and international markets, globalization should be a vehicle for improving the lives of the poorest people. We are in the most suitable position ever for ending world health crises like malaria, which still takes over 600,000 lives per year.[47] Global trade should mean the end of world hunger, yet more than nine million people die every year due to hunger or hunger-related causes.[48] Inexpensive laptops and Internet access should mean adequate education for all—perhaps the most important key to ending poverty. Yet in Pakistan, Mauritania, Afghanistan, and Iraq, literacy rates are below 50 percent. They are much lower in Swaziland, Botswana, and Niger.[49]

There is no doubt that the rapid increase of international interdependence in the global marketplace has improved the economies of the world's poorest countries, just as it has improved the economies of the richest countries. For example, Nobel laureate Muhammad Yunus tells the story of peasants-turned-entrepreneurs in Bangladesh who receive microloans so they can purchase materials to sell baskets.[50] Or tribal peoples in Malawi can purchase bundles of secondhand clothes imported from the UK, and resell the items in their small trade shops in the African countryside.[51] As remote villagers enter the global marketplace, education, health, and morale improves for them and their extended families.

Despite entry into the global marketplace, per capita income in many LDCs is decreasing, rather than increasing. During the 1990s, an important decade in globalization, the number of people living in poverty increased by 100 million. Forty-three percent of the world's population still lives on less than $2 a day.[52] However, this marks a significant decrease from 1980, when 70 percent of the world lived on less than $2 a day. This improvement is largely due to the burgeoning markets in China and India.[53] In the

---

47. http://www.who.int/features/factfiles/malaria/en/.

48. Food and Agricultural Organization, "What the New Figures on Hunger Mean."

49. Anderson et al., *International Studies*.

50. Yunus, *Banker To The Poor*.

51. Packer, "Susie Bayer's T-Shirt."

52. Stiglitz, *Globalization and its Discontents*.

53. Reeves, "Poverty and Inequality in a Global Economy," 142.

past three decades, we have also halved the number of children dying from preventable causes.[54]

Advocates of the poor (including former president Jimmy Carter) argue that the worst problem that has resulted during this era of globalization is the increasingly widened gap between the rich and poor. "The distance between the richest and poorest country was about 3 to 1 in 1820, 11 to 1 in 1913, 35 to 1 in 1950, 44 to 1 in 1973 and 72 to 1 in 1992".[55] Those who have been able to enter the global marketplace have benefited; those who encounter the barriers to globalization that I mentioned in an earlier section (civil wars, protectionism, unstable currencies, etc.) lag further behind.

The term "inequality" primarily sounds like a social justice issue—and income disparity is arguably unjust (2 Cor 8:13). But income disparity is also an issue of safety, affecting everyone (even the rich). Because of Hollywood, tourism, and the Internet, the poor and suffering are now more aware than ever of the affluence in other parts of the world. An awareness of inequality leads to lower morale, less social cohesion, homicide, drug use, shorter life expectancy, a decrease in innovation and creativity, mental illness, and corruption.[56] Inequality causes schisms, especially when the inequality is along ethnic lines. So while globalization should evoke the notion of unity, it may in fact be causing disunity. The United Nations has noted that "globalization is integrating economy, culture and governance but fragmenting societies . . . this era seeks to promote economic efficiency, generate growth and yield profits. But it misses out on the goals of equity, poverty eradication and enhanced human security."[57]

Perhaps the forces of globalization have not solved the problems related to poverty because they are powerless to do so. While the increased income disparity has coincided with globalization, we cannot conclude that there is a direct correlation between the two. Greenwald and Kahn have shown that nations are poor for a variety of reasons; and many of these factors cannot be directly influenced (for good or worse) by globalization.

> Since countries shape their own fates, there are limits to the benefits that even well-intentioned outside agents can bestow, whether in the form of material intervention—trade or aid—or policy advice. Access to global markets can stimulate local demand and

---

54. Ibid., 159.

55. United Nations Development Programme, *Human Development Report*, 38.

56. Wilkinson and Pickett, *The Spirit Level*.

57. United Nations Development Programme, *Human Development Report*, 38, 44.

local growth, but only if the firms function effectively and score high on productivity and quality. Material assistance may also provide benefits—reduce disease, lower infant mortality, extend life for adults—but it will not generate . . . developmental progress.[58]

But globalization has also had a positive effect in the lives of the poorest. It has encouraged central markets and foreign direct investment, which means people who would have never had access to education or capital are now becoming entrepreneurs. "For example, in 1950, only 8 percent of the world's total output crossed national borders; by 2007 this figure had climbed to almost 58 percent".[59]

Despite the global progress, there is no doubt that the gap between the richest and poorest continues to widen. We should not be surprised that globalization has been slow to improve the lives of the poor. Humans are greedy by nature (Jer 6:13; Gal 5:19–21). We need to look to the God of all resources—the God of the poor—for more adequate approaches to ending poverty. This approach will include a mix of market activities, technology, and political action.[60] To be a member of the kingdom of God is to be engaged in all of these activities. A study of globalization and culture will touch on these themes in economics, politics, material culture, as well as ideas (chapter 9); and it will build on the notion of culture itself, which is the topic of the chapter 5.

CONCLUSION

Enthusiasts of globalization envision a future with democratic states, free markets, and "one culture"—even if that means a bumpy road along the way. Consider Mark Pagel's optimism in this BBC article:

> Against this backdrop the seemingly unstoppable and ever accelerating cultural homogenization around the world brought about by travel, the internet and social networking, although often decried, is probably a good thing even if it means the loss of cultural diversity: it increases our sense of togetherness via the sense of a shared culture.[61]

58. Greenwald and Kahn, *Globalization*, 45.

59. Rundle and Steffen, *Great Commission Companies*, 53–54.

60. Asmus and Grudem, *The Poverty of Nations*.

61. Pagel, "Does Globalization Mean we will Become One Culture?"

This same inevitability of cultural oneness was coined (pejoratively) as "McWorld" by Ritzer.[62] However, in the twenty years since Ritzer predicted McWorld, we have discovered that there are many cultural, linguistic, religious, and political barriers to creating a homogenous (and bland) world culture. Globalization will never mean ubiquitous democratization and free markets—let alone a McWorld and the loss of cultural diversity—but it will mean the changing of cultures. This should not come as a shock to us: cultures are always changing.

Further, there have proved to be too many formidable barriers to globalization for us to believe that a McWorld is inevitable. For example, nation-states have repeatedly shown that they are too protective of their own interests to truly break down trade barriers and open the borders wide enough for the type of hyper-globalization that enthusiasts envision and critics vilify. Investors remain leery of foreign markets. Also, many of the world's 6,900 languages and 15,000 distinct ethnolinguistic groups have shown they are too resilient to succumb to the "one culture" of a McWorld. Religions, also, are too resilient; they solidify cultural barriers rather than breaking them down. Globally, there are multiple civil wars going on at any given time which hinder free markets and democratization.

So, as Veseth points out, much of the hype about globalization is globaloney.[63] We are certainly exporting Western innovations; but often these global trends are glocalized. Local cultures adopt Western language, fashion, technology, and even Christianity; and then hybridize these forms to fit local values and worldview. Consider McDonald's again to see how glocalization works:

> The McDonald's of Egypt is not the McDonald's of the United States. In the United States, McDonald's is a low-status, inexpensive, and convenient restaurant designed to serve frantically busy lifestyles, low budgets and the desire for places children can go with the parents. In Egypt, McDonald's is a high-priced, high-status restaurant that delivers food, caters parties, and is a favorite place for young cosmopolitan Egyptians to hang out.[64]

To put it another way, "Drinking Coca-Cola doesn't make Russians think like Americans, any more than eating sushi makes Americans think like

62. Ritzer, *The McDonaldization of Society.*

63. Veseth, *Globaloney 2.0.*

64. Anderson et al., *International Studies*, 112.

Japanese".[65] Culture runs much deeper than what we eat and drink, so these "surface structures" will be adapted by each society in a way that fits its own cultural logic. The "deep structures" of values, beliefs, kinship systems, and language patterns will persist as global trends are glocalized, since they are far more resilient than shopping preferences, clothing styles, etc.

The phenomenon of glocalization has helped us understand our role as World Changers. Ott has shown that glocalization and hybridization are, after all, more recent terms for the much more commonly used term in missions: contextualization.[66] Church leaders seek to "contextualize," or to make the gospel meaningful to the local cultural logic. In the twenty-first century, societies which used to be homogenous are changing as global trends (including Christianity) diffuse and are fit into a cultural context. Sometimes Christianity is glocalized in such a way that evangelical theology remains intact, but sometimes it is not. Still we have moved beyond an age where the debate is about whether Christianity should be introduced into local cultures at all, since Christianity is one of several global forces. On the other hand, from what we know of how hybridization works, we must dismiss portrayals of Christianity as a homogenous entity that will inevitably supplant local cultures. A McWorld is by no means a foregone conclusion, and neither is McChristianity.

To summarize an evangelical response to globalization, we live in an era of more cultural sharing than ever, and this has a potential for fostering a synergy that leads to stronger economies, better labor pools, better products. But it also means there will be increased conflict. Rather than withdraw and lose out, we must engage the world's cultures, which will help everyone thrive. And this cultural engagement is easier than ever in a "flattening" world.

REFLECTION AND REVIEW QUESTIONS

1. How would you respond to a peer who argued that globalization is hurting his culture or economy?

2. How have you experienced the synergy of working cross-culturally?

3. How does the "flattening" of the world affect you personally?

---

65. Huntington, "The West," 28.
66. Ott, "Globalization and Contextualization."

4. Why does globalization matter for Christians?

5. What could you say to allay the fears of someone who worries that too many manufacturing jobs are going overseas?

6. How can you use the momentum of globalization to care for the needs of the marginalized, the poor, and the suffering?

7. Describe the extent to which immigrants should adapt when living in your country. What biblical support informs your answer? Does the length of stay (tourist, student, permanent immigrant) affect the degree of assimilation or adaptation you would expect them to experience?

8. What characterizes the way a World Changer thinks about globalization?

CHAPTER 2

The gospel and the USA

A THEOLOGY OF CULTURE for this century must deal with theologically-charged discourse about God's blessing on particular nations. Scripture seems to make a good case that God chooses nations to bless (Gen 12, 17). The Israelites enjoyed many benefits as long as their society was founded on God's law: their armies were victorious; their land yielded abundant crops; their women were fruitful (Deut 28). This worldview of God blessing particular societies certainly shapes how we think about culture, multiculturalism, and international relations.

Two opposing voices are powerfully transmitted on the airwaves in the USA: we hear about "American exceptionalism" on the one hand, and on the other we hear anti-American sentiment. These opposing discourses are shaping how cross-cultural Christian workers respond to globalization. International perceptions and the self-perceptions of US-Americans have a definite impact on our cross-cultural strategies.

DOES EVANGELICAL THEOLOGY EMBRACE AMERICAN EXCEPTIONALISM?

The reason I have focused the discussion on the increasingly popular and controversial topic of American exceptionalism is that discourse of "God's blessing on a nation" seems to be largely limited to the USA. In fact, an Amazon.com search for titles on "God blessed Spain"—or Japan, or Korea, or France—turns up almost exclusively books on American exceptionalism![1]

1. Note that there is, on a smaller scale, a similar discourse about Canada's special divine blessings.

But not all evangelicals integrate their faith and patriotism. When I play Lee Greenwood's' song "I'm Proud to be an American" to my students (who hail from all over the world), the responses are usually polarized between pride and disgust. This suggests that there is, in fact, not "pride in every American heart" as Greenwald claimed. Evangelical views of America tend toward these two extremes: 1) the USA was founded on godly principles, but has gradually sunken deeply into depravity;[2] or 2) the USA is an exceptional nation that continues to enjoy tremendous wealth and global influence due to God's blessing.[3] A third voice is also present, but is in the minority among evangelicals, though it is garnering widespread support outside of the church: America was not particularly founded on biblical principles, and enjoys no particular status of blessing or exceptionality.[4]

In 2014, I surveyed 340 participants to see if there was a connection between evangelicalism and the view that the USA is particularly blessed.[5] I found that 43 percent of respondents, regardless of religious affiliation or citizenship, agreed or strongly agreed with the statement "God has specially blessed the USA—it is in a unique position and should maintain that position. It has its sin and problems, but also enjoys great wealth and freedom because of its Christian founding." When controlled for religious affiliation, 49 percent of evangelicals agreed or strongly agreed with the statement, whereas only 20 percent of those who identified themselves as "Christian but not evangelical" or as "no affiliation" agreed or strongly agreed. So evangelicals are twice as likely to believe in American exceptionalism as liberal or nonreligious folks. But it is by no means a foregone conclusion that evangelicals believe in American exceptionalism—they are about as likely to believe in it as they are *not*.

What seems to be a far more significant factor in determining one's view of American exceptionalism is time spent overseas. Only 32 percent of US citizens who had spent more than a year overseas (regardless of religious affiliation) agreed with the statement on American exceptionalism, compared to 51 percent of US citizens who never spent significant time outside of the USA. Of course, citizenship is also a factor. US citizens are

2. See Scarborough, *Enough Is Enough*; Starnes, *God Less America*.

3. See Carson, *America the Beautiful*; Gingrich, *Rediscovering God in America*.

4. See Hedges, *American Fascists*; Rudin, *The Baptizing of America*; Whitten, *The Myth of Christian America*.

5. I asked five acquaintances who each had more than 2,000 "friends" on Facebook to post the survey on their "wall." Respondents answered a survey on SurveyMonkey.

twice as likely as noncitizens to believe in American exceptionalism. Of US citizens, 46 percent overall agreed with the statement, compared to 23 percent of noncitizens (who lived outside of the USA). The most likely group to agree with American exceptionalism in this survey were evangelicals from the USA who had never spent significant time overseas—57 percent agreed or strongly agreed.

When Ronald Reagan was president, he remarked that he believed God placed the USA between the two great oceans to be a city upon a hill (referring to Matt 5:14). He and other politicians like Newt Gingrich argued for American exceptionalism. The term has been commandeered over the years to mean a number of things. What it first meant, when the French author Alexis de Tocqueville wrote about it, was not that US-Americans *deserved* to have a greater measure of wealth or blessings from God, but that they were unique because they were the only people (that Tocqueville knew of) who widely believed that the government existed to serve the people, and not the other way around.[6]

But today, many reimagine American exceptionalism to mean a sense of entitlement—that the USA should fight to maintain its place as a world leader. To see how the sentiment about American exceptionalism has changed in three decades, compare President Reagan's earlier comments to President Barak Obama, who said, "I believe in American exceptionalism, just as I suspect that the Brits believe in British exceptionalism and the Greeks believe in Greek exceptionalism."[7]

If, by asking, "Is the USA blessed?" we mean, "Is the nation wealthy?" the answer is an obvious "yes." Granted, the USA is by no means the wealthiest nation per capita, landing at number fourteen in the list of per capita income per country—earning nearly half of the income per capita of the country in first place: Qatar.[8] By conflating "blessing" with wealth, is Islamic Qatar even more especially "blessed"?

A country can be blessed, however one defines that—(i.e., economically, or whether many of its citizens have a relationship with Christ, etc.)—without necessarily being *uniquely* blessed. For example, some South Pacific nations have populations with 80 to 90 percent identifying themselves as Christians, and yet are very poor and are plagued by serious health

6. Tocqueville, *Democracy in America*.

7. Gingrich and Gingrich, "A City upon a Hill."

8. https://www.cia.gov/library/publications/the-world-factbook/rank order/2004rank.html.

problems. But are they blessed? Residents of some of the wealthiest countries, like the UK, Germany, and Australia, enjoy long healthy lives, but are among the worlds' most secular societies. Are they blessed?

So attributing the USA's (or any industrial nation's) position as a world leader or its accumulation of wealth to God's blessing is unhelpful from a historical, theological, and economic standpoint. From a theological standpoint, we see in Scripture that wealth can be both a blessing and a curse, and poverty can be both a blessing and a curse. From an economic standpoint, "God's blessing" of productivity is ambiguous. Is this blessing measured by the Gross National Product (GNP) or by some other measurement? Besides, good economic policies seem like a more likely path to development than chasing after an elusive "blessing." There are tangible policies and freedoms that are responsible for the economic productivity—the standard measure of wealth—in industrialized nations which can be put in place; blessing, on the other hand, is at the behest of the blesser. Note that God's blessing does not appear on Grudem and Asmus's list of seventy-nine factors that contribute to the wealth of nations.[9] However, God's command to create, work, and produce is essential to Grudem and Asumus's formula for the wealth of nations.

We will look more at biblical models for economics and politics in chapter 9; but it is important in this chapter on "The Gospel and the USA" to examine how we invoke "God talk" about our own nation-states. Is it tacitly ethnocentric to assume we have an extra measure of blessing over all other nations? Is it just for you to insist that your nation should remain more wealthy and powerful than all others? We'll look specifically at two issues of gospel and culture in the USA below: the supposed dilution of US culture, and anti-American sentiment.

DOES IMMIGRATION DILUTE US CULTURE?

As we have seen, globalization not only involves the exporting of US influence overseas; it also includes the way foreign-born residents are changing US-American culture. For many, this presents unprecedented opportunities for evangelism, as people from every tribe, nation, and tongue come to our cities, often for employment or education.[10] Enthusiasts of global-

9. Asmus and Grudem, *The Poverty of Nations.*

10. See George, "Diaspora"; Herppich, "Korean Diaspora and Christian Mission"; Wan, "Diaspora Mission Strategy."

ization recognize that this increase in international populations in the US means an increase in the labor pool, more potential buyers of real estate, and higher (as well as more competitive) enrollments at universities.

Others are far less enthusiastic. They conceive of US-American culture as homogenous, static, and ideal—unchanging, and practically perfect in every way. Any alteration would result in adulteration. They are afraid that immigrants "are going to take over." Immigrants are undoubtedly contributing to cultural changes in America, but not any more so than they have been for the past 200 years. There are currently 13 percent foreign born people in the USA,[11] and 18 percent speak English as a second language.[12] The time in US history when there were the most immigrants was 1890, when they made up about 14.8 percent of the population.[13] Granted, at that time, the immigrants were not coming from India or the Middle East; they came mostly from Western Europe. But they were no better received by ethnic majorities at that time than immigrants are today, and many were no more fluent in English than immigrants are today. And despite (or because of) the fact that the percentage of foreign-born US residents has hovered between 10 and 15 percent over the past 120 years, US-American culture—however one defines it—seems to have survived. There is no indication that the continual influx of immigrants to the US over the past 120 years has threatened the aspects of distinctly US-American culture that US-Americans value so highly. In fact, immigrants regularly solidify these values, while majority-culture US-Americans are increasingly challenging these traditional values.

WHY DOES THE REST HATE THE WEST?

While some US-Americans are touting American exceptionalism, others express anti-American sentiment—or more generally, anti-Western sentiment. And the reality of globalization makes the West more prominent, and also makes anti-Western sentiment more prominent. How can our Christian faith help us understand anti-Western sentiment? Is there anything such widespread disapproval of the West can teach us?

We might note, to begin with, that it is a bit strange to reify anti-Western sentiment as if it were something unique. Why not also speak of

11. Grieco et al., "The Foreign-Born Population in the United States," 2.

12. Shin, "Language Use and English-Speaking Ability," 2.

13. http://www.census.gov/population/www/documentation/twps0029/tab01.html.

anti-Eastern sentiment? Or anti-Southern sentiment? Or plain old anti-other sentiment? A recent BBC study of nearly 30,000 participants from twenty-seven countries showed that the US actually enjoys a 46 percent approval rating, number eight behind Germany at 59 percent, closely followed by the European Union, Canada, Japan, the United Kingdom, France, and Brazil. Countries with the lowest global approval ratings include North Korea at an approval rating of 17 percent, followed by Pakistan at 16 percent, and Iran in last place at 15 percent.[14] So there is plenty of anti-other sentiment to go around.

Nonetheless, somehow anti-Western sentiment is uniquely promulgated through film, music, novels and news broadcasts. In a recent qualitative study I conducted with nineteen missionaries and international participants, I discovered that often anti-Western discourse is more about branding one's self-identity than it is a reflection of one's actual feelings about the West.[15] That is, people in sub-Saharan Africa and Asia often speak negatively about Europe and the US as a way of separating themselves from the more popular uncritical sentiment. For example, if East Africans often think of Americans as benevolent sponsors, more "elite" East Africans will be critical of the US as a way of distancing themselves from their more "common" compatriots.

Anti-Western sentiment is also used to bolster nationalism. For example, South Americans who were sympathetic to communism in the 1970s and 1980s found it advantageous to contrast the supposed evils US capitalism against socialist economies.[16] In these cases, as with the examples of self-identity branding above, anti-Western discourse tells us more about local agendas than actual feelings people have about the West or Westerners.

But connecting anti-Western sentiment to self-branding or nationalism doesn't entirely let the West off of the hook. Meic Pearse has aptly studied some significant underlying causes of anti-Western sentiment. In short, Pearse argues that it is the recipe of enticement plus "anti-value" that makes the West seem so dangerous to global cultures. Hollywood, for example, idolizes gratuitous sex and consumerism—values that "traditional" societies find simultaneously disturbing yet enticing.[17]

---

14. BBC World Service, "Global Views of United States."

15. Nehrbass, "The Controversial Image of the US American in Missions."

16. Ibid., 6–7.

17. Pearse, *Why the Rest Hates the West.*

The shameful way that Western nations colonized much of the world in the eighteenth and nineteenth century is also an obvious contributing factor to persistent anti-Western sentiment. Western nations raped land of the natural resources and steamrolled over local religions, political systems, and languages. While the colonizers also brought hospitals, education, Christianity, and employment, the balance was far more in favor of the colonizers than the colonized. We cannot possibly take the time to go into detail about this aspect of history; but we must reckon with colonialism as we try to integrate our faith and global cultures. A theology of culture certainly also involves a theology of colonizer and colonized. In the globalized twenty-first century, a theology of culture certainly involves a theology of international relations, nationalism, and political identity.

CONCLUSION

Christians from any nation should be self-reflective about their feelings of patriotism and their attitudes toward immigrants. Rather than parrot the ideas of prominent religious leaders or politicians about exceptionalism or immigration, Christians should be careful to form opinions that are based on careful study of Scripture, world trends, and global cultures. In any case, claims about "God's blessing" on a nation should be formed carefully with clear definitions. Likewise, if we really wish to dialogue about the value of maintaining American culture (or whatever culture) we need to be clear about what actually comprises this unique culture; for when these terms are left ambiguous, claims about the "exceptional" quality (or the dilution of such qualities) lack punch. Those who have extensive exposure to many cultures are in a better position to develop a robust view of patriotism, in contrast to monoculturals.

REFLECTION AND REVIEW QUESTIONS

1. How would you describe American culture? Do your descriptions seem more like stereotypes, cultural metaphors, or cultural generalizations? Is the USA exceptional?

2. How does one's feeling of patriotism affect his or her ability to impact the world?

3. What is the responsibility of World Changers to the migrants in their area?

4. What would you say are distinct characteristics of your own national culture, and how do you feel about those distinct characteristics in light of a globalized world?

5. How have you seen globalization affect the marketplace in your region?

6. Give some arguments and data that discount the notion that globalization equals the inevitable exporting of US-American culture.

7. How have you experienced anti-Western sentiment, and how do you respond to it?

PART II:
Understanding culture and theology

CHAPTER 3

The role of culture in theology

WHEN I SPEAK TO groups about a "theology of culture" it quickly becomes apparent that I need to explain what I mean by *theology*. From my experience in Christian higher education, it seems Christians are often either well versed in biblical studies, but uncomfortable with the cross-cultural process; or they are well prepared in cross-cultural issues, but are not very prepared theologically. Here, I will explain what I mean by theology and evangelical theology, and will explain how an evangelical theology of culture can be developed.

Commonly, theology is described simply as "rational discourse about God."[1] But that definition hardly describes how we would develop an evangelical theology of culture. Grudem's definition better encapsulates the task: "Theology seeks to understand the God revealed in the Bible, and to provide a Christian understanding of reality" particularly creation and human beings.[2] Or we may accept a somewhat unconventional definition of theology: theology is seeing "the world according to God," as Greg Johnson put it.[3] A theology of culture involves seeing Culture and cultures God's way. Such a project may sound presumptuous; but why would we endeavor to see things any other way than God's? As I will explain in this chapter, evangelicals believe it is possible to see things God's way (though partially, and even imperfectly) because God has spoken through Scripture to humans (who bear his image) in ways that they can more or less understand. And the Holy Spirit gives us discernment (Heb 4:12) and guides us into

1. Geisler, *Systematic Theology*, 7.

2. Grudem, *Systematic Theology*, 17.

3. Johnson, *The World According to God*.

truth (John 16:13). If it were not possible to see things God's way, theology, as evangelicals define it, would be impossible. We would just be left writing down our own opinions.

Since I am developing an *evangelical* theology of culture here, I must also explain that by "evangelical" I mean one who agrees with the authority of Scripture, the need for salvation, and the atonement for sin accomplished by Jesus Christ's death and resurrection. A consensus of what it means to be evangelical has been worked out over the years, and is epitomized in the Lausanne Covenant.[4] Evangelical theology begins with the premise that God exists, has revealed himself, and the content of this revelation can be understood as we read the Bible.[5]

How do we actually attain "God's view of culture" though? To answer this, we need to explore a few questions about the interplay between theology and culture: 1) Is culture, as it is found in the Bible, prescriptive or descriptive? In other words, if we find culture in the Bible, does God mean for us to imitate it? 2) If theology is a cultural activity, is it possible to arrive at theological propositions that are more than *just* cultural ideas? And 3) can we learn theological truths from culture(s), or only from Scripture?

IS CULTURE IN THE BIBLE THEOLOGICALLY PRESCRIPTIVE OR DESCRIPTIVE?

There are many cultural elements recorded in Scripture that go directly against God's principles, so it would be entirely wrong to see all culture in Scripture as normative or "God's plan for culture." The culture of the patriarchs, for instance, involved polygamy, deceit, and divination—and we learn from Scripture that all of these elements are against God's plan (Gen 2:24; Exod 20:14,16, 17; Deut 18:10). In general, it is best to assume that historical narratives in Scripture are merely descriptive unless they explicitly say they are normative.

A simple reading of the Pentateuch would give us the impression that God revealed his plans for an ideal culture to the Israelites through the Law. It would seem that the political, linguistic, social, and public cultural life of which God approves must be that which is described in the Hebrew Bible. There is some merit to this argument. If the Old Testament is normative, is it culture as God intended? A corollary of this argument would be the far

---

4. Lausanne Movement, "Lausanne Covenant."

5. Grudem, *Systematic Theology*, 32.

more pervasive argument that the culture of the New Testament is normative for us today.[6] However, given the constantly changing nature of culture,
can we successfully reconstruct "the Old Testament culture" or "the New
Testament culture" in such a way that people in this day and age should
emulate it? Why would this recovery of New Testament culture not include
fishing in small boats on the Sea of Galilee and wearing linen robes? In
other words, if we emulate biblical culture, we must answer how much, and
which one?

Throughout history, numerous movements have tried to recapture an
imagined static "biblical culture," from the Hasidic Jews, to the Amish, to
the Church of Christ (noninstrumental), to "primitive Baptists." Perhaps
each of these movements successfully captures *some* of a *certain* biblical
culture (e.g., Hasidic Jews *do* often speak Hebrew, and they abstain from
shaving their sideburns; Amish initially lived on farms like the agrarians
of the Ancient Near East). These movements invariably adopt elements
that are much later than the biblical era, but which appeared earlier than
the Industrial Revolution. For example, Amish people and Hasidic Jews
wear clothing more reminiscent of the seventeenth century than the first
century. I do not intend to evaluate the authenticity of these "back-to-the-
Bible" movements here. Instead, I mean to show how a prevalent theme in
the Judeo-Christian tradition has been to envision a single, authentic, and
static God-approved culture. We want to live godly lives, and we wish could
just figure out what that looks like. What would we dress like? What would
we do for a living? What would we eat? Is there, in fact, a single culture of
which God approves—and is that in fact described in the Bible?

Today, most Christians live their lives as if the culture described in
the Torah is not normative. Without even developing a robust theology
of culture, we simply intuitively recognize that many OT norms regarding
holidays, cleanliness, social structure, economy, land use, etc., were God's
plan for the Israelites at that time, but not for us today. While many of the
principles are timeless (e.g., love God and others, care for the poor), the
specifics were embedded in a changing culture that is now extinct.

Also, while God seems to have given us the ability to run the "software" of culture, we don't have any reason to think that God prescribed specific norms of social organization, distribution of power, economic models,
etc. (chapter 9). Nor do we have a firm foundation for arguing that God
set specific cultural value dimensions such as collectivism, individualism,

---

6. Kruse, *New Testament Models for Ministry.*

hierarchy, egalitarianism, direct or indirect speech, or deduction or induction (chapter 10) within the cultural framework of ethnolinguistic societies. It is problematic to say that any specific cultural values, rites, beliefs, or social systems come from God. For instance, some would say democracy or vegetarianism more closely approximate God's original plan for culture. While some cultural practices in every society may closely approximate biblical practices and values, it becomes problematic to claim that any particular culture *in toto* is normative.

If we cannot look to "the biblical culture" to understand God's view of culture, is a theology of culture even possible? Yes, it is; but we must understand the theological task. Specifically, we must work out whether theology is just another cultural activity (like art or dance) or whether theology can actually attain propositional truths—that is, whether it can articulate "God's thoughts about things."

IS THEOLOGY MORE THAN JUST A CULTURAL ACTIVITY?

Thinkers outside of evangelicalism consider theology to be merely a cultural activity.[7] That is, claims about God in holy writings are only reflective of the *sitz im leben* of the authors—not of absolute truths. In this approach, theology is only of interest because it shows how cultural ideas play out in religious life.

Some thinkers who are located somewhere between evangelicalism and liberalism accept that absolute truths are communicated from God's revelation, but they also heavily emphasize the "truth" that can be found in nature, or within all humankind, through general revelation. These thinkers look for what theology can gain from secular culture, such as what we may learn from the Starbucks company[8] or from Hollywood films.[9]

Evangelicals, on the other hand, have higher expectations in the theological task. They may recognize (if they are truly honest with themselves) that theology does indeed reflect cultural ideals; but they stake their faith (and sometimes their lives) on the notion that theology also obtains truth beyond just "my truth or your truth." In fact a cornerstone of evangelical theology is the clarity and sufficiency of Scripture (2 Tim 23:15–17)—God

7. See Tanner, *Theories of Culture*; Tillich, *Theology of Culture*.

8. Sweet, *The Gospel According to Starbucks*.

9. Johnston, *Reel Spirituality*.

has spoken clearly through Scripture, and people from all cultures can know what he has revealed, if they have access to Scripture.

CAN WE LEARN THEOLOGICAL TRUTHS FROM CULTURE?

The doctrine of the sufficiency of Scripture raises an important question about the interplay between theology and culture. If we learn about God from his specific revelation in Scripture, can we learn anything about him from culture—that is, from the activity and wisdom of humankind? I have known a handful of evangelicals who were so enthusiastic about the sufficiency of Scripture that they purported to see no value in God's general revelation. They saw no need for anthropology or psychology, since God's truths are incompatible with human reason. But this posture does not describe the typical evangelical approach toward theology and culture. Evangelicals typically see human wisdom—what we might call a product of culture in this case—as illuminating and valuable, though subservient to Scripture. True, whereas liberal theologians tend to overemphasize the epistemic value of general revelation (God can be found by anyone in any context), evangelicals can be guilty of seeing general revelation as ancillary—an unnecessary appendix. While this may be an ostensible posture toward general revelation, evangelicals do not really treat creation like that. Evangelicals typically interact with culture—general revelation—to more fully understand God's specific revelation in Scripture.[10] Evangelicals have engaged in biology, history, philosophy, economics, psychology, and every other culturally produced type of knowledge precisely because we believe that God's truth can be found everywhere. We may not watch a Hollywood film to learn propositional truths about the faith, but we do expect that when we study Hollywood we will learn lessons about humans, persuasion, the theory of communication, and how context affects interpretation, etc.

And in fact the reason this present volume examines cultural universals (chapter 9) and cultural variants (chapter 10) is to see what we can learn about God and God's view of things in relation to human cultures. This is what I mean by the synergy generated though cross-cultural studies. If God is the author of humanity, then we will learn about him from his image in all its diversity.

---

10. Risner, "A Theological Justification."

SUMMARY

The main question of this chapter is "How do we arrive at God's thoughts about culture?" I have described an evangelical theology of culture as the interpretation of Scripture and creation (in this case, human cultures) in order to understand God's thoughts about culture.

Once we have understood theology to be the science of understanding God's revelation in Scripture, we are ready to work out our understanding of culture. It is only after both of these concepts are clearly defined that we can work out a practical theology of culture for the twenty-first century. In the next chapter, I will lay out various concepts of what culture is, and will conclude with an evangelical explanation of the concept of culture.

REFLECTION AND REVIEW QUESTIONS

1. Do you think there is a certain culture in Scripture that is normative? Why or why not?

2. In what ways does theology go beyond simply "a cultural expression of ideas?"

3. How can World Changers use the culture around them to develop their own theological understanding?

CHAPTER 4

An evangelical explanation of culture

CULTURE IS ABOUT NORMS in a society. We are certainly social creatures. God designed us to live in groups; so it is impossible to imagine humans without culture, any more than a piano without keys. Anthropologist Geert Hofstede likens culture unto the software that tells us how to respond to our environment around us. Culture helps us to look at the food, people, and building materials available to us—the "hardware"—and gives us instructions for how we should interface with that hardware.[1] Scholars are not in agreement, though, about why human existence necessitates culture in the first place, and various theories have been suggested over the centuries. In this chapter, I will critique some prominent explanations for why humans are cultural beings, and will suggest an evangelical explanation based on the nature of the Trinity. A biblical theory about the origin and function of culture is essential for evangelicals to develop as they seek to be World Changers in the twenty-first century.

WHAT IS CULTURE?

Until recent decades, the word *culture* carried the connotation of sophistication—"the best that has been said and thought in the world" as Matthew Arnold, a nineteenth-century British poet put it.[2] Someone who was "cultured" appreciated such amenities as fine wines, the opera, ballet, and Monet. Low culture within this taxonomy would consist of innovations like

1. Hofstede et al., *Cultures and Organizations*.
2. Storey, *Cultural Theory and Popular Culture*, 18.

folk music, hip hop, rave music, and graffiti. Recently, however, anthropologists and English speakers at large no longer associate "culture" with high-class Victorian European society.[3] Some might argue that this elitist sense of "culture" has come to disuse as "high culture" (however it was defined) has become extinct; but that is probably not the reason this sense of "culture" has come into disuse, as I will show below.

Before the 1960s, most Europeans and North Americans did in fact conflate the two definitions of culture. Many Westerners assumed (in line with Darwin's theory of evolution) that cultures evolved on an inexorable trajectory from "primitive" to "civilized." In fact, early anthropologists worked out definitive schemas through which cultures would pass from cooking on fires, to making bows and arrows, to cultivating crops, to pantheism, then to complex political systems, and eventually to democracy and monotheism.[4] In the days of imperialism and Manifest Destiny people assumed that "savages" (Pacific Islanders, natives of Africa, and natives of North and South America) had no culture, or very little of it. Basket weaving and carving were not seen as art—art was narrowly defined through European art forms in the Renaissance, like sculpture or oil paintings on canvas, etc. Chants and tribal dances were not considered music—music was performed by the orchestra. The 6,000 "minority" languages were not cultured—only the dozen or so languages of Western Europe were thought to have grammars. Therefore, our great-grandparents thought that "culture" (not conceived as Western culture, just "culture") would fill the societal and psychological void within benighted savages who heretofore had no "culture."

But since the mid-twentieth century, there has been a dramatic reversal in the discipline of anthropology. As anthropologists and missionaries have provided data from all over the world, we have discovered that cultures incorporate practically endless permutations of dance, language, art, social organization, and worldview, so no particular cultural norms arise as the "right way to do things." Now, the study of culture has a definite agenda of providing enough data from around the world to change popular thinking about culture. A century ago, scholars thought that, given the proper resources for enlightenment, the rest of the world would do things the way Europeans did. Anthropologists today would argue that there are so many

3. See Tanner, *Theories of Culture*, 4, for a discussion on how the notion of "high culture" was borrowed from Cicero, and later from French and German ideas.

4. See Morgan, *Ancient Society*.

variations of cultural norms that it is absurd to say there is one right way to believe, act, or think. European culture is not common sense, it is the common sense of Europeans—just as the ways people believe, act, and think in other societies are "common sense" for them.[5] So nowadays, we widely accept culture to mean "the acceptable practices, beliefs, and actions shared by members of a society."

Culture, though, is far too complex for such a simplistic definition. In fact, anthropologists have been searching for an adequate definition for decades, and have never agreed on one. "There have probably been more definitions of 'culture' than there have been anthropologists."[6] In fact, anthropologists question whether culture exists at all: If individuals are free to do what they want, to change, innovate, and deviate, then is there such a thing as culture?[7] And if we have corporate cultures, generational cultures, ethnic cultures, and can subdivide culture to the point that there is a motorcycle culture, or even a Harley-Davidson culture, and my culture and your culture, then "culture" becomes commandeered and confused to the point that it is no longer a useful concept.

But in reality, nobody—no less anthropologists—thinks we need to abandon the concept of culture, because it is the cross-cultural worker's most useful tool for understanding Others. So rather than abandon the tool, we need to sharpen it. Anthropologists have sharpened the tool of culture by generating more understanding about *characteristics* of culture in the past several decades. Below, I will explain specifically on how we must focus on the integrated, dynamic, contested, and symbolic characteristics of culture in order to develop an evangelical theology of culture in this century.

The integrated nature of culture highlights how virtually every cultural innovation is at some point a social, political, economic, and at its base, even a theological issue. Consider alcohol consumption in America. Drinking alcohol is not simply the act of taking in a liquid. Much drinking is done in social settings. People go to bars with drinking buddies. Our cultures tell us that there are proper drinks to be supplied at proper times of the day, and with certain types of meat, depending on the occasion. So drinking alcohol is not only a physiological act, but is also a social activity. There is also high-class and low-class drinking, so alcohol is tied to

5. Geertz, *Local Knowledge*, 73–93.

6. Monaghan and Just, *Social and Cultural Anthropology*, 11–12.

7. See Berger and Luckmann, *The Social Construction of Reality*.

status and role. In 2010, there were $400 billion in sales of alcohol, which generated $90 million in wages, plus $21 billion in taxes.[8] So drinking alcohol is also an economic activity. State governments regulate the sale of alcohol and set drinking ages. Our constitution prohibited alcohol in the eighteenth amendment then lifted Prohibition in the twenty-first amendment. So alcohol consumption is also a political activity. We have wine with Lord's Supper; but some denominations are teetotalers, so drinking can be a religious activity. A single cultural phenomenon like "drinking" is incredibly complex, involving economics, religion, politics, and status.

We can draw the *integrative* aspect of culture with a web, as shown in Figure 2. Material culture (the things we have in a society), politics, religion, social structure, economy, etc., are all tied to all other aspects.

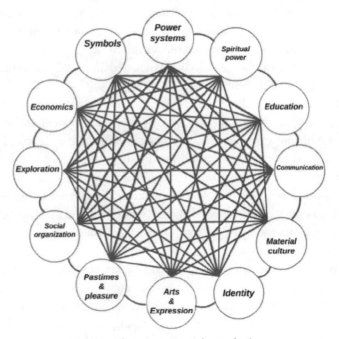

Figure 2: The interconnectedness of culture

However, there is an important aspect that the web metaphor fails to capture. The matrix of cultural subsystems are not entities that can exist on their own. They exist and thrive because they have an environment which generates, shelters, and feeds them. The interconnectivity of various

8. http://www.discus.org/economics/.

"systems" within culture can better be described as an ocean ecosystem.[9] Fish, plants, bacteria, and shellfish are unique organisms that depend on each other; but the saltwater is the environment that makes life possible for all of these organisms. What is this environment that allows these systems to grow and thrive? That is a highly debatable question. Some theorists believe the systems are sustained by an underlying worldview; others believe that these systems are kept alive by basic biological or psychological needs. Early thinkers thought the systems were the result of supposed genetic differences among the races.

To say that cultural systems all exist in a system with an underlying set of values is *not* to say that culture is ordered, cohesive, rational, or static. For example, cultural systems (economies, social structures, etc.) may thrive because of a cohesive underlying worldview, but these systems do not fit together like pieces of a jigsaw puzzle. They do not coexist peacefully any more than sharks and other fish do in the ocean. Cultures are dynamic, constantly changing as the people within those societies innovate and pattern behaviors that are diffused from other regions. As the political, economic, and geographic landscape evolves, so do cultural norms. So the various cultural subsystems can find themselves at odds with each other (consider the rift that often occurs between religion and politics).

Therefore, in addition to being highly integrated, we have discovered that cultures are dynamic or adaptive. We often (erroneously) talk about other cultures as if they have always been "this way" and will always be. Anthropologists refer to this mindset, pejoratively, as the ethnographic present. For instance, novices may characterize Native Americans as animistic or warfaring, without recognizing the drastic cultural changes that have taken place in Native American communities in the past 200 years.

The rapid cultural changes in this era of globalization have radically transformed the way anthropologists think about culture. In the early development of anthropology as a discipline, field workers would compile ethnographies to describe, for instance, Trobriand Islanders—or the Yanomami, as if the members of an ethnic group were homogenous. This monolithic characterization carried over to missionary strategies, so we would speak of the "way to reach the Karen of Burma" or "how to plant a church among Papua New Guinea highlanders" as if they are static and homogenous entities. However, due to high rates of migration and urbanization, even ethnic groups that were previously isolated are becoming quite

---

9. Howell and Paris, *Introducing Cultural Anthropology*, 38.

heterogeneous. We can no longer speak of "the Trobriand Islanders" or "the Maori" as if their cultural norms are uniform and static. As Rynkiewich has argued, cultural norms are often contested.[10] For example, within a given people group, we may be surprised to find elders who encourage a new egalitarianism and teens who support traditional hierarchical leadership. Some may be passionate about sending their children to school, others may reject European education. Some embrace working in a trade store, others prefer only to live off their subsistence farms. It seems like the moment we try to describe a culture, there will be dissenters who say, "It's not that way for me!"

Of course, culture has always been contested, but it is increasingly more so. For instance, there has always been some disagreement about what it means to be a US-American, but as more voices enter the dialogue about what it means to be a US-American, there is less agreement. There has been, then, a recent "loss of certainty" within the discipline of anthropology when it comes to analyzing and describing the world's cultures.[11] We are reticent to describe "what Japanese are like" in monolithic and positivist language, recognizing that there are not only multiple descriptions of Japanese, but that these images are often conflicted and regularly changing. But just because culture is contested does not mean we need to dispense with the concept all together. Consider the myriad of articles and books on Korean American culture[12] or African American culture; these indicate that—while there are detractors and exceptions—there are shared meanings and values among people who identify themselves as Korean Americans, or Africa Americans, and so on.

Throughout this book, I refer to cultural behaviors as "patterned" (others simply say these behaviors are "learned"). We speak and act the way we see others speaking and acting. Our beliefs are patterned after those around us. Language is the most obvious example: People who came from a home where a certain dialect was spoken tend to mirror that dialect, unless they find it more strategic to diverge from the minority speech community pattern. To take some other examples, Buddhists tend to be from Buddhist homes, or people with racist views tend to come from neighborhoods or social groups that breed racism. However, you might object, Buddhists don't always beget Buddhists; and racist parents do not always beget racist children. What does this mean for the argument that "everything we do,

10. Rynkiewich, *Soul, Self and Society.*

11. Ibid., 8.

12. Nehrbass, "Korean Missiology."

think, say, and believe (i.e., culture) is patterned"? This is precisely why anthropologists have carefully chosen the word "patterned" rather than "determined." While certain theorists in the nineteenth and twentieth century conceived of human behavior as culturally determined (or biologically, or cognitively determined), anthropologists recognize that culture is a strong force in shaping human behavior and beliefs; but it is not the sole force. For instance, we can recognize that criminals act counter-culturally because of other forces like psychological illness, the influence of drugs, or demon possession. Likewise, converts to Christ behave counter-culturally as the Holy Spirit breaks through their heretofore culturally patterned beliefs and practices.

Anthropologists have also learned that cultures incorporate symbols to express and even create meanings. Daily, we use culture to make and maintain an identity. This is probably the most popularly held defense for maintaining local cultures. When I ask members of minority cultures why they desire to diverge from the dominant culture, they typically respond like this: "Without my culture, how will I define myself within the group that is important to me?" So we use cultural norms like clothing, linguistic accents, and religious beliefs to signify to others (and to ourselves) who we are. A young member of a gang in Compton, California, for instance, doesn't just wear a certain ball cap and walk and talk a certain way because he is subconsciously patterning behaviors of others. He is deliberately fitting into a group (a culture) that gives him meaning. And the same is true for you when you choose to dress up for church, or to not split your infinitives or use other types of "bad" grammar. We all use culturally patterned symbols to express our identity—both to belong to the in-group and to distance ourselves from certain out-groups.

Culture, then, is more complex than an aggregate of "acceptable practices, beliefs, and actions shared by members of a society." These norms are integrated, patterned, contested, and symbolic. Below, I will examine some theories for why human nature depends so heavily on culture. Why is it the case that to be human is to be cultural?

The idealist explanation

I will begin with the "idealist" explanation, because even though it is not the oldest or most widely accepted theory of culture, it has been the basis of evangelical theories of culture for several decades. Evangelicals are concerned about ideas, about underlying doctrine, and the idealist explanation of culture says that behaviors and visible cultural artefacts stem out of an underlying worldview. After Hofstede et al.,[13] missiologists have thought of our cultural lives as an onion with several layers: on the outside, we have patterns of formality, language use, socializing, but if we peel the onion a bit, we will see deeper underlying values that explain those cultural norms, and if we peel the onion even deeper, we will discover an underlying worldview that shapes our more visible value systems, as well as the outward cultural lives. To use another metaphor, idealists are convinced that at the foundation of our cultural lives, there is an idea, such as "God is in control" or "society is supreme" or "there is no supernatural; life is meaningless," and the rest of our cultural lives are built on that foundation. The foundation may be unseen, but it is static, immovable. Consider the subsystems in American culture. We have a free market economy; our social structure permits us to marry whom we choose, and to locate our new household wherever we wish; our political system is a representative democracy; US-Americans choose whichever denomination or religious affiliation makes them happy. All of these cultural innovations were conceived and thrive because of the underlying worldview that the individual is of supreme importance. So within idealism, when we study, evaluate, and effect change in a culture, we not only look to the acceptable practices, beliefs, and actions shared by members of a society, we must try to discover the underlying and invisible worldview that upholds (or really, generates) those beliefs and practices.

Schaeffer[14] and Rookmaaker[15] were influential idealists and critics of culture. They both examined how visual arts and music have both reflected and perpetuated the underlying philosophical paradigms of the day. For example, in medieval Europe, art was often used for a hortatory purpose. In the period of secular humanism and the Renaissance, art idealized and idolized humanity, but typically refrained from teaching biblical concepts. Later, postmodernism and nihilism taught there are no absolutes and no meaning to life, and art became impressionistic or even totally abstract. The recurring theme within the idealist explanation of culture is that if we look to surface structures (art, clothing, socializing patterns) we can find an underlying worldview. To effect real change, rather than changing the

---

13. Hofstede et al., *Cultures and Organizations*, 7.

14. Schaeffer, *How Should We Then Live?*

15. Rookmaaker, *Modern Art and the Death of a Culture.*

surface structure, we would need to challenge the underlying worldview. Figure 3, below, shows the web of integrated cultural systems, with worldview at the center.

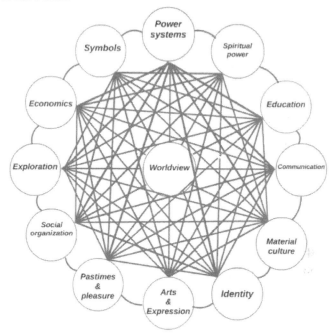

Figure 3: An idealist's concept of cultural systems

Evangelicals may be so familiar with this view of culture that they may miss the significance of accepting it as a theoretical approach. To be committed to the idealist explanation of culture is to diminish the role of biological determinism, or social functionalism, or behaviorism (described below). There are strengths to seeing how an underlying worldview is both supported by and perpetuated by surface cultural forms. However, idealists like Schaeffer and Rookmaaker saw worldview under every rock, and failed to recognize that sometimes, dribbles of paint on canvas are just that—they are not profound statements about the meaninglessness of life. And sometimes music, arts, and fashion are just fads—they are just *patterned*—and are not indicative of an underlying worldview. The more we are aware of the limited role ideals have in the shaping of culture, the more limited Schaeffer and Rookmaaker's approach becomes. Therefore we may look to other theories to add to understand the role of culture in our lives.

In fact, in the past fifty years, we have observed that not even world-view is a firm foundation. Even deeply held beliefs are contested, and changing continually. They are as influenced by social forces, market forces, and fads as other cultural systems. Therefore, rather than imagining worldview as the deepest layer of the onion, or the foundation of the house, it seems more plausible that ideas play *a part* in shaping the rest of our cultural lives. They are a part of the web.

The race/gene theory

The earliest recorded theory for the purpose of culture simply assumes that cultural traits are inherited just like biological traits. Westerners saw primitive peoples in Africa (and later the aboriginal peoples in Australia and the peoples of the Pacific) simply as savages who could not be civilized; they possessed inferior mental, social, and ethical capabilities. This notion persisted in the West from the ancient Greeks until the father of modern anthropology, Edward Tylor, proposed that cultural innovations evolve and are diffused, quite separate from genetic makeup.[16] If genes are at the core of cultural systems, then "races" are predisposed to have either kings or democracies, to have many gods or one god, to be either agrarians or merchants.

There is no good evidence that genes predispose people to certain arts, morals, beliefs, or market activities. There are very few academics who hold to the genetic theory of race, but it persists in popular culture. As the notion of race has been contested, the "genetic explanation" of culture has been contested as well. And as long as the notion persists, Christian thinkers will need to respond to it.

---

16. Harris, *The Rise of Anthropological Theory*, 140–41.

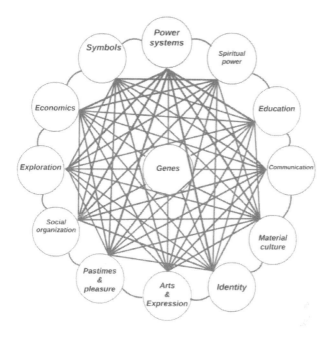

Figure 4: Cultural systems in the race/gene theory

The functionalist theory of culture

Since Edward Tylor's time (he was a contemporary of Darwin's), evolutionists have theorized that universal aspects of human behavior are tied to our survival. So politics, kinship, education, economies, and even religion must serve some sort of life-perpetuating function. If culture ensures that we can meet these basic needs, humans could not survive without culture. Anthropologists who have held this view are called functionalists, since they believe that the acceptable practices, beliefs, and actions shared by members of a society all serve a function.

Anthropologist Leslie White held this functionalist view for most of his career, arguing that "a custom is explained once we understand how it aids humans in adjustment to the material circumstances of everyday life."[17] Nowadays, however, we may not be able to quickly recognize the actual function of everything we do in culture. For instance, why do contemporary businessmen wear neckties? Or why do couples (in Western societies) kiss to show affection? Why must urban women wear high heels

17. Barrett, "The Paradoxical Anthropology of Leslie White," 988.

and lipstick in formal settings? Functionalists argue that if we look back far enough, we will discover that cultures are replete with vestiges of customs that "made sense" in the social context of our primordial ancestors. In colder climates, affluent men "tied" their necks with something like a fancy necktie, so the twenty-first century business suit is a vestige of something that used to have a function. Or Darwinists may argue that we kiss because in our evolutionary past, our distant bird ancestors fed each other by mouth. Women paint lips because in primordial times lips were a sign of fertility. And Neanderthals chose tall women over short women because they would survive longer, so modern women wear high heels to be more attractive.

In the middle of the twentieth-century British anthropologists de-emphasized the role that culture played in meeting individual needs, and instead focused on how culture perpetuated social structures (Hatch 1976, 201). So, whereas Malinowski focused on marriage as a means for fulfilling a biological need to have sex and procreate, social functionalists like Radcliffe-Brown and Durkheim looked at how social structures like exogamous marriage or monogamy strengthened political alliances or ensured food supplies.

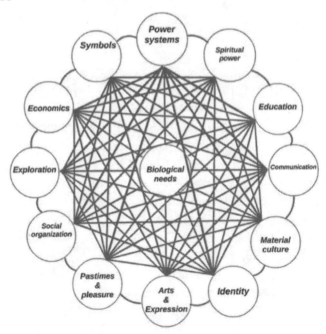

Figure 5: A functionalist's concept of cultural systems

Certainly, many of our cultural innovations do serve these basic needs in some way. Our political innovations keep us safe; social mores tell us how to get a spouse; economic systems ensure we will have food and shelter. The phenomenon of religion is a bit trickier; it has caused the greatest problem for modern functionalists. If religion is not essential for human survival, why is it ubiquitous? Elsewhere, I have given a synopsis of seven explanations offered by anthropologists for the pervasiveness of religion.[18] The theories are based on the presupposition that religion fulfills some sort of social or psychological function.

The difficulty with the biological-functionalist view of culture is that not all of the acceptable practices, beliefs, and actions shared by members of a society actually enable humans to meet the basic needs of life. Leslie White eventually took note of this with the American automobile industry. It is safer, cheaper, and better for the environment for us to use mass transit; but other parts of our economy and social life compel commuters to drive to work.[19] If cultural innovations serve a function, what do we do when competing innovations serve functions that are at odds with each other? Or when cultural innovations—which were supposed to meet functions—change drastically?[20]

The very complexity and multivocal struggle within culture causes us to doubt full-fledged functionalism. Consider marriage fidelity in the US. We have economic, social, and religious systems that reinforce heterosexual monogamy. But within our culture we also have social and entertainment systems that reinforce patterned behaviors of adultery, fornication, separation, etc. These competing voices are *all* part of our culture, but are at odds with each other. It would be impossible to trace such a complex and multivocal system to a utilitarian function. In short, in addition to meeting our needs, the competing customs within our culture cause us regular angst regarding the acceptable practices, beliefs, and actions shared by members of our society. As Paul said, "I do not understand what I do. For what I want to do I do not do, but what I hate I do" (Rom 7:15, NIV).

Likewise, social functionalism is contrary to the sensibilities of theists who see religious beliefs as propositional truth claims in and of themselves. We see religion as part and parcel of who we are as humans. But social functionalists see religion as a tool merely for lending legitimacy to social

18. Nehrbass, *Christianity and Animism in Melanesia*.

19. White, *The Concept of Cultural Systems*, 71.

20. Conn, *Eternal Word and Changing Worlds*, 103.

structures. For instance, social functionalists look to how myths are used to lend legitimacy to the power structures in society. However, in reality, people rarely describe their religious beliefs in terms how they meet the exigencies of social structures. It is far more common for insiders to take religious truth claims, rituals, and taboos at face value rather than see their religion as a method for social control.[21]

Functionalism serves as an excellent example of how naturalism (or materialism—a belief that there is no such thing as the supernatural) clouds our understanding of culture's purpose. An evolutionist's worldview requires that resilient traits (whether in body or mind) serve to ensure survival. Recent evolutionists have masterfully traced nearly every aspect of culture to our foundational need to perpetuate our "selfish genes" (Dawkins 1990). But if humans evolved from primates, we are severely over-programed. For survival, we need only enough culture to ensure that we can eat, find shelter, and reproduce sexually. However, the overwhelming evidence of human nature is that we not only seek sex but fulfilling marriages. We not only seek bananas and a roof over our heads, but enjoy reading Shakespeare (some of us do, anyway).[22] True, our cultural activities may serve a function, but this ultimate end is more about fulfillment than mere survival. We are most fulfilled when we are creating and socializing, not just eating and replicating.

The particularists' explanation

By this point, we have not adequately answered the question "Why does culture exist?" Idealism insightfully points out how worldview underlies many of our cultural systems, but can cause us to look for a worldview under every stone. Functionalism is a tidy theory that fits in the naturalistic worldview; but it fails to recognize the complexity and even irrationality of culture. One correction to functionalism is an approach in anthropology called particularism. Anthropologists such as Franz Boas have argued that customs are "fortuitous or random." Men wear neckties and women put on pumps and lipstick because there were endless possibilities available to humans for showing formality and status—and Westerners happened to innovate these particular conventions. Men may as well have been the ones to strap on high heels instead of women; and women may as well have worn

21. Hatch, *Theories of Man and Culture*, 247–51.

22. Cosgrove, *Foundations of Christian Thought*, 93, 141.

ties. In fact, cultural conventions regularly change and may even reverse. The significance of long or short hair on a man or woman is *particular* to time and space. It is not rational, and cannot be traced to a trajectory of evolution, nor to a utilitarian function. For particularists, while cultural norms help us make sense of our condition, they do not need to "make sense" themselves. We can record these customs in ethnographies, but cannot generate theories about humankind and our survival as a race based on these cultural particulars.

Particularists also emphasize the autonomy of culture; that is, culture is an entity *sui generis*, so our cultural norms cannot be reduced to biological or psychological needs. Boas's student A. L. Kroeber argued that culture was super-organic, taking on a life of its own.[23] At times, in fact, cultural innovations work against our biological needs (consider, for example, how a culture of promiscuity spreads viral diseases). Another of Boas's students, Ruth Benedict, theorized that culture had no basic sector; that is, the web of integrated cultural systems was so purposeless and autonomous, that there was no undergirding cultural system (neither worldview, nor biological functions, etc.) directing it.[24]

Instead, in this view (which has predominated American anthropology) cultures are all *particular* entities, with nearly endless permutations, influenced by the random process of diffusion and innovation.

23. Kroeber, "The Superorganic."
24. Hatch, *Theories of Man and Culture*, 127.

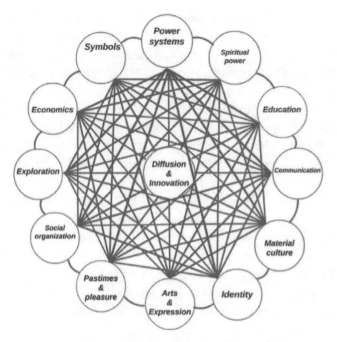

Figure 6: The particularists' concept of cultural systems

To make sure that you understand the difference between functionalism and particularism, try to determine whether the statements below come from a functionalist or particularist:

1. "While many cultures today give differing reasons for circumcising their boys, the custom is found in parts of the world because primitive peoples noticed the health benefits of removing the foreskin."

2. "Circumcision emerged in different cultures for different reasons. Other cultures use different types of body marking, and for different reasons."

The first statement is made by a functionalist, who assumes a utilitarian and material benefit for everything we do within culture. The second statement, made by a particularlist, shows the importance of studying each culture on its own terms. Jews circumcised because God told them to (Gen 17); some South Pacific Islanders circumcise their five- to seven-year-old boys because "it will make the boys tough." US-Americans circumcise boys because "everyone else does it."

The limitation of particularism is that there are not endless and random possibilities for human culture. This theory fails to recognize a long list of cultural universals (discussed in chapter 9). There are indeed commonalities in human cultures which result from humans bearing the *imagio dei*.

The semiotics/structuralist explanation

Structuralists view culture as the "symbolic expression of the human mind."[25] Some structures common to the human psyche require humans to organize themselves in society, to express themselves symbolically. Some theorists would place symbols at the core, as the basic cultural system that directs the rest of our cultural lives. Sapir and Whorf would have placed language at the core, since their research focus was on how language shapes cognition, worldview, and the rest of our lives.[26]

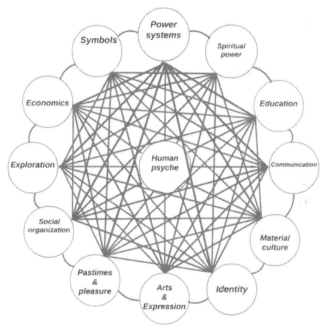

Figure 7: A structuralist/semiotic concept of cultural systems

25. Moore, *Visions of Culture*, 228.
26. Carroll, *Language, Thought and Reality*.

The inclusivist explanation

The inclusivist explanation of culture embodies all of the other theories listed above: culture is simply the acceptable practices, beliefs, and actions shared by members of a society, regardless of *why* or *how* those practices, beliefs, and actions came to be. This includes cultural innovations that are simply patterned for no other apparent reason; it includes those innovations which meet a psychological, social, or biological need; it includes innovations that are born out of deeply held worldviews; and it includes cultural patterns that help us decipher the symbolic messages around us to have a sense of shared meanings. So the inclusivist is not contra any of the previous theories; it realistically recognizes that there are many explanations for the various innovations we find in any society.

Figure 8: An inclusivist concept of cultural systems

The shortfall of the inclusivist definition is that it is atheoretical—it does not attempt to explain human nature. Is there a way to balance our biological needs, the structures of our human psyche, and to generate a theory of culture that has enough explanatory scope?

The Image Bearing explanation

By this point, I have described a number of limitations with the various explanations for why we have culture in the first place. The biological, psychological, and behaviorist explanations leave us with a very low view of culture—culture becomes a minimal need, or a necessary evil, rather than something which is rooted in the very nature of God. By extension these views leave us with a low view of humans, reducing them to functions and processes.[27]

This low view of culture has even been part of missiological thinking as we talk about "functional substitutes" as if cultural innovations are necessarily tied to biological or social functions. Rather than abandon these partially flawed theories, we can redeem them by understanding that God has indeed created humans with biological, psychological needs and culture is God's mechanism for meeting those needs. But if we accept that culture is about being in God's image, then it is much more than a vehicle for just meeting basic needs. Culture is about being human. So in order to answer "What is culture?" we first need to answer "What is a human?" or more precisely, "What does it mean to bear God's image?"

What does it mean to bear God's image?

When systematic theologians ask about the nature of human beings, they are exploring, "What does it mean to be in God's image?" Questions about the nature of humanity belong to a specific branch of systematic theology that is referred to as theological anthropology. Anthropologians (theologians of anthropology) focus primarily on what it means that humankind was created perfect, because God cannot create an imperfect creation.[28] Jesus, the perfect God-man, is the model for this inquiry. Anthropologians also look at the essence of humankind: the relationship between the human body, soul, spirit, and heart (or inner person).[29] In a broader sense, they are concerned with the role of humans in respect to creation at large, as well as questions of race, free will, sexuality, and economics.[30] An evangelical

---

27. Conn, *Eternal Word and Changing Worlds*, 117.
28. Grudem, *Systematic Theology*, 22.
29. Geisler, *Systematic Theology*, 50–53.
30. Cortez, *Theological Anthropology*.

theological anthropology recognizes that humans are tempted, but are morally accountable, and because of the fall, currently exist in an abnormal state.

There are substantive, relational, and functional aspects of being in the image (or shadow or reflection) (Hebrew: *tzelem*) and likeness (Hebrew: *demuth*) of God. Theologians have described three possible explanations for what it means that we are in God's likeness: 1) we share characteristics, like rationality; 2) we are relational, and in relationship with God; or 3) we function in ways that God does. I cannot develop each of these ideas here, but I will point out that my argument that bearing God's image means cultural behavior emphasizes the *functional* image. We function in ways that God does, as we rule, create, express, and relate to others, and even rest. Of course, functioning in God's image does not mean that we *mirror* his image. The cultural ramifications of the fall are that we function in cultural systems (economics, social structures, expression, etc.) but are immensely creative in the way we corrupt each of these systems.

If we employ any number of definitions of culture, it would be accurate to say that culture is rooted in the very nature of God. Culture is fundamentally about communicating, creativity, society, and norms. And the Trinity is eternally engaged in these activities we call culture. The Father, Son, and Holy Spirit communicate—though the Trinity is not confined to any particular language. God has tremendous (unlimited) creative potential. The Trinity has recently been described as a society of three, eternally existing in communion.[31] Jürgen Moltmann, who focused especially on the social aspect of the Trinity,[32] understood that this view of God would have political and social implications—that is, it would have to do with culture.[33] And God has norms of behavior we see reflected in his Law (Ps 119).

T. F. Torrance has masterfully tied the act of creation/culture, as well as its purpose and design, to the Trinity. "The very plurality of God serves as the basis for the unified and creative agency of God".[34] The Father, Son, and Holy Spirit fellowship in creative activity. Humans, as image-bearers, are mediators or stewards of the order of creation, and that is really what

31. Leech, *The Social God*.

32. Moltmann, *The Trinity and the Kingdom of God*.

33. Unfortunately, the metaphor of the Social Trinity can admittedly be hijacked by any social agenda. Specifically, socialists coopt the notion of a perfect heavenly society and mandate that the people of God, as representatives of the Trinity, must reconstruct this perfect society. See Chapman, "The Social Doctrine of the Trinity."

34. Flett, *Persons, Powers and Pluralities*, 18.

culture is about: "'The creative re-ordering of existence' . . . . This is by its very nature a socio-cultural activity."[35]

Granted, the eternally existing culture in the Trinity is not perfectly analogous to culture on earth. Our cultures seem to be inextricably linked to the environment in which we live, and it would require linguistic gymnastics to say that God exists in an environment.

If culture is rooted in God, is it necessarily good?

It is extremely important for World Changers to work out their understanding of the origin of culture, since this foundation affects our attitude toward our own culturally patterned beliefs and practices, as well as our approach toward other cultures. In my work as a missionary and professor, I have repeatedly heard people defend their own cultural norms with a simple argument about the divine origin of culture, which I will call the "God created culture hypothesis":

1. God created everything that exists.

2. Culture exists.

3. Therefore God created culture.

Once they have shown that God created culture, they can argue:

1. Everything God created is good.

2. God created culture.

3. Therefore culture is good.

The purpose of the argument is to understand our customs and beliefs (culture) as integral to how we were created—as if we cannot help but be "this way." As a missionary in the South Pacific, I observed this apparently flawless line of reasoning being used to defend such cultural norms as democracy, marriage of cousins, the use of magic and sorcery, and dietary practices. Islanders told me, "Magical rain stones exist, and God made everything, so he must have wanted us to use stones to cause rain." Or, "Everything God made is good, so it's good to eat bats." While some of these cultural norms may be good or at least acceptable, we know intuitively that not everything in culture is good, and that not all cultural

35. Ibid., 114.

norms were directly created by God. To take two examples, some cultures institutionalize inequity (e.g., the caste system in India) and some exhibit brutality (e.g., female genital mutilation in Somalia). How can the logic of the "God-created culture" hypothesis be corrected in light of this?

The first correction is to undercut premise (1), that God created everything. We can challenge that notion with another commonly accepted line of reasoning:

1. Sin exists within culture.

2. God did not create sin.

3. Therefore God did not create everything that exists within culture.

This conclusion does not prove that God *didn't* create culture; but it challenges the notion that "if something exists, God created it that way." Of course, the original "God created culture" hypothesis can be modified:

1. God created all *good* things.

2. There are good things in culture.

3. Therefore God created the good things in culture.

But we still need to examine this conclusion, since it is contrary to our experience. One man's "good" is another man's "awful." And nobody really thinks that the things we appreciate in culture (music, foods, rituals, pass times) really come directly from God. Consider these possibilities:

1. God created the good things in culture.

2A. Jazz is a good part of culture.

2B. Marrying your parallel cousin is a good part of culture.

2C. Democracy is a good part of culture.

2D. Eating grub worms is a good part of culture.

3. Therefore God made jazz music, marrying parallel cousins, democracy, and eating grub worms.

While you may not agree that jazz is good, millions of people worldwide do regard it as good. Often, Westerners think of marrying cousins as wrong, but tribal Christians point out that marriage between parallel cousins is not forbidden in the Pentateuch.[36] While some believe that

---

36. Leviticus 18 only forbids sexual relations with a man's stepchildren, aunt, sister, or

democracy is the biblical model for government, others would say that God did not create a certain government (other than, perhaps, the theocracy from the time of the exodus through the period of the judges). True, God made grub worms, but the jury is still out on whether or not they are good to eat. So while we can say with certainty that God is not responsible for the sinful parts of culture (e.g., widow emollition), we cannot say with certainty that God created the good parts of culture, since so many "good" patterns are objectively neutral. Eating cows, for instance, is seen as wrong in some cultures and good in others.

At this point, it would be good to remember a simple definition of culture that I offered earlier: the acceptable practices, beliefs, and actions shared by members of a society. The "God-created-culture" hypothesis makes God responsible for everything (perhaps everything good) shared by members of a society. This would include our music, diet, forms of government, social norms, etc. Most would agree that God did not directly make music; though he made us with the apparent universal desire to make music, and certainly gave us (some more than others) the ability to do so. God may have created the original language(s), but we cannot say that he created the modern languages. For example, the English language evolved over the past 700 years as the result of contact between French, Dutch, German, and other languages. But God gave us the capacity—and even the need—for speaking and modifying language. To provide another example, God did not create pizza but one could easily argue that God gave humans the raw materials for making pizza, the creativity, drive, and physiological capabilities for doing so—and even the disposition to assign a meal like pizza as more appropriate for informal meetings at night than for business meetings in the morning. The world's cultures are very much human creations. They are perhaps humankind's most impressive example of God-given creativity. But the capacity for creating culture is of divine origin. Put another way, God made humans to be culturative[37]—to exist within culture.

What is human nature?

But some will still find it disturbing to say that God did not create something—especially something as fundamental to the human race as culture!

half sister, daughter-in-law, sister-in-law, granddaughter, or step-granddaughter; Deuteronomy 25:5–6 commands a man to marry his sister-in-law if his brother dies.

37. Hegeman, *Plowing in Hope.*

Perhaps if we move away from the abstract notion of "culture" to the concrete reality of *cultures* (i.e., the acceptable practices, beliefs, and actions shared by members of a society) we can agree that God did not create *cultures*. At least, God did not create the cultures known to us today. But he has created humans with a fundamental need and capacity to be innovative within a cultural framework.

As we consider God-given culturative nature of humans, we need to visit God's original commands to humankind, which are called the "cultural mandate." In Genesis 1:28, God told the man and woman to "fill the earth and subdue it." Does that mean humans were created to worship, or to work? The answer is probably "yes—both." Worship is implied in Genesis 1–3, but the purpose of work is expressly stated: when God set Adam and Eve in the garden of Eden, he commanded them to work. True, the hard work by the "sweat of the brow" was a curse because of Adam and Eve's sin (Gen 3:19). But before the fall, God said, "Fill the earth and subdue it" (Gen 1:28, NIV). To subdue (Hebrew: *kabash*) is to take for the enjoyment and benefit.[38] Later, in Genesis 2:15, we see the first explanation of God's purpose for humans: "The Lord God took the man and put him in the Garden of Eden to work it and take care of it" (NIV). And Genesis 2:19 underscores this culturative activity—humans (expressly not God) created a foundational part of their culture (i.e., language) as Adam named the animals.

But why is this mandate to "fill, subdue . . . tend and guard" called the "cultural mandate"? Over time, the Hebrew word *'âbad* (tend) conflated the notions of "work," "serving," and "working," which can also refer to serving God.[39] Similarly, the Latin word *colere* simultaneously came to mean "worship" and "work." We get the English words "culture," "cultivate," and "cult, cultic" (related to worship) from a single Latin root.[40] So the term "cultural mandate" refers to when God mandated humankind to do culture (*colere*)—with all its connotations of worship and work. Working the land was a way of serving the Lord as was sacrifice or prayer. Unfortunately, English speakers have since forgotten the connection between these concepts of work and worship. "By the end of the nineteenth century, culture began to be used to denote more generally the whole way of life of a group or society" rather than to work or worship.[41]

---

38. Kline, *Kingdom Prologue*, 69; Risner, "A Theological Justification," 81.

39. J. Barber, *The Road from Eden*, 520.

40. Hegeman, *Plowing in Hope*, 14, 17.

41. Ibid., 14.

Why would work be so central to worship? Because work, like all of culture, stems from the nature of God. Banks has studied sixteen metaphors of God the worker in Scripture,[42] including God as composer and performer (Deut 31:19, Jer 48:31–32, 36), metalworker (Isa 1:24–26, Mal 3:2–3), potter (Job 10:8–9; Isa 31:9, 64:8), garment maker and dresser (Job 10:10–12, 29:14), gardener and orchardist (Ezek 31:8–9), farmer (Hos 10:11) and winemaker (Isa 5:7), shepherd and pastoralist (Ps 23:1–4, 77:20; Mic 2:12–13), tentmaker and camper (Exod 26; Job 9:8), a builder and architect (Pro 8:27–31, 24:3; Job 38:4–7; Isa 28:16–17, 54:11–12).[43]

But even if there were not linguistic evidence linking work and worship, we can see a metanarrative in Scripture that when God created humans, their task was more than the direct acts of worship, such as singing hymns and expounding Scripture. If you are like me, this understanding of work/worship excites you—you were created to work: to create, build, dream, explore, change, solve, serve, and even rule! While prayer and praise are essential to a life of worship, so is the work of filling the earth, ruling over it, tilling it, and guarding it. And ever since Adam and Eve, humans have creatively worked out their own cultural norms for doing those tasks. Culturally patterned social systems enable us to fill the earth through kinship associations. Culturally transmitted economic systems have to do with tending the earth, harnessing its resources and redistributing them. The various cultural expressions in arts and architecture are examples of our culturative nature. We take Earth's resources and rearrange them in ways that make sense within our own culture. Why else would God have put that gold, bdellium, and onyx in the garden (Gen 2:12), except for Adam and Eve to excavate the minerals and make something of them?[44] The garden of Eden was not the absence of culture, but the beginning of culture.[45]

We may uncritically assume that since the first humans were in a primitive garden, we are "meant to live in nature." This notion is actually influenced by evolutionary biology, which teaches that humans were hunter-gathers for hundreds of thousands of years, and have not lived in civilization long enough to adapt well to advanced societies.[46] So, the reasoning goes, modern humans have a continual angst, since we are "de-

42. Banks, *God the Worker*.

43. Stevens, *The Other Six Days*, 113.

44. Crouch, *Culture Making*, 165.

45. Van Til, *The Calvinistic Concept of Culture*, 139.

46. Brown, *Human Universals*, 100.

signed" (by evolutionary forces) to live in small bands, yet we find ourselves in cosmopolitan settings. However, in reality, it seems that we humans are hardly suited for the sort of lifestyle the in which the animal kingdom exists; and given the cultural mandate, it would be a tremendous abdication of our obligations to God to return permanently to the garden. God told us to make something of the world! We may enjoy trips to the wilderness for fishing and camping, but even folks who live in the most undeveloped nations rely on their settled hamlets for purpose, cooking, and shelter.[47] We were made to enjoy the garden and the city—even the Walmarts and McDonald's. Culture is God's original plan for humanity.[48]

And our culturative nature has caused us to endlessly innovate religions, ethical systems, ideas about beauty, the self, and the use of time and space. In chapter 9 I will explain that humans universally function within social, ethical, economic, and political systems. These systems vary greatly, but we all have an innate dependency on each of them. By arguing that God created humans to be culture dependent, I mean that God gave humans the ability to respond to our environment, to innovate, and to adopt the innovations of others. Put another way, God gave us the ability to create culture. We do this all the time—passively as we respond to changes in the environment, and actively as we innovate and spread these innovations. Note that while this view is similar to particularism (i.e., cultures are the product of endless creativity) the difference is that the "Image Bearing" theory recognizes that God is the model of our cultural activity; but our cultures are also fallen, and need to be restored.

This argument for the human origin of cultures (as opposed to the "God Creates Culture" hypothesis) should be very freeing for us, rather than disturbing or controversial. It should allow us to stop holding so tightly to so many of our culturally patterned behaviors and beliefs as if we were bound to them. As the antiquated usage of culture/cultivate implied, the acceptable practices, beliefs, and actions shared by members of a society—culture—is cultivated in us; it is not innate. And since our culturally patterned systems are not innate, they can change, and appear in tens of thousands of permutations across the globe.

How, then, can we summarize an evangelical explanation for the origin of culture? I propose that we abandon the syllogisms all together, and focus instead on some propositions:

47. Crouch, *Culture Making*, 111.

48. Ibid., 175.

1. God created humans with the capacity to interact with their environment in a way that will cause them to flourish.

2. Since it was God's intention that humans will be culture dependent (culturative), our requirement for cultural activity (politics, economics, religion, material needs, socializing) is good.

3. God created humans with innate abilities, which include the ability to govern, produce and distribute resources, form associations (including marriage), and express themselves symbolically with arts and language.

4. Sometimes the human innovations within a culture are good, and sometimes they are sinful. These human societies kept getting things wrong—wrong in kinship, wrong in economics, wrong in worldview— which is why God kept sending prophets and eventually his son to correct them.

Figure 9 (below) organizes cultural innovations around the central idea that humans, as image bearers—are culture creators.

Figure 9: "Image Bearing" explanation of culture

What is the eternal value of culture?

If culture is fundamental to God's nature, then how much continuity is there between cultures (earthly ones) and heaven? To deny the continuity between creation and the new creation is to risk falling into the sort of dualism that pits earth against heaven: If you see this world as unworthy of being perpetuated, you probably see this world as evil and the next as good. Christian thinkers have tried to steer clear of dualism, though sometimes they slip into it. If creation is good, and culture is practically inextricable from creation, we must understand there is a high degree of continuity between this creation (culture and all) and the next.

But this raises the question, in what way will there be culture(s) in heaven? Some have argued that there is biblical evidence of what we know of culture in heaven, based on some enigmatic verses in Revelation:

- "Their works do follow them" (Rev 14:13, KJV).
- "The nations will walk by its light, and the kings of the earth will bring their splendor into it" (Rev 21:24, NIV).

Crouch has suggested that what we are seeing in Revelation 14 and 21 is a redeemed or transformed version of culture.[49] This interpretation allows us to maintain a high view of culture; however, the notion of cultural continuity between earth and heaven in these verses is still fuzzy. What sorts of works will follow us into heaven? What splendor will these kings be bringing into the New Jerusalem? And will they really be kings in heaven? These two verses in a highly symbolic book like Revelation do not provide enough support for the notion that earthly cultures will be transferred into heaven. But there is certainly ample evidence in Scripture that our cultural nature is eternal—we will always be working, creating, ruling, socializing, and speaking. Therefore, we will certainly have culture! Our non-corporeal but nonetheless culturative selves will engage in arts and singing and dancing and feasting.

There is another image of people "from every nation, tribe, people and language" in Scripture (Matt 24:14; Rev 7:9, NIV) which gives some erroneous the impression that there is ethnocultural continuity between earthly cultures and eternity. The "nations" are apparently represented in heaven, in these verses. An interpretive problem immediately presents itself: Which nations? Does this mean only nation-states recognized by the

49. Ibid., 169–170.

United Nations? What about nations that have gone extinct, like the Otto-man Empire and Babylon, or nations that have reinvented themselves, like Egypt and Greece? What about nations that are yet to be born? It is quite problematic to link *ethne* (translated as "nation" in the passage above) to modern nation-states.

Some think they have cleverly solved this problem by explaining that the Greek *ethne* should be rendered "ethnic group" rather than "nation."[50] Unfortunately, rather than solving a problem, this interpretation further reinforces an error in popular evangelical theology of culture. Think of the difficulties in interpreting *ethne* as ethnic groups: Is the child of an African American father and Korean mother a member of a distinct *ethne*—yet another *ethne* that must be evangelized and will be included in the "all cultures in heaven" list? Would reaching a Korean-African American be considered as one new *ethne* or two or three *ethne*? What about people like Tiger Woods—"Cabalasians" who have numerous ethnicities in their background (as, in fact, we all do)? Are they included as a distinct *ethne*? Are Caucasian Americans in the twenty-first century—with the innumer-able combinations of Scandinavian, Mediterranean, and Eastern European ancestry—to be understood as a single *ethne*? If we extend *ethne* to mean "however people identify themselves ethnically" or "all possible ethnic per-mutations" then we are left with so many possibilities that we may as well just say "all people." In fact, that is exactly what many theologians conclude: we must interpret "every tribe and nation" as a metaphor for many people from all over the world.[51]

This way of looking at *ethne* may seem like splitting hermeneutical hairs, but it has profound implications for an evangelical theology of cul-ture in the twenty-first century. It should radically change the way we think about race and ethnicity. Ethnic boundaries are gradients and porous, not defined and static. Now, even if the Greek term *ethne* means "all people," in *practical terms*, I would still maintain the conventional missiological wisdom that the best way to reach "many people from all over the world"

---

50. USCWM, "Who are the Unreached?"

51. Some scholars have suggested that *ethne* in Matthew refers only to Gentiles. There are times when context does indicate this rendering. However, in these eschatological verses, the meaning seems to be extended to all people (see Meier, "Nations or Gentiles"). Note that *ethne* is rendered twelve different ways, depending on context, in popular Eng-lish translations: nation(s), people, country (or countries), province, Gentiles, heathens, pagans, peoples, world, foreigners, mankind, race (see Muthuraj, "The Meaning of Eth-nos and Ethne")—but *never* as "ethnicity."

is to focus on their self-identified ethnic groups! But those lines are always shifting and are contested.

SUMMARY

After examining theories of culture, I have argued that while there is some explanatory scope for the functionalist, idealist, structuralist, and particularist theories, the only comprehensive explanation for why being human requires being culturative is that culture is rooted in the nature of God. He creates, rules, communicates, and is social, and he made us to do the same. At this point, as we work out a biblical theology of culture, we still need to explore what culture was like for humans at the time of creation—from Eden to Babel. That is the subject of the next chapter.

REFLECTION AND REVIEW QUESTIONS

1. What were the weaknesses of the genetic theory of culture?

2. In what way do you see work and worship connected?

3. If you had to choose between biological or social functionalism, idealism, structuralism, or particularism as the primary instigator of human culture, which would you choose?

4. If World Changers saw their culturative nature as part of bearing God's image, how would that change the way they interact with their world?

CHAPTER 5

God and the origin of ethnicity and culture

A CENTRAL THESIS OF this book is that to be in God's image is to function in cultural ways; God is not a-cultural. Even if no human cultures ever existed, we know that the persons of the Trinity have been expressive, social, creative, productive, and so on. In the past century, anthropologists and missiologists have debated whether it is possible to speak of culture as an entity *sui generis*, existing eternally somehow in the world of ideals, beyond human existence, regardless of whether it manifests in actual *cultures*. For instance, language cannot exist as an abstract form, it only exists as *languages*. Likewise, there is no abstract eternal politics—only actual human political systems. And the same is true for social organization, music, art, etc. So it may seem equally strange to conceive of culture in general as existing as an eternal "ideal" outside of actual cultures. But what if we locate culture within the character of the Trinity? Then culture does exist outside of temporal, human existence; albeit not as an abstract. It is eternally a lived reality as God communicates, acts, rules, and creates. The realization that God is cultural in nature significantly elevates our view of culture; however, it also raises questions about whether God endorses a particular culture. Or are they all relative? Is God so transcendent that he is above all cultures? Or so immanent that he is found in all of them? Rooting culture in God's nature requires us to work out a theology of cultural diversity and cultural pluralism. We will address these questions below.

IS GOD ABOVE CULTURE?

Missiologist Charles Kraft tried to address the problems of ethnocentrism, relativism, and the transcendence and immanence of God by referring to God as supra-cultural.[1] For Kraft, God is above human culture, but he works *through* culture. However, even though Kraft has a high view of culture, he may not have realized that by referring to God as supra-cultural, he denied the continuity between God's creativity and our own as culture makers.[2] In short, Kraft failed to recognize that it is precisely our cultural activity—the way humankind "shapes and crafts the already-existing world" —that epitomizes how we uniquely bear God's image.[3] I believe that if Kraft would agree with Crouch's definition of culture as "making something of the world" then he would agree that God is absolutely cultural! True, if we limit our understanding of culture to the "non-biologically transmitted heritage of man" (viz. Tylor) or "learned behavior patterns," and "glasses with distorting lenses [which] filter through this perceptual screen" (viz. Keesing and Keesing) then we will see God as supra-cultural rather than culturative. But to root culture *a priori* in human society is to begin with a low view of culture—and to miss out on all that God has planned for our lives through culture.

But what Kraft meant by calling God supra-cultural was really that God does not endorse or embody a super-culture (on Earth, anyway) that is normative for all times and places. Instead, God has adapted his prescriptive linguistic and behavioral patterns over time—even as recorded in the Bible. Take circumcision, for example. God mandated the custom for the Israelites (Gen 17) and then released the Christian Gentiles from the rite (1 Cor 7:19; Gal 5:2–11). God provided for the Israelites to be governed by their own judges and kings, by foreign governments, and later by more foreign governments, and finally, much later, became a modern nation-state. Or consider divorce: God forbade it (Mal 2:16), and yet allowed for some exceptions (because our hearts are hard—Matt 19:8); he created man to take one wife (Gen 2:24), yet instituted levirate marriage (Deut 25:25–26).

So we see what missionary-anthropologist Eugene Nida called "relative relativism in the Bible."[4] This leniency regarding cultural norms has caused theologians to be careful about ascribing any particular culture (or culture in general) to God. Sixty years after Nida's work was published, the term "relativism" has taken on such confusing or negative connotations that Nida may easily be misunderstood. Nida was simply agreeing with

---

1. Kraft, *Christianity in Culture*, 123.
2. Crouch, *Culture Making*.
3. Hoekema, *Created in God's Image*; Risner, "A Theological Justification," 80.
4. Kraft, *Christianity in Culture*, 128.

Hebrews 1:1: "In the past God spoke to our ancestors through the prophets at many times and in various ways" (NIV). God has not been limited by language, societal norms, or governments. He has worked through any and all ethnolinguistic cultures. But it is not as if God uses culture mechanically or impartially as a tool the way a carpenter uses a hammer or saw. Rather, God works through culture because the creativity, expression, governance, and socializing are fundamental to who he is as a relational, communicating Being.

DID GOD CREATE AN ORIGINAL CULTURE, AND WAS IT THE IDEAL CULTURE?

A strand of Christian thinkers have historically assumed that after God created Adam and Eve, the two of them lived within the linguistic, cognitive, and social constructs of the Israelites as recorded in the time of the patriarchs Abraham, Isaac, Jacob, and Joseph. Since the book of Genesis was originally written in Hebrew, some have imagined Adam speaking in Hebrew, giving the impression that Hebrew was in fact the first language, and even the language of God. (Note that while the Gospels were written in Greek, Jesus and his disciples neither spoke Hebrew nor Greek on a regular basis, but Aramaic. So it seems that there is more than one divine language! Maybe there is more than one divine culture!) Certain medieval rabbis and theologians were so convinced of the Hebrew-Adamic link that they theorized newborns were born knowing Hebrew, and subsequently lost their ability to speak the language as they were socialized into the language and culture of their parents. (We now know that children would not speak *any* language if they were denied contact with speakers of a language.)

Discovering this original language/culture was a dominant theme in early British anthropology and linguistics. To give an odd example, in the seventeenth century, John Webb, a member of the Royal Society, built a case for Chinese as the "purest version of Adamic Hebrew" since the Empire of China had remained so isolated for millennia.[5] Today, the theory of Hebrew as the *ursprache* (first language) has been largely abandoned.[6] But if we are to connect human cultural activity with God's cultural nature, we must at least puzzle over these questions.

---

5. Livingstone, *Adam's Ancestors*, 10.
6. Keil, *Biblical Commentary on the Old Testament*, 175.

To connect the first culture described in the Bible to creation is to tacitly endorse that archetypical culture, however it is defined—and wherever it is located—as *the* right culture. Africans, Pacific Islanders, Chinese, and Germans, Swedes, Ethiopians, Belgians, Icelanders, etc., all lay claim to the oldest, most unadulterated linguistic, religious, and cultural capital of the original man and woman.[7] But we need to keep in mind a few observations which challenge these proto-cultural folk theories:

- Earthly languages change all the time—in matter of years, not centuries. If Adam's language was the *ursprache*, by the time of Noah, the world's languages had evolved over numerous generations to the point that nobody remembered how Adam spoke. Further, we do not know how similar Noah's descendants' language was to that of Adam, and after Babel, we have no clue what language Terah, Abraham's father, spoke.

- Cultural norms change within each of our lifetimes. Ideals about matchmaking, occupations, and other forms of expressive culture (like those found in Gen 4:21, 22) are constantly challenged and re-invented. That's the nature of culture.

- Given the constantly shifting nature of language and culture, how could we pinpoint a certain time in the past and select *that* particular time as the heavenly endorsed culture?

- If we were to recover this hypothetical heavenly endorsed culture, we (because of our cultural nature) would have changed it so drastically within ten years, we would need to re-recover it.

- The only constant we see over time is our need to constantly change our culture—to make it anew.

- Cultures were not homogenous as the books of the Bible were being written. Which Israelite culture is normative? The time of the patriarchs? Israel in slavery? Israel in exile? Israel as a conquering nation? Israel as an institutionalized monarchy? Israel as a disintegrating kingdom? Israel as it was oppressed by Assyria, Babylon, and Rome? The political and social organization changed dramatically, as did the material culture of the Israelites, over two millennia as the Bible was being written. Like all cultures, the biblical culture was continually in flux.

7. Hodgen, *Early Anthropology*, 306; Livingstone, *Adam's Ancestors*, 116.

Nonetheless, Eden, with its society of two, was culturally homogenous. Or did it have culture at all? Some Christian thinkers assume that culture has its roots in the fall, not in Eden. Bradshaw, for example, conceived of culture as only necessary *after* the fall. Clothing, economics and politics were only necessary to provide for human flourishing once the garden of Eden was no longer a viable habitat.[8] So *kosmos,* for Bradshaw, is fallen human culture.[9]

But Adam and Eve had social structures with status, roles, and rituals. Their lives were guided by ethics (don't touch the tree, for starters—Gen 3:3), and worked within an agrarian economy. The pre-fall society certainly had language and ritual. And God's command to Adam and Eve was to go out and create more of these cultural innovations. So there is a sense in which God is responsible not only for the culture-dependent nature of humans, but apparently for an actual primal Edenic culture in which the first humans lived. What language did they speak? What were their social norms? It may seem pointless to speculate about Adam and Eve's original language and culture, but the ramifications are quite profound. Judeo-Christian movements throughout history have felt that if they could grasp the pre-fall culture, we could indeed live pious lives on Earth. For example, some argued that if man and woman would live according to the proper order of creation, relationships would be harmonious; or if we would stop building cities and return to a lifestyle in Edenic nature, we would be more fulfilled. The reasoning seems to go like this:

1. God created Adam and Eve with a specific culture.

2. What God creates is perfect and timeless.

3. Adam and Eve's culture was that of the Ancient Near East through the time of the patriarchs.

4. Therefore God intends for us to live like Adam and Eve: simply, as agrarians and herders, speaking Hebrew, arranging marriages, and so on.

In contrast, this book argues that while God certainly did create Adam and Eve with an original culture in Eden, his plan was not for that culture

8. Bradshaw, *Change Across Cultures,* 71.

9. Note that elsewhere, Bradshaw uses *kosmos* to refer to all of creation (see ibid., 171).

to remain static or for it to be normative. Instead, he made humans to be constantly reinventing culture in endless varieties.

IS CULTURAL DIVERSITY GOD'S PLAN?

The amount of literature on promoting multiculturalism, even within the Christian workplace,[10] reveals the value that we are increasingly seeing in diversifying (culturally). Unfortunately, not everyone sees cultural diversity as a plus. Having taught on culture to numerous audiences around the world, I have encountered two objections to "diversity." First, some people come from fairly monocultural backgrounds and are either afraid of other cultures or even presuppose an amount of cultural superiority. "They should just learn English," or "We have more freedoms here in America" are typical statements from monocultural folks. A subculture in the US holds to "American exceptionalism" (see chapter 2), conceiving of the US as particularly and uniquely blessed above all other nations.[11]

Some detractors of "diversity" are not against multiculturalism per se, but see diversity as an agenda which is hollow or self-defeating. They mainly point to research that indicates that cultural heterogeneity reduces interpersonal trust and causes people to disengage from society.[12] The more that civilizations meet each other, the more clashes there will be, as a result of differences in ideology and religion.[13]

Part of the ambivalence evangelicals have about multiculturalism comes from our interpretation of the tower of Babel in Genesis 11. Because the confusing of languages and subsequent scattering of nations appears to be a punishment, Christians may tend to paint multiculturalism in a negative light. Our argument may look like this:

1. Linguistic and cultural diversity did not exist at the time of Noah's family (because there were only eight people) and in immediately subsequent generations.

2. Cultural diversity was a result of the sin at Babel.

---

10. Priest and Nieves, *This Side of Heaven*; Roembke, *Building Credible Multicultural Teams*; Silzer, *Biblical Multicultural Teams*.

11. B. Carson, *America the Beautiful*; Rauchway, *Blessed Among Nations*.

12. Putman, "E Pluribus Unum."

13. Huntington, *The Clash of Civilizations and the Remaking of World Order*; Rundle and Steffen, *Great Commission Companies*, 78.

3. God does not will sin.

4. Punishment, as the result of sin, is not God's original plan.

5. Therefore, cultural diversity was not God's original plan.

However, remember that God's problem with the tower of Babel was hubris (Gen 11:4), and his *solution* was diversity in location, land, and subsequently culture.

Sometimes we build a theology of cultural diversity by arguing that diversity is extended to heaven. The argument is mostly based on the book of Revelation, in passages like Revelation 7:9–10, which say heaven includes "every nation, tribe, people and language" (NIV). We reason erroneously as follows:

1. Cultural diversity exists in heaven.

2. God's will is done in heaven.

3. Therefore it is God's will (and not an accident) that cultural diversity exists.

4. If it is God's will for diversity to exist, and God's will is carried out, then diversity will continue to exist.

However, as I showed in a previous section, it is asking too much of the passage to take "nation, tribe, people and language" as proof of cultural diversity in heaven. The emphasis here is more on the fact that God's grace is extended to all of humanity rather than on the eternal permanence and static identification of ethnic categories.[14] The passage shows that God's promise to make Abraham the father of many nations (Gen 15:5, 32:12) has been fulfilled.[15]

So if we are to build a theology of diversity, it is more advisable to find evidence of cultural diversity through the Old and New Testament than to use Revelation 7:9–10 as a proof text. Even a cursory reading of the Psalms shows God's interest in people from all backgrounds and languages (see Ps 2:8, 33:12, 67:1–7). In fact, numerous theologies of mission have shown God's interest in all people groups throughout the Old Testament.[16] Despite Jesus' enigmatic argument that he was sent to the Jews, his ministry was

---

14. Trial, *Exegetical Summary of Acts.*

15. Hughes, *The Book of Revelation*; Mounce, *The Book of Revelation.*

16. Köstenberger and O'Brien, *Salvation to the Ends of the Earth*; Richardson, *Eternity in their Hearts*; Verkuyl, "The Biblical Foundation."

notably multicultural. The plot of the book of Acts is that the church will expand from Jerusalem to the ends of the earth (Acts 1:8). The historical narrative moves along as God's grace extends to the southernmost part of the known world, Ethiopia (Acts 8:26–30), and then to the Greeks, ethnic minorities in the Mediterranean, and on to Rome. Diversity is a major theme in Acts, including (and often blurring the lines between) linguistic, ethnic, and religious diversity.[17]

This multiculturalism is in the DNA of the church; as Andrew Walls put it, the cross-cultural process has been the lifeblood of the church.[18] Some theologians have even suggested that cultural diversity is rooted in the Trinity.[19] A revised, exegetically substantiated line of reasoning would look like this:

1. Cultural diversity on earth is a reflection of what it means to be in God's image.

2. God's working out of salvation history has always been multicultural, because all people are in God's image.

3. Because it was God's will to create people in his multicultural image, multiculturalism is God's will.

To summarize my answer to the question about whether diversity is God's plan, we must recognize that there are several practical reasons for intentionally embracing multiculturalism. First, the world is on an inexorable trajectory of multiculturalism, so those who fight it will be left behind. Second, there is a synergy created by fusing the value orientations of other cultures, and on drawing from the rich wisdom of various cultures' pasts, which would be missing in a monocultural workplace. Last, an authentic recognition of diversity is only possible when one understands the character of God, who is the author of humanity in all its diversity.[20]

---

17. Barreto, *Ethnic Negotiations*.
18. Walls, *The Cross-Cultural Process in Christian History*, 67.
19. Campbell, *A Multitude of Blessings*.
20. Parler, *Things Hold Together*, 218.

DID RACE COME FROM NOAH'S SONS, OR BABEL— AND WHY DOES IT MATTER?

Granted, God created Adam and Eve to function in ways that bear his cultural image. But how did the single race and culture of this primeval society of two ripen into a world with such diverse cultures and ethnic physical features? Folk explanations for the *ethne* have been offered for millennia, and as Livingstone pointed out: "These questions had the profoundest implications for everything from the cultural politics of human anatomy to biblical hermeneutics, from the justification of the slave system to the regulation of republics."[21] Here, I will limit the discussion to four theories of the origin of the *ethne* that have been formed by Judeo-Christian thinkers over the years. The earliest (and most easily refuted) theory was the theory that ethnic diversity comes from Noah's sons.

Noah's Sons theory

Before historical linguistics burgeoned as an academic field, some Caucasian scholars[22] as well as some African American ones[23] conjectured that there were three "great races:" Mongoloid, Caucasoid, and Negroid. Other taxonomies had four, five, or ten racial groupings,[24] which were imagined to have firmly defined boundaries (See Figure 10). Or, if the boundaries were fuzzy, the races at least embodied prototypical characteristics. For example, Europeans would have agreed on prototypically African-looking hair, or Asian-looking eyes. Note that many other "great races" were arbitrarily ignored in this model: there was often no category for Amerindians, Polynesians, Western Asians, North Africans, or Dravidians from South India, to name just a few. There was a prototypical "Mongoloid" Asian race, but just who fit this category was unclear. Were Japanese, or Koreans, or Southeast Asians also "Mongoloid?" What about Kazaks and Uzbeks? If they were Mongoloid, were they thoroughly located within this boundary, or at the periphery? Which Chinese fit the description of Mongoloid? Just the majority Han people, or also the hundreds of ethnic minority groups in the region?

21. Livingstone, *Adam's Ancestors*, 79.

22. Morton, *Crania Americana*.

23. Delany, *Principia of Ethnology*, in Livingstone, *Adam's Ancestors*, 185.

24. Paris, "Race," 22.

Figure 10: Early conception of races as distinctive categories

By some strange rule of association, it was popularly imagined in previous centuries that if there were three races, these must be descended from the three children of Noah: Shem, Ham, and Japheth. By the seventh century, this was part of popular culture, as seen in a "T-O map" drawn by Bishop Isidore. The map depicts the known continents at the time—Africa, Asia, and Europe—with the names of Noah's children on the continents. Shem is in Asia, Japheth in Europe, and Ham in Africa.[25] This folk etymology of the origin of ethnicities is still articulated by some today.[26] And always in this schema, Ham is the one in Africa, cursed with black skin either for the sin of Cain[27] or for the sin of Ham's son Canaan (who sinned by seeing his father's "nakedness" in Gen 9:22).

There are numerous problems with the "Noah's sons" theory. First, the biblical story of Noah contains nothing about the origins of ethnicity. Second, as I discussed earlier, there is no biological evidence for three prototypical races. Humans have an endless variety of physical features. The most disturbing part of the theory is what Livingstone[28] has termed the "bio-theology" that develops out of this hermeneutic. It suggests that pigmentocracy is God's plan.

Polygenetic theory

While the typical reading of Genesis infers a monogenetic lineage through Adam, a number of thinkers have proposed polygenesis over the years in order to answer the question of race and ethnicity: if humans are so

25. Livingstone, *Adam's Ancestors*, 6.

26. Abrams, "The Origin of Race"; and http://www.bible–history.com/maps/2–table–of–nations.html.

27. Livingstone, *Adam's Ancestors*, 121; Lumeah, "Curse on Ham's Descendants."

28. Livingstone, *Adam's Ancestors*, 197.

different across the globe, can they really share a common ancestor? For early Christian thinkers, polygenesis meant that the Bible only told the story of the (usually white) descendants of Adam, while other races—no less created by God—are not "one blood" with Adam's line. This theory had varying political, theological, and intellectual ramifications. For some, polygenesis proscribed interracial marriage, and legitimated slavery and the caste system, as each (supposedly homogenous) race was suited for a certain geographic and social space. For others, polygenesis harmonized science and theology. And as naturalists began to publish findings about the geological record, theologians found difficulties with explaining how the human race could only have been around for only a few thousand years, as the lineage of Adam to Jesus seemed to put Adam in the fifth millennia BC. Polygenesis seemed to offer an explanation for the appearance of many races suddenly, miraculously, 6,000 years ago.

One form of polygenesis, argued by Samuel Kneeland and Charles Hampton Smith,[29] uses the same three great races theory as the Noah's Sons theory: God created three original couples: Caucasian, Mongoloid, and Negroid. However, Kneeland and Smith argued these races emerged separately, and long before Adam's day. So this differs significantly from the Noah's Sons theory in that its reliance on polygenesis undermines the "unity of humankind" in Acts 17:26. Some pre-Modern thinkers were unsure whether the inhabitants of places outside of Europe were even human beings. Did they have souls? If they were not descended from Adam, were they cursed as Adam was, after the fall?

Note that an acceptance of polygenesis also requires Noah's flood to be local, not global. A global flood would mean that all humans—of all ethnicities—alive today stem from the line of Adam's descendant Noah; but polygenesis conceives of the separately created "great races" as having endured over the millennia despite Noah's (local) flood.

As with the other theories of race, proponents of polygenesis turn to historical linguistics for evidence. William Lane's taxonomy of language included two protolanguages, one primeval, and the other Semitic. If the two protolanguages have no common ancestry, the theory went, then humans must have separate origins.[30] Lane (ethnocentrically and erroneously) portrayed all non-Semitic languages as monosyllabic, and therefore simplistic, and therefore inferior.

29. Ibid., 97–99.
30. Ibid., 102–103.

So while some thinkers were trying to build a taxonomy for "great races" that descended from Adam, others solved the question of the origin or ethnolinguistic peoples by relegating Africans (and later natives of the Americas and the Pacific) to non-Adamic or even nonhuman status.[31] In the eighteenth and nineteenth century, proponents of polygenesis considered monogenesis to be a politically motivated polemic, rather than an exegetical or theological argument. If Africans shared a common ancestor with Anglos, then the slave trade was inhumane. We can see that at times both proponents of monogenesis and polygenesis have used a theology of race and ethnicity to promote their political agendas.

Gradual dispersal theory

Today, Christian thinkers, along with almost all anthropologists[32] and linguists (not to mention biologists) reject the "three race" typology. It is now nearly universally asserted that there is one human race, with fuzzy boundaries between the thousands of ethnolinguistic groups. There is no prototypical Asian, or Caucasian, or African. This is even more the case in the twenty-first century, when more and more children of multiethnic couples find it impossible to describe their race. For example, *National Geographic* reported on the millions of US-Americans in the 2010 census who fit the "other" category.[33] Among them were a man who identified himself as Blasian: half African American, half Korean; another was a woman who was half Chinese, a quarter Swedish, and a quarter French, but checked the box for "Chinese."

To be far more accurate about race and ethnicity, we may depict the singular human race as a gradient, with blurry boundaries and no particular center (see Figure 11). Does this mean we should do away with the notion of ethnicity all together—since ethnic identity is fluid, contested, and constantly changing? If there is no prototypical Asian ethnicity—only contested ideas about what it means to be Asian—does that mean there is no such thing as Asian? Not at all. Ethnicity continues to embody shared meanings and identities for people around the globe, so we need to continue to understand how it shapes people's behavior and identity.

31. Ibid., 26–51.
32. Smay and Armelagos, "Galileo Wept."
33. Funderburg, "The Changing Face of America."

Figure 11: Ethnicity is a fuzzy set, with obvious differences but no clear boundary

If we move beyond the notion of fixed boundaries of race, then how can theology inform our understanding of the origins of ethnic diversity? Within orthodoxy, there are really only two possibilities:

1. The physical features, languages, and cultures are the result of slight variations in the human physique and culture due to isolation of gene pools[34] after God confused the languages at Babel.

2. God created physical features, languages, and embedded cultures to some degree miraculously, either immediately after Noah, or else at Babel or at some point afterwards.

This first explanation, which I will call the Gradual Dispersal theory, has been around since 1788, offered by Samuel Smith in *Essay on the causes of the variety of Complexion and figure in the Human Species*.[35] Human skin tones, hair, nose shapes, etc., have undergone slight changes just as the languages and cultures have, since societies began migrating from Babel. Tribes migrated, according to language, and their gene pool became isolated for a time, allowing certain recessive traits to become emphasized, or allowing genetic changes to flourish. Now, we know that languages change rapidly, but it is debatable how quickly features like melanin levels can change in a period of several thousand years. So the Gradual Dispersal theory of ethnicity may require a human race to have been created much earlier than the Young Earth creationists hold to.

But how much do we actually know about the dispersal of the ethnolinguistic peoples at the time of Babel? Very little, it turns out. From Genesis 10, we read that Ham's descendants went along the Mediterranean

34. And other popular possible factors include the influence of the latitude, humidity, diet, intermarriage, etc.

35. Livingstone, *Adam's Ancestors*, 74.

and into North Africa. The Cushites migrated to the Arabian Peninsula, Egypt, Ethiopia, and the Sudan. Mizram's descendants traveled to North Africa and Crete. The descendants of Shem went to the Persian Gulf, Persia, and the Arabian Peninsula. Folk explanations of the "table of nations" extrapolate these antiquated terms, and proceed to interpret the text with all sorts of modern ethnic and national labels, locating modern ethnolinguistic groups in certain regions using modern geopolitical labels. However, we need to read Genesis 10 and 11 together to get an idea whether the "table of nations" provides an explanation for the geographic distribution of *ethne* in post-Babel times and on to today.

First, it is difficult to tell whether the Table of Nations in Genesis 10 happens chronologically before or after Genesis 11. Genesis 10 describes a wide and gradual movement of tribes, apart from any overt action on God's part like we see in chapter 11. But Genesis 11:1–2 says that the world spoke one language and then settled at the plain of Shinar. Westerners, who are used to reading stories chronologically, would get the impression that all these migrations of peoples across the Middle East and North Africa in chapter 10 are subsequently undone in 11:1 as "the whole world" apparently moves east and settles at Shinar. And certainly any etiology of cultural or national groupings in chapter 10 would be undone by 11:8, as the peoples are dispersed apparently *a second time* in 11:8 through more supernatural involvement (remember, following a chronological interpretation, the first gradual dispersal was recorded in chapter 10).

But note that OT and NT stories are not always told chronologically; the authors make certain information prominent by foregrounding. In this case, the author may be "getting ahead of himself" by telling in chapter 10 how people gradually scattered across Eurasia and North Africa *after* God confused their languages. And then in chapter 11, the author may jump back in the story line, *before* the scattering of the people groups, to fill in the details about the tower and supernatural judgment. Note that Genesis 10:10 says Nimrod founded Babel (without any further explanation); and explains in chapter 11:9, after God confused the languages, how Babel came to be founded and named. So Genesis 10 and 11 must be read as a unit to make sense. To put it another way, Genesis 10 tells the same story of dispersal as chapter 11, albeit with a very different focus than the story of Babel in chapter 11.[36] Chapter 10 tells the "who and where" and chapter 11 tells the "how and why."

36. Von Rad, *Genesis*.

Now, the verb "scatter" in Genesis 11:8 seems active—as if God actively scattered the nations by plopping them down "over the face of the whole earth" (NIV). But the overwhelming commentary consensus, as early as Josephus in the first century AD, is that the scattering was passive—"on account of the [different] languages."[37] God was responsible for scattering the nations, but indirectly, the same way that I am responsible for baking a cake. The gas oven is the active agent in baking, but I am ultimately responsible for the result. As Waltke put it, God "forced [the ethnolinguistic groups] to separate."[38] Note that virtually all major commentators including Matthew Henry, NICOT, Gill, Barnes, Pulpit Commentary, and Ellicott agree with Josephus's secondary-agent rendering.

Just as proponents of polygenesis turned to historical linguistics to buttress their argument, the Gradual Dispersal theory can be supported by a reconstruction of protolanguages. Historical linguist Quenten Atkinson has suggested a single *ursprache* which originated in Africa, and gradually became more morphed as humans migrated up through Europe, across Asia, the Pacific, and eventually to the Americas. Atkinson's data, however, relies only on one feature of speech: the amount of phonemes (meaningful speech sounds). Atkinson's thesis is that as languages developed the phonemes became simplified. The language with the most phonemes (that is, the oldest) has been found in Africa, with 141 phonemes; and the language with the fewest (eleven) is in South America—presumably the last migration of human societies.[39]

Biblical scholars and linguists find problems with the *ursprache* theory. First, Babel tells a story of much wider linguistic diversity than this. Second, there is no good reason to think that languages with more phonemes are older than languages with few ones. And phonemes are only one of many, many features in a language—it is almost arbitrary to single out phonemes as the criteria for tracing linguistic variations back to a protolanguage. Why not look at the complexity of the lexicon? Or why not single out verbal affixes as the marker of historical changes in language, as William Lane did?

37. Josephus, *Antiquities 1.5.1*.
38. Waltke, *Genesis*, 184.
39. Naik, "The Mother of all Languages."

Divine Scattering theory

The *prima facie* reading of Genesis 11 is that God rather suddenly created not only distinct languages at Babel, but also *miraculously* scattered (11:8) these distinct ethnolinguistic groups across the "face of the whole earth" (NIV). These language communities would have quickly developed enough cultural information to allow for their languages to make sense within their new environments (e.g., the Inuit possess a culture and language in their tundra homeland that is different than that of the Pacific Islanders).

This is fairly different from the Noah's Sons theory, since it does not limit the *ethne* to three imagined racial boundaries, and does not attempt to explain who is the descendent of whom. It also envisions a rather immediate peopling of the nations (hence allows for a young earth schema), whereas the Noah's Sons and Gradual Dispersal theories can involve a gradual migration and even Old Earth creationism. But one's interpretation of Genesis 11 depends on how he understands the Hebrew word *'eretz*, ("earth" in the NIV). The Hebrew term usually means "land" and "all over the land" may as easily mean "all over the Ancient Near East" as "all over the face of the earth." If *'eretz*, in Genesis 11:8, means "God caused the people to be scattered all over that land" we end up with a very different interpretation than English speakers would get from their English "the whole earth gathered . . . and God scattered."

But how many *ethne* would the "divine scattering" entail? The field of historical linguistics can give us a far more complex picture of how Babel relates to the peopling of the continents and the emergence of distinct *ethne*. To do this, linguists compare grammatical features and cognates of neighboring languages to see how ethnolinguistic groups share a common ancestor. Typical language family taxonomies list about a dozen protolanguages scattered throughout the Earth, giving the impression that perhaps ethnolinguistic diversity had around a dozen distinct origins. For example, a lecture from the University of Texas divides language families into the following categories: Indo-European, Semitic, Hamitic, Altaic, Niger-Congo, Austronesian, Uralic, Sino-Tibetan, Austro-Asiatic, Japanese and Korean, and "other."[40]

However, the "other" category is problematic, because they are found in little pockets all over the world, and are unrelated to each other. We cannot steamroll over the "other" category to reduce historical ethnolinguistic

---

40. http://www.utexas.edu/depts/grg/adams/old305b/geolinguistics/305lect12a.htm.

roots to a neat dozen any more than we can steamroll over the world's distinct physical features to fit the *ethne* into a neat three or five or ten "races." As historical linguists trace the family tree of the world's languages, the trail stops not at three (contra the Noah's sons or polygenetic theories), or even at a dozen, but at 218 irreducible language families.[41] That is, we cannot find any common ancestor between these 218 language family groupings to demonstrate how they are lexically related to each other. The grammatical and lexical differences between these languages are so significant that it is almost as though God implanted protolanguages on the hearts of early ethnolinguistic people groups. As Babel suggests, these distinct ethnolinguistic groups are geographically dispersed on all six continents. Creationists who hold to a Young Earth theory would probably envision a miraculous shifting of skin tones at this point in prehistory.

However, just as there are problems with the use of historical linguistics to buttress the other theories of ethnicity, relying on irreducible language families is problematic. Note that lexicons can change drastically as ethnic groups willfully isolate themselves from neighboring groups. Plus, languages which are lexically differentiated may still share grammatical features. And speakers of many of these isolated languages share *physical* features of the neighboring languages, which suggests common ancestry regardless of what language they speak.

Ramifications of the theories of ethnicity

By this point, we have not arrived at a conclusive explanation for the origin of ethnicity, but we have certainly ruled out some unacceptable explanations and now we are more aware of the issues and ramifications of our theories. The theology of ethnicity, place, and Babel affects our view of the *ethne*; and in a globalized world, the *ethne* are a part of our daily work and life. From the story of linguistic and even ethnic variation at Babel, we may conclude that there is a sense in which God is ultimately responsible for the diversity of cultures. But what was God's role? We've looked at four ways to answer this question. Table 1 summarizes the theories and the ramifications.

41. Lewis et al., eds., "Ethnologue."

Table 1: Comparison of four Christian theories of ethnic diversity

	Time-frame and agent	Proponents	Theory (or theories)	Ramifications
Monogenesis	Sudden, miraculous	Bishop Isidore; Morton, Delany	Noah's Sons theory: "Three Great Races"	Allows for a literal reading of Genesis, but requires imposing an external interpretation on the text Technically defends the unity of humankind, but causes readers to attribute cultural differences to God's will or even God's punishment
	Sudden, miraculous	Prima facie reading	Divine Scattering theory: God created distinct ethnolinguistic groups at Babel, and placed them in geographic contexts	Defends the unity of humankind and preserves dignity of all ethnicities, since none is singled out as cursed or blessed. Literal reading of Genesis High view of sovereignty of God Allows for Young Earth theory God is responsible for original cultural and linguistic forms Explains why there are hundreds of protolanguages Ethnic boundaries were originally distinct, but have become blurred through diffusion
	Gradual, natural	Josephus; Samuel Smith; Most major commentaries	Gradual Dispersal Theory: Languages were confused at Babel, but physical, cultural and subsequent linguistic distinctions are the result of geography, microevolution, diet, diffusion, and migration.	Defends the unity of humankind and preserves dignity of all ethnicities, since none is singled out as cursed or blessed. Requires some literary explanation for the chronology of Genesis 10 and 11, and an interpretive rendering of "scattered" in Gen 11:8 Ethnic boundaries have never been distinct Does not allow for Young Earth theory, unless one holds that distinct ethnic features can emerge rapidly

	Time-frame and agent	Proponents	Theory (or theories)	Ramifications
Polygenesis	Natu-ralistic polygenesis	Samuel Morton, Josiah Nott, Alexander Winchell	"Races for places" (see Livingstone, p. 95).God created distinct human species with certain dispositions. Theistic evolution: Humans evolved, but God miraculously implanted the soul in Adam and Adam's descendants	Pre-Adamic races either have no soul or were not affected by the fall, so were not in need of conversion Certain races are inferior, destined to be slaves Requires nontraditional reading of Scripture (esp. Rom 1:15) Requires a local flood, wiping out only one race (usually Caucasian) Sees races as "pure" and interracial sex as wrong
	Divine Polygenesis: Young Adam, Old Earth	Isaac La Peyrère, Louis Agassiz, Charles Caldwell, Samuel George Morton, Edward William Lane, Samuel Kneeland, Charles Hamilton Smith, John Harris, William Buckland, RA Torrey	Pre-Adam Civilizations: Civilizations existed before Adam, which explains why archaeologists have found prehistoric human settlements before Adam's day; but all human ethnicities today are descended from Adam	Requires nontraditional reading of Scripture (esp. Rom 1:15) Allows for a harmony of geologic time + literal reading of Scripture Allows for a global flood which wiped out all of these prehistoric civilizations

Finally, God's plan was always that people would fill the earth and create endlessly diverse ways of living, so Babel was not as much a punishment as it was God's way of ensuring that his original plan—the creation mandate—was carried out.[42] In Genesis 10:18 and 10:32, the scattering or "spreading abroad" was "blessed, sanctioned, and willed by Yahweh. It is part of God's plan for creation and the fulfillment of the mandate of 1:28."[43]

---

42. deClaisse-Walford, "God Came Down." For an alternate interpretation—that cultural and linguistic diversity are a "monument to sin"—see Ross, "The Dispersion of the Nations."

43. Bruggemann, *Genesis*, 98.

The Gradual Dispersal theory comes closest to recognizing the observable reality that the boundaries between the *ethne* are blurred, and that societies have always been changing and moving. Or to look at it another way, the Gradual Dispersal theory is the theory that aligns best with the principle that God has made humans to be culture makers.

HOW MANY CULTURES/PEOPLE GROUPS ARE THERE?

If ethnicity is a fuzzy set, how many people groups are there? It depends how you count. Often, cross-cultural training books attempt to describe national cultures, as if there is a homogenous culture within the borders of the nation-state.[44] This would give the erroneous impression that the world has about 220 people groups because there are 220 or so countries (again, depending on how you count). However, many people groups span across national boundaries (like the Kurds in Turkey and Iraq), and other nations have hundreds of distinct people groups within their boundaries, like Nigeria or Indonesia. We speak of entire blocs of people like "Middle Easterners" or "Asians" as if the culture is homogenous. In fact, the Joshua Project is now recognizing sixteen "affinity blocs" which share language groupings, religious background, and perhaps a similar political history.[45] If by culture, or people group, we mean distinct languages—not dialects— there are about 7,000. However, some of these languages, like English, are shared by people with very different ways of organizing themselves politically, religiously, and socially. Perhaps the best tally we have nowadays for people groups is from Joshua Project, which says that there are about 15,000 distinct ethnolinguistic peoples, when we take into account a shared set of meanings and values. We will look at ways cross-cultural theorists have tried to explain the origin of these differences in the next chapter.

SUMMARY

I have argued here that cultural activity originates from God, but it is methodologically, theologically, and practically flawed to contend that any particular culture is prescriptive or uniquely endorsed by God. Instead, God's plan is for human societies to be diverse. Even though the dispersal at

44. See, for example, Morrison et al., *Kiss, Bow, or Shake Hands*.
45. http://joshuaproject.net/help/definitions.

Babel was a punishment, that does not mean that cultural or ethnolinguistic variation is against God's plan. In fact, biblical descriptions of the kingdom of God and of heaven include ideals of cultural and linguistic diversity.

Various theories of race and the origin of ethnic differences have been proposed over the years. I have shown how the theories that put humans into bounded, distinct, and static racial categories are flawed at a biological and theological level. Scripture does not give a clear account for the origin of ethnic differences, but polygenetic theories and the theory that races came from Noah's sons are problematic. The Gradual Dispersal theory maintains the unity of humankind while recognizing God's plan for diversity.

REFLECTION AND REVIEW QUESTIONS

1. Do you see God (and heaven) as cultural or super-cultural?

2. In what ways is it worthwhile to reconstruct a primal (biblical) culture, as Adam and Eve must have experienced?

3. Which theory of ethnicity seems most plausible to you? Polygenesis, Gradual Dispersal, Noah's Sons, or Divine Scattering?

4. How would you answer the question, "How many races are there today?"

5. If World Changers adopt the gradient view of ethnicity, rather than the bounded-race view, how would that affect the way they interact with their world?

CHAPTER 6

The gospel and cultural differences

WE HAVE WORKED THROUGH theories of race and the origin of the ethno-linguistic peoples, but a central question in the study of culture has been "Why are cultures different?" Anthropologists and cross-cultural theorists have developed a number of explanations for cultural differences. Below are five predominant theories that we'll critique in this chapter:

1. Genetics—different "races" are predisposed.

2. Unilineal evolution—cultures evolve along a trajectory from savage to barbarian to civilized.

3. Functionalism—cultural innovations serve a biological or social function.

4. Culture-trait theory—Cultures vary to the extent that cultural innovations diffuse across the globe.

5. Environmental determinism—cultures evolved due to a society's immediate environment and food supply.

GENETIC DETERMINISM

The notion that cultural differences are related to *race*—biological differences (presumably due to divergent evolutionary paths)—was widely believed in the nineteenth century, and continued to be perpetuated through the 1960s. And with the great leap forward in our understanding of genetics, the conventional wisdom in the West has continued to be that culture is tied to genetics. Way and Lieberman for instance, have tied the individualist/collectivist dyad to prevalence of a certain "social sensitivity" gene in certain populations.[1]

However, the prevalent rhetoric that "Africans are born that way" or "Asians are genetically like this" is almost never tied to evidence. For example, there is little empirical evidence to support the notion that Japanese are genetically predisposed to focus on shame rather than guilt; or that Caucasian genes are tied to punctuality or African genetics are predisposed to a loose reckoning of time rather than a precise one. We tend to tie culture to genes because people from the same gene pool seem to share a similar culture.

The genetic argument becomes even more bizarre when we look at how it is applied to Latin America. One may say that Latin Americans are genetically (take your pick of a certain adjective)—let's say, hot-tempered. Virtually all Latin Americans are of mixed decent—with some Amerindian and some European ancestry, and many (especially in Brazil) also have African descent. Which genes explain the fiery temper—the European, African, or Amerindian? Or is it some sort of synergistic change that happens when the genes are mixed together? There can be no genetic explanation for the attribution of "fiery temper" to ethnicity.

Genes are vastly inadequate for explaining cultural differences. For example, they do not account for how so many Germans moved from pagans to Lutherans to agnostics in the past 700 years while many of their genetic cousins, Spaniards and Italians, turned to Catholicism and still many of *their* genetic cousins, Arabs, embraced Islam.

While cultures are not directly related to genetics, it is true, in some limited senses, that culture affects physiology. And physiology can in turn have an effect on future cultural developments. For example, our culture affects how much we eat, what we eat (there are culturally specified dietary rules and expectations for how varied the diet will be), who we eat with, and how large our meal portions will be. These cultural norms over time will affect the health, height, lifespan, and fitness of the majority of people within a culture. Those physiological shifts can in turn have an impact on cultural innovations such as the height of doors, size of automobiles, length of the work day, and so on. This link between physiology and culture is undoubtedly part of the "evidence" that has led to the persistent misconception that culture is somehow genetic.

---

1. Way and Lieberman, "Differences?"

UNILINEAL EVOLUTION

Early anthropologists like Lewis Henry Morgan[2] and Edward Tylor[3] theorized that cultures were different because they were all at different stages on the evolutionary trajectory from primitive to civilized. Primitive peoples must have started out animistic. They gathered fruits and went hunting. Their social organization centered around the clan. As societies developed into a middle stage, which Morgan called Barbarism, people began farming. Their social organization became more stratified and centralized, as did their religion. They were polytheistic, and appointed priests to perform sacrifices. Then, as societies developed further, they shifted toward a monarchy and eventually a democracy. Their religions became monotheistic (and eventually entirely secular, or naturalistic). In this schema, the aboriginal peoples of Australia, Amerindians, Melanesians, and sub-Saharan Africans are classified as "primitive." The polytheistic peoples of India and East Asia were considered further along the evolutionary trajectory. And the Anglo society from which Morgan and Tylor came represented the height of evolutionary stages. Interestingly, Morgan believed that this inevitable cultural evolution was "part of the Supreme Intelligence to develop a barbarian out of a savage, and a civilized man out of this barbarian."[4]

Since the 1940s, anthropologists in North America and Europe have rejected the notion of unilineal evolution—not because they reject evolution *per se*, but because the unilineal scheme simply does not fit the data. In the mid-twentieth century, anthropologists discovered that there are thousands of distinct ethnolinguistic people groups, with their own cultural developments. They cannot be neatly fit into a paradigm of cultural development. Each society has its own particular religious system, its own politics, its own economic and social organization. The realization that cultures must be studied in their own context, rather than fit into an evolutionary scheme, is called particularism (see chapter 4).

FUNCTIONALISM

The limitless permutations of human social organization, diet, religion, etc., have baffled scientists who begin with Darwinian presuppositions. If

2. Morgan, *Ancient Society.*
3. Tylor, *Primitive Culture.*
4. Morgan, *Ancient Society*, 554, in Moore, *Visions of Culture*, 29.

the most basic instinct in the animal kingdom is to survive, why do we paint Sistine Chapels, compose music, or relate epoch-making poems? Each scientific discipline has come up with a partially satisfying answer. Psychologists like Freud proposed that our culture fulfills fundamental psychological needs.[5] Social anthropologists like Durkheim and Mauss[6] argued that culture perpetuates the society: survival of the fittest *at the social scale*. In each of these schema, cultural innovations must serve a purpose related to survival, or else they would be spurious, and would necessarily erode away. Culture, then, must serve a function. Functionalists like Malinowski have argued that any cultural innovation must serve one of seven basic survival needs:

1. Metabolism (so we eat)

2. Reproduction—the survival of society (kinship, marriage)

3. Bodily comfort (technology, economics)

4. Safety

5. Movement—recreation

6. Growth—initiation rites

7. Health

Malinowski referred to these needs as the Permanent Vital Sequence.[7] Functionalists, operating from Darwinian presuppositions, say that cultural differences result from the multiple ways people have answered life's basic questions. We can readily see that societies have various answers to the basic question "What will I eat?" It should be no surprise that they have also developed, over thousands of years, various (sometimes competing) answers to the other basic questions, "How will I be safe?" and "Whom will I marry?" In fact, in the mid-twentieth century, anthropologists reckoned that there were only six basic answers to the question, "Whom will I marry?" so they forced the world's kinship systems into these six basic categories. Since then, we have discovered that even kinship systems are malleable and fuzzy.

---

5. Freud, *Totem and Taboo.*

6. Durkheim and Mauss, *Primitive Classification.*

7. Malinowski, *A Scientific Theory of Culture and Other Essays.*

CULTURE-TRAIT THEORY

Another important piece of the explanation of cultural differences has to do with the way cultures have changed over time. Cultures are different *today* because societies responded to innovative changes in different ways. And those innovations were introduced at different rates, throughout different centuries, in different parts of the world. While from an evolutionary perspective, the various cultural innovations are all different answers given for some basic *functional* questions about survival, these innovations are not limitless. They are bounded by the local environment and the accumulation of previous cultural knowledge that has been passed on or diffused from neighboring peoples.

For example, it turns out there really is more than one way to skin a cat. If you surveyed "cat skinning" throughout the cultures in the world, you might find half a dozen or even scores of ways to do it, but the various methods would be limited by the local resources, the historical sharing of knowledge, and the cultural systems (religion, politics) in that area. And if you think skinning a cat is detestable, that attitude is also culturally patterned. Remember that hundreds of millions of people in India think it is abhorrent that you eat beef; and hundreds of millions of Muslims and Jews throughout the world find it detestable that you eat pork. Cultures are full of traits that have presented themselves due to unique histories and geographies, and to proximity of other cultures where innovations can be shared. These innovations may be technological, religious, political, and so on. Diffusion of such innovations include the introduction of Chinese food to the USA, and the subsequent "glocalizing" of Chinese food as Chinese American chefs created chop suey.[8]

The culture-trait theory recognizes that cultures have been changing since the dawn of humanity, due to a process known as the diffusion of innovations. Let's say Ug the cave boy grew up using a rock as a hammer. But Ug was a clever boy, and thought outside of the box (which may be anachronistic, since boxes didn't exist yet in this hypothetical society). So Ug tied a rock onto a stick, and invented the first hammer. Then Ug's brothers started doing the same. Over time, this innovation diffused, as perfume diffuses throughout a room. The use of this primordial tool spread first to

---

8. http://blog.ted.com/2013/04/13/ted-weekends-traces-the-origin-of-the-all-american-chinese-take-out/.

the rest of the clan, then throughout the tribe, and ultimately across linguistic, political, and social boundaries.

But if we glance back at the history of the world, innovations did not diffuse with equal rapidity or scope. Brits knew of tomatoes in the Mediterranean, but were late adopters of the so-called love apple. Gen Xers adopted laptops early, but Baby Boomers prefer tablets. Christianity spread rapidly in South America and the Pacific, but has barely taken hold in Japan or the Middle East. The English language has been adopted by one sixth of the world's population, while hundreds of tribal languages are in danger of extinction. So while we know that cultures change through the diffusion of innovations, what affects the speed of the change process? What hinders or fosters change?

Everett Rogers's study of the diffusion of innovations proposes that there are five criteria which affect the adoptability of an innovation:[9]

- Relative Advantage
- Compatibility
- Complexity
- Trialability
- Observability

The easier it is to pick up an innovation, taste and smell it, and see if it's "okay," the more likely it is for a society to adopt that innovation.

Rogers's study focused primarily on industrialized societies, and on the adoption of technological innovations. In addition to Roger's criteria, a more comprehensive model for culture change must take into account cross-cultural theory, including: time orientation (past or future, long term or short term); rates of migration and urbanization; fate versus personal efficacy; collectivism vs. individualism. These value orientations are examined from a biblical perspective in chapter 10. Since evangelicals are highly interested in transforming culture, much attention has been given to the theology and practice of culture change.[10]

---

9. Rogers, *The Diffusion of Innovations.*

10. Hiebert, *Transforming Worldviews*; Lingenfelter, *Transforming Culture.*

ENVIRONMENTAL DETERMINISM

The differences among races or ethnic groups are based on patterned be-haviors and are also contingent on (that is, limited by) the environment.[11] Biologist Jared Diamond's (1999) somewhat myopic argument is that the world's cultural development over the past millennia has been almost ex-clusively determined by geography. Papua New Guineans, Diamond argues, could have been the peoples who would have dominated the globe, if their society had been situated in the Fertile Crescent (the Middle East) with its access to grains and cattle. Their luck (or misfortune) of being situated in New Guinea with taros and sago palm has inhibited them from experienc-ing an agricultural revolution that would have led to the division of labor and specialization in other fields such as metallurgy.

Tylor and later anthropologists Leslie White, Julian Steward, and Mar-vin Harris formulated this view called the Materialist theory (or cultural ecology). It argues that the environment—especially the source of food—"is a creative as well as a limiting factor behind culture."[12] In short, the mate-rialist's view works like this: hunter-gatherers' kinship would be organized along simple bands, and they would be animists. Agrarians and pastoralists would have more complicated tribes and perhaps polytheism. Industrial societies would have complex social networks and would be monotheists. Certain environments, the theory says, would inevitably and predictably lead to certain cultural types. So the Inuit in the tundra regions, or the Akie hunters in Tanzania, and hunter/gatherers all over the world, were destined to develop loose bands, and to be animistic. More arable regions, regard-less of where they are found, would eventually develop into polytheist and peasant societies. Corollaries of this theory are technological or economic determinism: cultures vary depending on the resources available to them.

Environmental determinism has been a minority theoretical position in American anthropology since Franz Boas's particularism (chapter 4) supplanted earlier nomothetic theories. However, the theory has not alto-gether disappeared, since there is some obvious merit to it. We note that animism does seem to be found in hunter-gatherer societies, and that (be-fore European contact) these societies did not organize into concentrated urban centers, specialize in labor, or accumulate capital.

---

11. Rynkiewich, *Soul, Self and Society,* 39.
12. Hatch, *Theories of Man and Culture,* 119–20.

Are there really "hot" and "cold" cultures?

One way that environmental determinism is manifested at a popular level is a meta-dyad of "hot and cold cultures." Lanier, for instance, described a number of ways in which hot climate cultures (e.g., Southeast Asia, Africa, and tropics) differ from cold climate cultures (e.g., Northern Europe, USA, and Canada).[13] Lanier's distinctions include (to name a few): hospitality, use of property, being or doing, collectivism or individualism. Lanier argues that hot climate cultures tend to be collectivist, high context, and hospitable. Cold climate cultures tend to be individualist, low-context in communication, more reticent to provide hospitality, and more private in the use of property.

The notion of hot and cold cultures goes back to Ibn Khaldun in the fourteenth century, who maintained that hot cultures are passionate and expressive while cold cultures are reserved.[14] Later, the French political thinker Montesquieu argued that those in cold climates have circulatory systems which lead them to be savvy and hard workers, while those in the tropics are lazy, gloomy, robbers and liars. Livingstone has called this tradition the "imperialism of climate."[15] The ramifications of such typologies of culture and climate are immediately obvious to contemporary readers: we may attribute all accepted cultural components to people who come from our own environment, and attribute all deplorable behaviors and attitudes to geographic spaces that we also deem to be substandard.

What explanation can materialists or environmentalists give for how "hot climate cultures" differ in these ways from "cold climate cultures"? Picture European civilizations developing over the past several thousand years, with the nuclear family huddling over a fire, just hoping to make it through the winter. They only venture outside to hunt or gather. The village only comes together for specific tasks; but for many hours socializing is done in small units inside modest houses. Nuclear families begin to identify themselves with their own house, property, and plot of land. Meanwhile, as societies are flourishing in tropical climates, life is spent outdoors. Most public interaction is social, rather than simply task-oriented. Life becomes about "being" rather than "doing." Property—in fact everything in life, including the daily decisions in life—is shared.

---

13. Lanier, *Foreign to Familiar.*
14. Moore, *Visions of Culture,* 1.
15. Livingstone, *Adam's Ancestors,* 55, 64.

This hyper-environmental determinism is highly reductive. It is wildly inaccurate to lump all "warm climate" cultures into one category, as if the excess of one thousand ethnolinguistic groups in Africa shared a unified culture, along with the Pacific Islands, India, Southeast Asia, and South America. Not only does the "warm climate" include more than 10,000 distinct ethnolinguistic groups, but (as Lanier pointed out) nation-states may contain both severely warm and bitterly cold climates, as Chile does. Do we expect to find individualistic, task-oriented, private, hierarchal tribes up in the Andes and collectivist, event-oriented, public, egalitarian tribes in the warmer parts of Chile? No; in Lanier's model, all of Chile (with the rest of Central and South America, with all its cold and warm climates) are lumped together as warm climate cultures (along with all of Africa, the Pacific, etc.).

Despite its inaccuracies, the notion of "warm and cold climate cultures" is still commonly used in cross-cultural training. It is not particularly helpful in describing *specific* cultures, but it is indeed helpful for showing North Americans and Europeans a number of ways in which they differ from cultures outside the West. Westerners tend to be highly individualistic, private, and task-oriented, whereas in "the East" (that is, the eastern hemisphere, to cover Asia, Africa, and the Middle East) people tend to be collectivist, public, and event-oriented. In fact, the bifurcation has often been conceived in *other* environmental terms: the West versus the East, or West vs. the Two-Thirds World,[16] rather than "hot and cold cultures."

Now, "East" and "West" are as imprecise as "hot and cold," since South America fits the broad cultural descriptions of "Eastern" culture, though it is in the Western hemisphere. And the predominant national culture in Australia, though situated in the eastern hemisphere, is "Western." What East/West signifies is more precisely exposure to the industrial revolution. All cultures, Pearse supposes, were collectivist, people-oriented, public, hospitable, and polychronic before the industrial revolution.[17] It was only after families moved off the farms, and began working long hours in the factory, that we began depending less on the extended family and more on money, status, and work. The economic environment—including the food supply—in postindustrial nations has caused cultures to become more individualistic, whereas developing nations continue to allow (determine?) cultures to be collectivist as food production is done collectively.

16. D. Elmer, *Cross-Cultural Conflict.*
17. Pearse, *Why the Rest Hates the West.*

While the "hot/cold culture" form of environmental determinism is flawed, we cannot dismiss the materialist explanation altogether. Human cultures are shaped by food supplies and climate just like they are shaped by biological needs, psychological needs, structures of the human brain, and by the diffusion of cultural innovations. However, there are serious problems any time we pit half of the world's cultures against the other half, imagining that all cultures in the East are one way, in contrast to the West. It is best to accept environmental determinism as one explanation for cultural innovations, but to avoid reducing cultures to dyadic categories like East/West or hot/cold. Instead, we must begin by studying each culture on its own, as particularists do. This will allow us to see what themes emerge from within the culture. After that, we can theorize about the ramifications of those cultural themes in a globalized twenty-first century.

CONCLUSION: THE IMAGE BEARING THEORY

For Christians, the existence of limitless permutations of human cultures is not enigmatic at all; these differences serve as further evidence that we bear God's image of creativity. Given that God created us to be culturative, cultural innovations are no surprise. We do not need to find the social *function* of a necktie, or a white wedding dress; we do not assume there is a necessary biological function that resulted in circumcision or tattooing. We understand that cultural innovations are the result of our relentless culturative nature. We are not surprised that Spanish has a unique word *Friolero*, for people who are particularly sensitive to cold weather, or that some Indonesian societies keep corpses in their house for several months before burial, or that traditional Chinese bound women's feet. Because bearing God's image means an endless creativity, we are not surprised to find 15,000 distinct ethno linguistic groups throughout the world. In fact, such innovation is exactly what we would expect from humans that are made in God's image.

Table 2 summarizes six explanations for why cultures are so different from each other. Note that these explanations are not mutually exclusive. In other words, if we accept the Image Bearing theory, we do not need to reject wholesale the theories of functionalism or the culture-trait theory. We may easily reject unilineal evolution, and we can see that functionalism is severely near-sighted: if we are just machines that function to perpetuate our genes, we are seriously over-designed. As Francis Schaeffer put it, if evolutionary forces caused us to be merely gene-perpetuating machines, humans are like a river that rises above its source.[18] In other words, the expressions of culture carry a level of complexity and desire that far exceed functions that are basic to human survival. However, these theories hold some amount of sway because each of them has varying degrees of explanatory scope.

Table 2: Six theories that explain cultural differences

Theory	Proponent(s)	Idea
Genetic determinism	Way & Lieberman	Genes are responsible for cultural differences
Unilineal evolution	Morgan, Tylor	All cultures evolve from savagery to barbarism to civilized
Functionalism	Malinowski, Mauss, Durkheim	Cultural innovations serve a biological or social function
Culture-trait theory	Rogers	Cultures evolve over time as innovations are diffused across cultural boundaries
Environmental determinism	Diamond	Human cultures evolve based on their access to grains, cattle, and other natural resources
Image Bearing theory	Crouch, Calvin, Van Til, Kuyper, Hoekema	Cultural differences are expected since God created us to be creators

REFLECTION AND REVIEW QUESTIONS

1. Which theoretical explanations of culture most resound with you, and which seem most implausible to you?

2. How have you seen culture meet biological or functional needs?

3. What is the limitation of speaking of East vs. West (or hot/cold) cultural differences?

4. What do World Changers need to understand about cultural differences, in order to affect their world?

18. Schaeffer, *Francis A. Schaeffer Trilogy*, 95.

CHAPTER 7

An evangelical approach toward evaluating and changing cultures

BY THIS POINT, I have argued that a theology of culture for the twenty-first century involves embracing multiculturalism. But this raises a difficult question for evangelicals. If we embrace multiculturalism, is it right to try to change culture—especially the sinful parts? Further, how can we evaluate other cultures, with the plan for changing them, without being ethnocentric?

ARE SOME CULTURES BETTER THAN OTHERS?

In chapter 5, I explored whether the first culture (Adam and Eve's) was normative—or whether some later culture recorded in Scripture (Israel under the judges or monarchy; the New Testament church) was normative. A major reason we need to work through these questions about Adam and Eve's culture, or whether OT culture is prescriptive, is that many Christians over the centuries (not just in Western nations) have assumed their culture was better than others' because their own culture was apparently more approximate to the biblical culture—however that was defined. In fact, evangelicals sense the urgency to demarcate cultural standards from a biblical perspective, not so they may denigrate others, but to allow them come closer to God. In the twenty-first century, can evangelicals actually maintain that one culture is better than another—and if so, how can they do this without being bigoted or ethnocentric?

Since creation, humans have been fighting over land, power, and resources. But the justification and even the impetus for such atrocious warfare has often been based on attitudes of cultural supremacy. The civil war in Sudan, which took more than two million lives, was motivated in part by cultural differences. This is true for Hitler's extermination of Jews (as well as many others), the civil war in former Yugoslavia, and the ethnic cleansing in Rwanda and so on. Xenophobia, the fear of people from other cultures, is found in the highlands of Papua New Guinea, the urban centers of Asia, as well as in the West. This pervasive fear of the Other is not always manifested in war—sometimes it comes out in the form of prejudice, stereotyping, racial slurs. No matter how educated, nice, or Christian we are, we continue to be ethnocentric. That is, we presuppose that our own culture is the standard by which all other cultures shall be evaluated.

Let's suppose you took a trip to Papua New Guinea (PNG) to learn about an indigenous culture. As you walked along a trail, you encountered a naked boy who appeared to be about three or four years old. He strolled along the trail apparently without a care in the world, carrying his machete in one hand and a piece of boiled taro in the other. When an emaciated dog appeared from nowhere, you observed the boy as he swatted the dog's muzzle with the blunt end of his machete—apparently for no other reason but to hear the dog yelp. You might make the following judgments:

- He should not be traveling alone, and should be supervised.
- He should be wearing clothes.
- He should not be carrying a machete.
- That dog should be better fed, and should be better supervised.
- He is being mean to that dog.

Because you probably grew up in a culture where young boys do not run naked, carry machetes, travel alone, or swat dogs to hear them yelp, you probably never encountered such a sight in your own society. So you assumed that Papua New Guineans—or everyone everywhere—agreed with your own ideas about supervision, care of animals, and wearing of clothing. You expected cultural sameness. And when you encountered such a radically different approach to supervision, clothing, and care of animals, you may have made the following conclusions:

- Papua New Guineans don't care for their children.
- Papua New Guineans are mean to animals.

So expecting cultural sameness is not only disorienting, it is also responsible for a sense of cultural supremacy. This is how ethnocentrism works: we expect cultural sameness, and evaluate other cultures through our own culturally patterned values.[1] But in tribal areas in PNG, children may typically walk from one village to another without encountering strangers or dangers. And the machete is a normal tool for walking on trails. Dogs are swatted proactively to keep them from becoming too aggressive.

Nowadays, many of us are "multicultural" enough to recognize the flaw of ethnocentrism. We try instead to lean toward cultural relativism. But we are wary of embracing full-fledged relativism. In fact, contemporary anthropology *presupposes* cultural relativism, in part to intentionally mitigate the problems of ethnocentrism. But there are two distinct things we can mean by "cultural relativism." One definition is that "culture is relative to context."[2] In other words, ideas about morality, "politeness," "respect," etc., are relative to a specific culture. Let me supply a controversial example. If the anthropologist notices southerners in the US saying "yes sir" or "yes ma'am" she would not conclude that southerners are more polite than west coasters; instead, she would note that each society uses the proper cultural markings relative to its own setting. West coasters have other ways to mark politeness.

Virtually all of the acceptable practices, beliefs, and actions shared by members of a society are relative to a specific context. We would not expect people from far away continents to have the values we have, or enjoy the same foods we enjoy, or believe the same things about God that we do, any more than we would expect them to speak the same language that we speak. We know better than to expect cultural sameness. So when someone from another culture receives a gift from us without saying "thank you" or shows up an hour late to a meeting, we do not think to ourselves, *These people are rude!* Instead, we conclude, *Ah, of course! Ideals about punctuality or gratefulness are culturally relative.* Cultural relativists reason that if cultures are the result of human beings reacting to their environment, as people adopt innovations at various rates, it is senseless to evaluate any given culture based on the norms within another culture. In the end, the cultural relativist says that the various cultures in the world are all somewhat different

---

1. Storti, *The Art of Crossing Cultures.*

2. Brown, *Human Universals*, 65; Howell and Paris, *Introducing Cultural Anthropology*, 31.

answers to the same basic questions in life such as *What will I eat, How will I be safe, Where will I live*, and *Who will I marry*?

Another related (yet distinct) conceptualization of cultural relativism argues that "no culture is better than any other." As Bennett defined ethnorelativism, "There is no absolute standard of rightness [or] 'goodness' that can be applied to cultural behavior. Cultural difference is neither good or bad; it is just different."[3] Note that one could hold to the former definition of cultural relativism here (i.e., culture is relative to context) without holding to the latter (i.e., no culture is better than another). That is, it is possible to acknowledge—even expect—people from different cultures to have different values and standards *without* arriving at the conclusion that there are no standards at all.

We may not be surprised, though, to find that many Westerners prefer the latter definition of cultural relativism (no external standard by which we can evaluate cultures), since most Westerners no longer believe in objective standards. Over the past forty years, US-Americans have increasingly been won over to philosophical relativism—the belief that truth is what you make it. In 2001, the Barna Group reported that 78 percent of US-Americans agreed with the statement "there is no such thing as absolute truth." Only 13 percent of people under the age of thirty-six believed in absolute truth.[4] Since the vast majority of US-Americans are philosophical relativists, we may expect them to be relativists in relation to cultural differences as well. That is, we would expect them to believe that "no culture is better than any other." However, in daily life, US-Americans' philosophy (relativism) often is misaligned with how they really behave (ethnocentrically). Many of our neighbors, and maybe we ourselves at times, assume that our own culture is better than the Other's culture.

Since this latter definition of cultural relativism presupposes philosophical relativism, it has limited usefulness in a Christian approach toward culture. We do in fact have an external standard by which we can evaluate culturally patterned beliefs and practices: God's revelation in the Bible. However, I suggest that even as we dismiss philosophical *relativism* as philosophically flawed, we must embrace cultural *pluralism*. Cultural pluralists and relativists both observe the *plurality* or endless variety of cultures throughout the world, which have developed over time due to geography, diffusion, and innovation. The pluralist takes note of endless

3. Bennett, "Towards a Developmental Model," 46.
4. Barna Group, "How America's Faith has Changed Since 9–11."

varieties and uses this data to explain and engage cultures. He assumes that all cultures make sense within their own cultural logic. He expects people to behave the way their cultural norms teach them to, rather than like his own. He's not surprised by different values and patterns, and when he sees different beliefs or practices, he wants to know how those norms are consistent within the Other's cultural logic.

But it is at this point that the relativist and cultural pluralist diverge. Cultural pluralists assume that all cultural artifacts (things people do and think in a society) make sense when understood within their own cultural context. The relativist, on the other hand, uses the same observation of cultural pluralism as further proof of philosophical relativism. Margaret Mead, for instance, wanted the (fabricated) data that Polynesian girls are sexually loose[5] to supply proof for her philosophical commitment that there are no universal standards of sexuality—or of anything else.

Culture-minded missionaries have long known that they should avoid ethnocentrism, but have wanted to maintain the prerogative to evaluate all culture—their own and the Other's culture. This distinction between relativism and cultural pluralism should allow us to reconcile these two seemingly conflicting agendas. To put it another way, we can say that cultural pluralism is descriptive, whereas relativism is prescriptive regarding attitudes about these differences.

Determine whether the statements below reflect relativism or cultural pluralism:

1. "Various cultures promote different views about sexual immorality, so there is no such thing as 'proper' or 'improper' sexual behavior."

2. "Various cultures promote different views about sexual immorality, so in order to understand and work with people in a given culture, we need to study their own views within their specific historical and geographic context."

The first comment reflects relativism, and is problematic for evangelicals. The second reflects cultural pluralism, and is the sort of approach toward culture that is essential for Christians to be effective in the multicultural twenty-first century.

Cultural pluralism is meant to teach us that many of our judgments about the way other people do things are hasty, arbitrary, or contradictory. For instance, many US-Americans think it is disgusting for Chinese people

5. Mead, *Coming of Age in Samoa.*

to eat dog meat. Many US-Americans think it is chauvinistic for Afghani women to be veiled, for Indian marriages to be arranged. "Yet common American practices of premarital sex, eating pork, private ownership of land, male circumcision, making pets of dogs, talking to strangers about intimate family problems (including, through television talk shows, to millions of strangers), and putting criminals to death are just as disgusting, immoral or oppressive in the eyes of many other peoples."[6] To make this observation about cultural pluralism is not to take a stand on the "right" way to arrange a marriage or the right type of meat to eat—it is just to point out that it is erroneous to expect cultural sameness. For every practice or belief that we think "they" are wrong, "they" think the same about us.

While "cultural pluralism" wasn't exactly the context of the Sermon on the Mount, Jesus' words are relevant here: "Do not judge, or you too will be judged" (Matt 7:1, NIV). Kraft's term "cross-cultural perspective" is meant to embody the same attitude as what I have described as cultural pluralism. "This is a perspective that always takes into account the fact that there are a variety of culturally governed perceptions of any given segment of reality".[7] Christian cultural pluralism, or Kraft's "cross-cultural perspective," is meant to mitigate our tendency toward tacit ethnocentrism. That is, this perspective should keep us from expecting cultural sameness.

When I present cultural pluralism to audiences, they commonly have two objections. First, they will cite examples of societies that *must* be worse. "Don't Eskimos leave their elderly out to die?" Or, "What about the headhunters?" Note that these nearly apocryphal accounts of ruthless "Eskimos" and "headhunters" are never placed in a specific time and place, such as the Intuits in the nineteenth century, or the Shuar in Peru during the twentieth century. Such imprecision makes it impossible to verify the inherent "badness" of these hypothetical "bad" societies. Despite our inability to locate when and where, specifically, these degenerate societies exist, we are certain they must be out there. And this must be data that disproves full-blown cultural relativism.

Anthropologists have responded to this sort of objection to cultural pluralism in two ways. First, many anthropologists are opposed to the reduction of cultures to monolithic caricatures such as "headhunters" or "cannibals." There may be instances of such behaviors in certain parts of the world (and at certain times in history), but these societies are much

6. Anderson et al., *International Studies*, 123.

7. Kraft, *Christianity in Culture*, 48.

richer in their complexity than a simple stereotype would suggest. Second, contemporary anthropologists have questioned the pervasiveness of such blatantly awful behaviors. Reports of headhunting and cannibalism during early European contact may have suffered accretions and exaggeration.

Another common objection Christian college students have to the idea of cultural pluralism is related to the degree of exposure a culture has had to the Bible. "Aren't cultures that interacted with Christianity for 2,000 years more likely to reflect godly standards?" This is undoubtedly the case, as Cunningham has argued.[8] Many cultures have a version of the golden rule, or at least the "silver rule" (don't do to others what you don't want them to do to you), but cultures that have been exposed to Christianity tend to place high values on self-sacrifice, unconditional love, justice, and equity. Similarly, Kraft has argued that while there is no culture which can be considered normative for all people at all times, there are cultural forms (perhaps democracy and free markets) that more easily facilitate Christianity.[9]

Sherwood Lingenfelter, while not disagreeing with the tremendous benefits cultures will acquire as they encounter God's word, attempted to reconcile cultural pluralism with a Christian perspective.[10] To the extent that all cultures are human constructions, they are as fallen as the human race. All cultures are equally unimpressive in God's sight in that they have sinful elements in their politics, economics, social structure, and worldview that must be redeemed. Everything we say, think, and do as members of the human race is only corrupt, continually (Gen 6:5). To the extent that cultures approximate the "common grace" that God has extended to all humanity, they are viable options for image bearers to follow in answering life's questions.

In summary, it is possible to avoid ethnocentrism without embracing the wholesale adoption of postmodern relativism. But our theology of culture in this century must be sufficiently informed about ethnicity, the lived experience of people from other cultural backgrounds, and the theory of culture and culture change, to bring us to the realization that it is fallacious to expect people in other societies to think, act, or behave the same way we do. While it is unsuitable for Christians to embrace philosophical relativism, we must at least embrace what Rynkiewich calls methodological

8. Cunningham, *The Book that Transforms Nations.*

9. Kraft, *Christianity in Culture*,108.

10. Lingenfelter, *Transforming Culture.*

relativism. "One cannot know and understand another culture while at the same time judging and condemning it. Therefore, these things should be taken in stages. One should withhold judgment at least for a given period of research and study until the culture is described, analyzed and understood."[11] And, Rynkiewich points out, as the early church expanded cross-culturally, it worked out a theology of cultural pluralism. For instance, Paul argued for pluralism in diet and ritual cleanliness in Romans 14:13–23 and 1 Corinthians 8:1–13.[12]

Last, the question of whether some cultures are better than others can really be taken several ways. If the question means, "Are there some societies that more closely approximate God's plan for culture" then the answer is yes—those which have had more prolonged and profound contact with God's revelation than others typically approximate biblical norms better than those which have had little exposure to the Bible. But if the question means "are there some societies where the sum total of shared beliefs and actions are better than others" the question is impossible to answer. How can we decide if the art, food preferences, music, social organization, economic practices, hospitality norms, etc., are all, in totality, better than others? But we may take the question to mean something else: "Are there some *cultural features* which are better than others?" And that is a more practical and answerable question, which I will address below.

Can we evaluate cultural features without being ethnocentric?

The problem with attempting to evaluate every feature in a culture with the criteria "Is it biblical?" is that there are many things we do which are not in the Bible, but which are acceptable: speaking English or Japanese, using computers or chopsticks, going jet skiing. To solve this, theologians have suggested that we could use an overarching categorical imperative to evaluate cultural norms such as "only norms which promote human flourishing."[13] This categorical imperative is useful because it can be used to evaluate social, religious, or technological features. And based on the history of thought about human flourishing from Aristotle to Aquinas, humans flourish when they live according to the way they were created—when they function as image bearers. However, the problem is that Confucius

11. Rynkiewich, *Soul, Self and Society*, 29.

12. Ibid., 30–31.

13. Volf, *A Public Faith*.

and Aristotle could speak about human flourishing, virtue, and "the good" without talking about God and the Bible; and nowadays, "human flourishing" sounds suspiciously amenable to secular humanism. The "chief end of man," as the Westminster Catechism put it, was not merely "to flourish" but "to glorify God and enjoy Him forever." Let us aim for cultural activity that allows us to enjoy God without idolizing culture.

Kraft points out that the criteria we use for evaluating cultural features will depend on what sphere of culture we are evaluating. For instance, we may evaluate technological features based on efficiency, or on availability. We would evaluate social structures based on their ability to connect people to each other. We could evaluate religious features on their ability to connect people to God.[14]

D. A. Carson has suggested that for evangelicals to critically evaluate culture(s), they must recognize that 1) everything that is detached from the centrality of God is evil; 2) God has given common grace and good things to all societies; and 3) God gives out relative degrees of punishment, depending on the degree of rebellion.[15] Carson's criteria recognize that cultures serve a legitimate purpose, as long as they make God central. That is, insofar as cultural components function to reflect God's image, in all the diversity of that image, those features are positive. Our rule of thumb for evaluating culture would be, "How do I see God's image reflected or distorted here?"

To summarize my answer, no, it is off-track to think of the sum total of one culture as better than the sum total of another. But yes, it is absolutely possible to evaluate cultural elements without being ethnocentric. Evangelicals seem to be more comfortable with the notion of evaluating culture than they are with avoiding ethnocentrism. In order for World Changers to engage in culture change and cultural evaluation without falling into stereotyping and ethnocentrism, they need a firm grasp of theology, on the one hand, and cross-cultural studies on the other. And the only way to avoid ethnocentrism while making evaluations is to limit the areas we evaluate. It *would* be appropriate to evaluate spheres of culture (chapter 9) like the political, social, economic, and religious structures from a biblical perspective. But it is impossible to escape ethnocentrism if we evaluate areas that are simply preferences like time reckoning, power distance, or speech directness (chapter 10).

14. Kraft, *Christianity in Culture*, 92–93.

15. D. A. Carson, *Christ and Culture Revisited*, 73–74.

WHAT IS THE DIFFERENCE BETWEEN MAKING CULTURAL OBSERVATIONS AND STEREOTYPING?

Cross-cultural theorists try to categorize cultures in order to describe them. The task of any science and the science of culture, in its quest for knowledge, requires some amount of labeling as well. When scientists label any aspect of creation (from chemical elements to geometric proofs) there is always a measure of controversy. But this controversy is seriously elevated when it comes to putting labels on human cultures. How can we categorize and label, without stereotyping? What's the difference between bona fide scientific categories within cultural studies and plain old-fashioned stereotypes?

Do you assume that Asians are good at math? That Irish love to drink? That Brits cannot cook? What stereotypes have you heard about Caucasians? About African Americans? Or Latinos? We have seen the danger that labeling human cultures can cause: The sentiment that Jews were greedy and dirty was an image the Nazis leveraged to cause many German citizens to passively accept the extermination of millions of Jews. And there have been scores of instances of ethnic cleansing since then, usually strengthened by stereotypes. Ethnocentrism led to numerous genocides in the Balkan states during the twentieth century. Also during that time period, a civil war raged in Rwanda that led to nearly a million deaths along socially constructed ideas of ethnicity.

Do the dangers of stereotyping mean we cannot make *any* generalizations about other cultures? Or even about our own? Not at all. The discipline of cross-cultural studies is built on generalizations or cultural tendencies. In fact, these sorts of cultural comparisons comprise the main theoretical framework of cross-cultural studies. For instance, you may read in an international business article that Japanese people prefer indirect speech, or that South Americans are more interested in relationships than deadlines. How do these generalizations differ from stereotyping? Is labeling Japanese culture as "indirect" any different than labeling Asians as "good at math"?

There are several criteria which distinguish solid cross-cultural theory from stereotypes. Stereotypes are not backed by quantifiable data (how do you define "good at math"?). And they are ambiguous (what does "love to drink" really mean?). The table below summarizes the basic differences between stereotypes, which we try to avoid, and cross-cultural comparisons, which are essential to cross-cultural studies.

Table 3: The differences between stereotypes and cross-cultural comparative data

	Stereotypes	Cross-cultural comparative data
Definitions	Ambiguous	Clearly specified
Cultural designation	Extremely broad, such as "All Africans" or "Asians."	Specific, such as "Laotians" or "Urban Brazilians."
Purpose	To simplify a complex issue	To explain an issue in its complexity; used to understand the cross-cultural process
Tone	Can be positive or negative	Are typically value-neutral
Scope or incidence	Uttered as if this is true for ALL people in a society	Recognize that there are tendencies within a society, but that not all individuals conform to the general tendency
Basis or proof	Anecdote; hearsay. Accuracy cannot be verified.	Qualitative and quantitative research methods; use of contemporary cross-cultural and anthropological theory

Based on the above table, determine whether the following eight comments are stereotypical or based on cross-cultural theory. For each answer, select one of the criteria above to explain *why* it is a stereotype or a plausible cultural generalization. Note that not all stereotypes are negative.

1. Many Saudis expect more small talk before a business meeting than US-Americans do.

2. Arabs refuse to do manual labor.

3. Ninety percent of US-Americans believe in God.

4. US-Americans are greedy.

5. The reverence that most Thai feel toward their king Bhumibol Adulyadej can be surprising to US-Americans, who value egalitarianism over meritocracy.

6. Thai women are promiscuous.

7. Chinese are great at running businesses.

8. The income gap between indigenous poor Filipinos and rich Chinese businessmen in Manila has led to numerous instances of violence.

While cultural generalizations may be grounded in data, they are still problematic: surely not everyone in a society conforms to the cultural generalization. For instance, a study of societies in the South Pacific may indicate that tribal peoples often make decisions as a group. But a critic might ask, "Aren't there plenty of selfish Pacific Islanders who hoard their property, work only for themselves, and ignore the clan's wishes regarding whom they marry?" This is where we see the main difference between stereotypes and generalizations. Stereotypes begin with a theory about people in other cultures, and require individuals to fit the profile. They are not based on data, and they have the pretense of being true of all people in a society. In contrast, cross-cultural theorists look for patterns as they work with real people in real contexts, and then they form generalizations. These generalizations explain cultural tendencies, but theorists don't expect these tendencies to be true of all members of a cultural group. For example, the generalization that Asians are past-oriented and value the elderly is not *true* in the sense that it describes all Asians. It is *true* in the sense that it is based on broad comparative studies of certain Asians in their specific contexts.

Before living overseas for a decade, I was suspicious of the types of cultural generalizations that cross-cultural theorists make. I remember reading Lingenfelter's report of a foot race on the island of Yap, in Micronesia.[16] The man who was ahead kept turning around and slowing down. Lingenfelter asked some cultural informants why the man kept turning around, and they responded that the runner would be ashamed to run on ahead and leave everyone in the dust. Lingenfelter explained that Yapese are group-oriented, and do not want to be singled out. *But aren't there plenty of Yapese who will ignore the collectivist nature of Yap society, and think only of themselves?* I wondered. Part of my skepticism was the result of my monoculturalism. I expected cultural sameness: I had a hard time believing that collectivist societies actually exist. Having lived in a collectivist society from 2002–2012, I now find Lingenfelter's account to be highly plausible. There may be some selfish athletes in Pacific societies—but there is also a general tendency to preserve the honor of the group rather than "get ahead."

16. Lingenfelter, *Agents of Transformation*, 106.

But part of my initial skepticism about the cultural generalizations generated in cross-cultural studies was due to my misunderstanding of the way theorists form these generalizations. When we say that Latin Americans have a loose reckoning of time (ROT), we don't mean that they are incapable of punctuality. Nor that there are people in Latin America who are never punctual. We mean that there are culturally based preferences. Latin Americans will show up on time for a movie in the cinema, lest they miss the film, though some are more likely to show up on time than others. But in general, there is a culturally patterned preference in Latin America for socializing to not be based on the clock. Similarly, tribal peoples are relationship-oriented, but they still know how to get a task done. Also, Hindus and Muslims believe much of life is directed by fate or the will of God; but many obviously understand personal efficacy as well (as evidenced by their enrollment in universities).

So as you work through the thirteen value orientations in chapter 10, remember that these are *general tendencies* that describe culturally patterned *preferences*. They are not monolithic and rigid descriptions of all people within a society.

SHOULD WE TRY TO CHANGE CULTURE?

After categorizing and evaluating cultural norms, the next logical step, at least for World Changers, is being part of changing culture. This, too, is tricky, since our desire to change the Other can often be rooted in our own misunderstanding, rather than in a deep understanding of both Scripture and the Other's culture.

For a time in modern history (roughly 1860 to 1960), a number of anthropologists argued that Westerners should study other cultures, but should not try to change them. This became a dogmatically held position, called "salvage anthropology." These anthropologists wanted to "salvage" indigenous cultures before they were lost to the prevailing national cultures. The position even permeated popular culture in the West. As I was studying at the University of California in the mid-1990s, my peers regularly challenged me, "Why are you going to go into the mission field to try to change those people? They have been existing happily for thousands of years! What makes you think your way of life is better?"

Now, many anthropologists—especially applied anthropologists—recognize that salvage anthropology was both naïve and irresponsible. It was naïve because it failed to recognize that cultures never remain constant. Societies have been adopting innovations since the beginning of time, and will do so increasingly due to globalization. It was irresponsible because people groups in underdeveloped nations have minimal power (referred to as "agency" in anthropological circles) to protect themselves. They may desperately want to adopt education, political stability, or technology, but have few resources to do so. Change is precisely what they need and desire.

There are too many blatantly disturbing social problems to pretend that the world's cultures should be left alone. Can't anthropologists use the theory of culture to improve the lives of the hungry? Of those suffering from Malaria and AIDS? Of women who are kept out of formal education or even beaten? The question in the field of anthropology is no longer whether we should be part of the change process, but which issues we will tackle, and what role we will take. Issues range from industrial mines in aboriginal lands, to vernacular education in former colonies, to the environmental effect of indigenous farming practices, and so on.

For Christians, as well, the question is not as much "Should we change culture?" as "*How* do we change culture?" We take it as a given that the kingdom of God *will* change cultural values. Making disciples of all nations will result in a new worldview, transformed ethics, and restored social relationships.

SHOULD OTHER CULTURES CHANGE US?

If we are truly cultural pluralists who want to avoid ethnocentrism, we would understandably turn the question of changing culture on its head. Should we seek to have other cultures change us? Over the years, I've seen trainers promise students that their cross-cultural training (CCT) courses will "challenge students' assumptions." This objective is so ambiguous that it is difficult to gauge whether the goal has ever been obtained; and it is impossible to gauge whether such a goal is even worthwhile in the first place. If by "challenging their assumptions" the trainers mean they hope students will alter their own ideas of right and wrong, change their beliefs about God and the supernatural, realign allegiances, and revise values about punctuality, hospitality, or productivity, etc., this goal seems highly unattainable. And it may not be a worthy goal. How does the trainer know that there is something deficient with the students' preconceived ideas about right and wrong, God, the supernatural, allegiances, etc.?

On the other hand, a more modest interpretation of CCT's goal of "challenging assumptions" would be that students will complete their cross-cultural studies course with an understanding that most of what they assumed about the right way to do things, the right way to act or think—is culturally determined rather than "common sense." This is a worthwhile objective. And while still fairly lofty, it may be an attainable goal.

But the short answer is yes—we should embrace the way other cultures do change us. If we are not allowing cultures to change us, we are not receiving all the benefits God has in store for us from the cultural synergy. And as I have argued throughout this book, the world's cultures are already changing us profoundly.

SUMMARY

Here, I have offered "cultural pluralism" as an antidote to full-fledged relativism. I have shown how cross-cultural theory can be generated to explain cultures, without falling into the trap of stereotyping. And I have argued that since cultures are dynamic, and since the world is in great need, it is fitting for World Changers to accept the challenge of changing cultures, and of letting cultures change them.

REFLECTION AND REVIEW QUESTIONS

1. How can a World Changer evaluate aspects of a culture without being ethnocentric?

2. What is the difference between cultural pluralism and Christian cultural relativism?

3. What change do you want to help foster in a given society?

4. What ways would you like to see your own culture changed due to the influence of other cultures?

CHAPTER 8

The gospel and the role of Christians in culture

AT THIS POINT, IT should have become clear that my thesis is that Christianity has *everything* to do with culture.

1. Culture is the acceptable practices, beliefs, and actions shared by members of a society.

2. We cannot escape being participants of cultural activity, and one society cannot have "more culture" than another.

3. God created us for cultural activity, and all these activities are our part of our service and worship of the Lord as long as they are according to God's plans.

4. Therefore, God wants to be lord over all the practices, beliefs, and actions shared by members of a society.

5. Therefore, a theology of culture is really a theology of all of the practices, beliefs, and actions shared by members of a society.

And so it becomes apparent how ambitious it really is to develop a theology of culture, for it becomes a theology of *everything*! A theology of culture would involve, as Eagleton put it, everything "from pig farming to Picasso, from tilling to splitting the atom."[1] "Not only did the gospel make an appeal to all, it claims all of man."[2] A theology of culture is central to a systematic theology, since its central research questions are: Who is God, and who are humans, and how do they relate to God? Stephen Long goes so

1. Eagleton, *The Idea of Culture*, 1.
2. Van Til, *The Calvinistic Concept of Culture*, 68.

far as to say that theology is fundamentally about cultural anthropology[3] since the minute God acts in history, it is cultural.[4]

The problem is that evangelicals in industrialized countries generally love their lives on earth (i.e., culture) but feel guilty for doing so, since we typically frame the gospel in spiritual terms. How do we reconcile our God-given culturativeness with Jesus' obvious concern for us to *not* be in love with the world (i.e., culture)? Niebuhr referred to this frustrating tension as the church's "enduring problem." How can we be faithful to God while still effective in engaging the world?[5] In short, theologians have argued that God designed us to be engaged in this-worldly culture, neither leaning toward asceticism nor hedonism. We need a theology of culture which embraces cultural activity without idolizing it.

> We ought neither to despise nor deify creation, but we must use it in the service of God as one of his good gifts (1 Cor 7:22, 31) . . . God's world, the created universe, is an object of love and of joy. This is the place where God wants man as his cultural creature, and man has no right to shun the world, or to hate it, for he would thereby deny his calling and be a rebel.[6]

John Piper, this generation's foremost thinker on the "enduring problem" put it this way:

> Money is given to you so that you might use money in a way that shows money is not your treasure, Christ is. Food is given to you so that you might eat it in such a way that it would be plain food is not your treasure, Christ is. Friends, family, are given to you so that you might live with them in such a way that it will be plain to the world they are not your treasure, Christ is. Computers, toys, houses, lands, cars, are given to you so that you might use them in such a way that it would be plain to the world these are not your treasure, Christ is.[7]

As the church has tried to solve this "enduring problem" it has run into numerous challenges. How does the church's response to cultural life differ when it is a persecuted minority versus the dominant repository of political power and influence? How does the church engage in cultures that have

3. Long, *Theology and Culture*, 19.

4. Ibid., 24.

5. Parler, *Things Hold Together*, 35.

6. Van Til, *The Calvinistic Concept of Culture*, 194–95.

7. Piper, "Treasuring Him."

backgrounds in polytheism, animism, secularism? Should the Christian have a political contribution? Do the visual arts have to do with the Christian's faith? Is economics a theological activity?

For instance, some students asked Pastor Tim Keller why the evangelical church is so involved in the debate about same-sex marriage, whereas mainline churches seem to be going with the cultural tide. Keller tried to explain to the students that the various responses are really indicative of how we conceptualize the Christian's role in wider society. Those who see the church as having a major role to play in wider cultural life also want the church to be involved in politics and social issues. How we envision our role in wider society (some would say, in culture) influences how we answer those questions.

Theologies of culture, then, are not static; they are worked out for each generational and cultural context. We'll examine some of the more influential responses to the "enduring problem" below, beginning with pre-Christian notions of the dilemma and solutions proposed in those religious systems.

PRE-CHRISTIAN ANSWERS TO THE ENDURING PROBLEM

One of the world's oldest religions, Hinduism, had no enduring problem with reconciling this-worldly life and piety. Hinduism merged theology and culture so thoroughly that the two are virtually indistinguishable. Sexuality, eating, dancing—these were both cultural and religious. Buddhism (as a philosophy, not as it was eventually lived out) went to the opposite extreme, divorcing culture from theology. Buddhist priests withdrew from culture; there was no place for religion in secular life, as religion did not offer any answer for day-to-day problems.[8] Could it be that our notion of this dualistic dilemma between culture and piety is not part of the Christian worldview at all—but reflects pre-Christian answers to the enduring problem?

8. Corduan, *Neighboring Faiths*.

JESUS' ANSWER TO THE ENDURING PROBLEM

Throughout his life, Jesus thoroughly combined culture and piety, especially in the Sermon on the Mount, which Van Til fittingly called the "canon of culture." Jesus expected godly folks to be involved in the cultural systems of health, politics, economics, etc. He said "people do not live by bread alone," (Matt 4:4, NLT) but he broke bread with his disciples (Matt 26:26). Granted, economic, health, and political systems would need to be radically reformed under the kingdom of God. But Jesus' answer was not a withdrawal from the world; it was to enact just laws and to care for the poor. It was not to despise material wealth but to use it for good.

Others, including Niebuhr, see Jesus' theology of culture as enigmatic. His declaration "my kingdom is not of this world" (John 18:36, NIV) has been sorely misunderstood to mean that he has no interest in this world. Jesus' command not to worry about tomorrow or store up wealth (Matt 6:19–22) seemed to indicate that Jesus was uninterested in this world. In fact, Niebuhr argued that Jesus took theology completely out of culture,[9] causing cognitive dissonance for the church over the past 2,000 years.

So our theology of culture must establish Jesus' view of work and productivity, family, eating, relaxing, socializing. Jesus' full participation in human life as the incarnate God certainly indicated his high view of culture. Remember that he was not the ascetic that John the Baptist was, and he was criticized for that (Matt 11:18). It seems that by Jesus' day, the enduring problem was already plaguing the religious: one could not be a prophet and also engage in this-worldly culture.

JOHN AND PAUL'S ANSWER TO THE ENDURING PROBLEM

At times Paul, too, seems to despise this world. "The wisdom of this world is foolishness in God's sight . . . no more boasting about human leaders" (1 Cor 3:19–23, NIV). We see hints of asceticism in Col 2:20–23 and Rom 14:23. Paul told the church in Ephesus, "Our struggle is not against flesh and blood" (Eph 6:12, NIV). And when Paul told the church in Corinth not to be yoked together with unbelievers (2 Cor 6:14, NIV), he seemed to be encouraging this exclusivism that Niebuhr called "Christ against culture." But Paul was not encouraging withdrawal from cultural life; rather, he was

---

9. Niebuhr, *Christ and Culture.*

warning the church not to yoke themselves with the hateful philosophy of popular culture.[10]

And what of Paul's admonishment, "Do not be conformed to this world" (Rom 12:2, ESV)? It really comes down to how we interpret Paul's use of *aionos* (see the next section). Paul was not criticizing involvement in cultural life, but rather a mindless mimicking of this *generation*.

However, we also see a high view of cultural involvement in Paul's letters. He esteems marriage (1 Tim 4:3), the human body (1 Cor 6:19), proper use of wealth (1 Tim 6:10–18), and he certainly encouraged work (Col 3:23; Eph 4:28; 1 Thess 4:11, 5:14; 2 Thess 3:10; 1 Tim 4:1–5). So a balanced view of Jesus and Paul's approach is a posture of profound cultural involvement, which at times ran counter to the prevailing cultural norms.

What does "the world" mean in the New Testament?

In order to make sense of Jesus', John's, and Paul's multivocal response to the role of the pious in this-worldly culture, we need to understand their various renderings of four Greek words which are all rendered at times as "the world" in English. But "the world" takes on different meanings in different contexts. In one sense, the world is "the mass of mankind as alienated from God through sin."[11] In another sense, the world just means the material universe. In another sense, it means all human beings. And at times, it means something more like "this generation."

The New Testament employs four Greek words and four general renderings for "world." Unfortunately, there is not a one-to-one correlation between each Greek lexeme and the probable interpretation. The authors did not feel it was necessary to systematize the use of these terms, so a lexeme like *kosmos* must take on more than one meaning. Even the Apostle John, in Jesus' high priestly prayer (John 17), used *kosmos* with various senses. Table 4 shows the various ways that these Greek words can be rendered.

10. Van Til, *The Calvinistic Concept of Culture*, 210.

11. Ibid., 195.

Table 4: Comparison of the possible meanings of four terms rendered "world" in English, in the Greek New Testament

	Masses Alienated from God; the earth	All people (whole world, all the earth; nations/ kingdoms of the world; savior or reconciliation of the world)	The universe, (material rather than heaven— foundation/ creation of the world; gain the world)	Generation (end of the age)
Primary Greek lexeme	*Kosmos* John 1:10,14:30, 16:11 16:33, 17:9, 14, 24 1 Cor 1:21; 2:12, 3:19, 4:9, 13, 5:10, 6:2, 11:32 Heb 11:7 Jas 4:4 1 John 2:15, 16; 4:5; 5:19	*Kosmos* Matt 5:14; 13:35, 38; 26:13 Mark 14:9; 16:15 Luke 12:30 John 1:9; 3:16–17, 19; 4:42; 6:14, 33, 51; 9:39, 12:19, 47; 17:6, 18 Rom 11:15 1 John 2:2	*Kosmos* Mat 25:34 Mark 8:36 Luke 9:25; 11:50 John 13:1, 14:27; 17:5, 13, 24 Rom 1:20 Gal 4:3 1 Tim 6:7	*Aionos* Matt 12:32; 13:39, 40, 49; 24:3; 28:20 Mark 4:19; 10:30 Luke 1:70, 18:30, 20:34–35 John 9:32, Acts 15:18 1 Cor 3:18 Tit 2:12
Secondary Greek lexeme	*Aionos* Gal 1:4 1 Cor 2:6	*Aionos* Luke 16:8 1 Cor 1:20	*Aionos* Matt 13:22	*Kosmos* James 2:5
Tertiary Greek lexeme	*Oikoumene* Acts 17:31 Rev 12:9	*Oikoumene* Matt 24:14 Luke 2:1, 4:5 Acts 24:5 Rom 10:18 Rev 3:10		*Oikoumene* Heb 2:5
		Ge Rom 10:18		*Kairos* Mark 10:30 Luke 18:30

So when John says "Do not love the world or anything in the world. If anyone loves the world, love for the Father is not in them" (1 John 2:15,

NIV) he means don't love the sinful ways of this generation. When Jesus says "my kingdom is not of this world" (John 18:36, NIV), he means "my kingdom is not constricted by time and space as this material universe is." When Jesus is the savior of the world (1 John 4:14), he is Savior to the masses of humanity.

Since the discourse of the enduring problem centers on these verses, a biblical theology of culture must take into account the polysemous nature of these Greek lexemes rendered "world."

NIEBUHR'S ANSWER TO THE ENDURING PROBLEM

Niebuhr's taxonomies for Christ and culture have framed the discussion on the Christian's role in the world for the past fifty years. Niebuhr argued that three main postures toward culture have characterized the church: Christ against culture, Christ of culture, and Christ above culture (which contained three subgroups). Note that within each of these camps, the voices were multifaceted, and Niebuhr recognized that no single individual or movement completely embodied one of these three approaches at the total exclusion of the other two. The postures were tendencies, not absolutes. Or in Niebuhr's terms, they are motifs rather than "types."

Christ against culture

Niebuhr described the Christ against culture motif as a withdrawal from the wider society. St. Augustine (fourth century) pitted the city of God against the city of man—Jerusalem against Babylon. Augustine attacked Greco-Roman civilization, and abhorred nature: the arts, philosophy, and science had no place in Christendom. Sexuality was sinful, philosophy could not attain knowledge. Reason was fallible, since God alone is the ground of our certainty.[12]

The Donatists (fourth century) advocated withdrawal from the world. And much later Thomas a Kempis (fourteenth century) was a champion of *contemptus mundi,* "contempt for the world." Niebuhr's quintessential example of this motif was Leo Tolstoy, who, despite his wealth, had no interest in government, economics, philosophy, arts, or science. Exclusionists—those

---

12. See ibid., 74. Interestingly, though, Niebuhr did not consider Augustine to be emblematic of the Christ-against-culture motif.

who exclude the church from the world—saw involvement in the world as an either/or choice. You are obedient to Christ or you are lawless. There could be no middle ground. The church was in exile. To be a friend with the world was to be an enemy of God's (Jas 4:4).

Exclusionists (in this sense of the word) make bad citizens. If Christians withdraw from political, social, and economic life, should it be surprising when a Stalin or Hollywood successfully fills the void in economics, the arts, and political influence?

Christ of culture

"Christ of culture" was the posture of the Christian church that became so enjoined to society that you could not distinguish one from the other. Niebuhr's main examples were the liberal theologians of the nineteenth and twentieth centuries. These thinkers made an attempt to harmonize Christianity with popular culture—especially the popular denial of the supernatural, miracles, and the exclusivity of Christ. Jesus was reduced to the great hero of human culture. Niebuhr also called this posture Culture-Protestantism, found within the conciliatory or mainline churches. But an infiltration of popular cultural values into the church can arguably also be found within the prosperity gospel or even fundamentalism.

The decline in membership in mainline churches is indicative of a problem inherent in the Christ of culture posture. Contrary to what liberal theologians forecasted, people are attracted to Christ because of how he was engaged in culture yet critical of it. As Livermore showed with several examples, Jesus both embraced and protested the culture of first-century Palestine.[13] In an effort to be winsome to Westerners in the nineteenth and twentieth centuries, Culture-Protestantism actually deterred people from going to church. Why go to a church that asks nothing of me, and that doesn't teach me anything different from what my state university or my programs on television teach?

Even Niebuhr sensed a problem with the Christology of Culture-Protestantism. "It is not possible honestly to confess that Jesus is the Christ of culture unless one can confess much more than this."[14] Culture-Protestantism is still around, and continues to address the enduring problem by embracing, rather than protesting, Western-dominant values and norms.

13. Livermore, *Cultural Intelligence.*
14. Niebuhr, *Christ and Culture*, 115.

Christ above culture

If Christ was neither against nor of culture, then, Niebuhr explained Christ must be above it. Niebuhr saw three permutations of the Christ above culture motif: the synthesists, dualists, and conversionists.

The synthesists, Niebuhr explained, saw this world as a training ground for heaven. Clement (third century) argued that "God admonishes us to use indeed, but not to linger and spend time with secular culture."[15]

By this point in the book, the failings of the synthesists' approach should be clear. We cannot dichotomize God and this-worldly culture since our culturative nature is precisely what it means to be in God's image; and this world is, after all, God's very good creation.

The dualists, Niebuhr explained, saw Christ and culture in paradox. Humans are both righteous and sinners.[16] We live in an age of law and grace. We experience the continual struggle between flesh and spirit, as Paul described in Romans 7. For the dualists, culture was neutral—just a vehicle for transmitting ideals. At times, the culture will evidence the values of the redeemed; at times it will carry the values of the depraved. So Christians need not withdraw from wider society; they must remain faithful to Christ within it.

Martin Luther (sixteenth century) was Niebuhr's prototypical dualist. Luther recognized that Christians may aspire to be builders, physicians, carpenters, lawmakers. "Living between time and eternity, between wrath and mercy, between culture and Christ, the true Lutheran finds both tragic and joyful."[17] And Niebuhr explained, the only resolution we will find to this paradox is when we are taken up to be with Christ in heaven.

The conversionists employ the third posture within Niebuhr's Christ above culture motif. In my experience, evangelicals who have only passing knowledge of Niebuhr's taxonomy assume that they align with this approach of "Christ transforming culture." It takes a keen reader of Niebuhr to realize that his version of Christ transforming culture is about a hopeful humanism, where humankind is corrupt, but not inherently bad. The human race is on an inexorable trajectory where people will turn toward God as King.[18] There is no historical consummation, only human progress as the

15. Ibid., 128.
16. Ibid., 157.
17. Ibid., 178.
18. Ibid., 209, 214.

result of humans living godly lives.[19] What Niebuhr "meant by transformation is so inadequately defined that it is virtually indistinguishable from the Western doctrine of progress."[20]

So each of Niebuhr's motifs seem to fail to answer the enduring problem. In fact, there are a number of ways in which Niebuhr has been challenged. I will list three below.

Limitations of Niebuhr's approach

The most immediately obvious problem with Niebuhr's taxonomy is that it does not employ a consistent definition of Christ (Neibuhr's Christ is at times Jesus of Nazareth, at times a metonym for "the church," and at other times anything that points men to God). Likewise, Niebuhr could not find a consistent definition of culture. He variously described culture as social activity, human achievement, work, worldly values, or the total activity of humankind.[21]

Additionally, Niebuhr never conceived of a God-directed cultural life; culture was inherently against God.[22] One can see the danger here, of defining culture as only human activity. Christ, then, becomes super-cultural, which calls into question the incarnation.[23] Since Niebuhr's Christology was Docetic rather than Nicene, Christ could not be reconciled with culture. Christ must have been other-worldly.[24]

Another limitation of Niebuhr's taxonomy is its failure to incorporate the approaches of the majority world church. How has the persecuted evangelical church in China defined its role within wider society? What do African theologians say about the enduring problem? Do Niebuhr's motifs also describe the church in South America? In the Pacific? Niebuhr's church was ethnocentrically confined to the Western church in power.

A more theoretical problem with Niebuhr's answer to the enduring problem is his hermeneutic. Certainly, a theology of culture will be formed by one's view of Scripture. Literary critics, who see Scripture as wholly the product of human composition, expect the Bible to have conflicting answers

19. Parler, *Things Hold Together*, 53.
20. Gorringe, *Furthering Humanity*, 16.
21. D. A. Carson, *Christ and Culture Revisited*.
22. Carter, *Rethinking Christ and Culture*, 39.
23. Tennent, *Invitation to World Missions*, 160–163.
24. Carter, *Rethinking Christ and Culture*, 26.

to the enduring problem. Since human authors will contradict each other, there can be no reconciling of ideas from book to book in the Old or New Testament. Historical-critical scholars have a similar low expectation on the Bible's ability to give us a unified theology of culture. If the books reflect only the milieu at the time of composition, the multiple answers to the "enduring problem" may not be reconciled. On the other hand, evangelicals, committed to a metanarrative of Scripture (since it is inspired by one divine Author), seek to find an explanation for these seemingly paradoxical approaches.

But Niebuhr—probably best characterized as neo-Orthodox—had a low view of Scripture. For him, "the biblical language is true when taken symbolically and false when taken literally."[25] He did not come to Scripture with an expectation of a metanarrative or with unified parameters for delimiting orthodoxy. Instead, he just found various paradigms in various books. There were no heresies for Niebuhr, just competing paradigms. Evangelicals, on the other hand, try to construct a unified (albeit complex) picture of what the Bible says and means for us today.[26] For the evangelical, there are not conflicting traditions of Christ and culture in the Bible; instead, we find complementary narratives for defining our complex role within wider society.[27]

Table 5 represents the connection between hermeneutics and the enduring problem.

Table 5: Hermeneutics and the enduring problem

Literary-critical	Historical-critical	Evangelical (Metanarrative)
The Bible has conflicting or paradoxical solutions to the enduring problem There is no way to reconcile the various approaches.	The *sitz im leben* of various Bible books led to multiple, conflicting solutions to the enduring problem. There is no way to reconcile the various approaches.	The Bible is neither conflicting nor paradoxical. It deliberately gives various approaches to the problem to help us approach it in various situations in our life. The various approaches can be reconciled if we understand that there are different connotations to "world."

25. Parler, *Things Hold Together*, 41.

26. Ibid., 42.

27. D. A. Carson, *Christ and Culture Revisited*.

CALVINISTIC ANSWER TO THE ENDURING PROBLEM

Calvin's answer to the enduring problem was to conceptualize all of creation (culture)—work, civic life, the arts, etc.,—under God's sovereignty. Looking back, this may seem like an obvious solution. But it was actually seminal. "Calvinism is momentous in the history of Christian thought for thoroughly sweeping away the dualistic cosmologies and theologies of the past that pitted one part of creation against another, and replacing them with an ethical view of life that sees the whole of creation as an object of God's sovereign redemption."[28] I have referred to Calvin and Calvinists (such as Van Til and Kuyper) dozens of times, since their contribution to an evangelical theology of culture is immeasurable.

Henry Van Til's solution was association with culture, but without apostasy.[29] "We ought neither to despise nor deify creation, but we must use it in the service of God as one of his gifts."[30] Christianity is the way of restoring people's daily service to God through cultural activity.[31] So Van Til argued that there is no Niebuhrian dichotomy between Christ and culture—it is simply a matter of our duties. We must continually ask, "What is our duty to God, to society, to family, to the state?"

PACIFISTS' ANSWER TO THE ENDURING PROBLEM

In the twenty-first century, as the world becomes increasingly hostile to Christianity, another major deficiency in Niebuhr's taxonomy arises. Niebuhr did not imagine a "culture-against-Christ" scenario, he was only aware of a situation that was the other way around. Niebuhr was confined to the paradigm of Christendom, where the church had enjoyed power over Western Europe for 1,600 years. Meanwhile, Christianity struggled as a minority voice in other parts of the world. Yet Niebuhr framed his categories as if theologians could *choose* their posture toward culture or the wider society. "The relationship between Christ and culture . . . or more narrowly . . . between the church and the state. . . . is a luxury reserved for those who have options."[32]

28. J. Barber, *The Road from Eden*, 252.
29. Van Til, *The Calvinistic Concept of Culture*, 23–24.
30. Ibid., 194.
31. Ibid., 154.
32. D. A. Carson, *Christ and Culture Revisited*, 224.

In his monolithic tendencies, Niebuhr lumped those who removed themselves from wider society—whether pacifists, monastics, or ascetics—into the same category. However, the manner, extent, and reason for withdrawal from the dominant culture varied greatly for these exclusionists. For example, the Anabaptists did not withdraw from cultural life, they were forced out.[33] Therefore, Anabaptists severely criticize Niebuhr for characterizing pacifism as "Christ against culture." For example, Tertullian (second century AD) would not serve in the military, so Niebuhr considered him to be emblematic of this motif. Niebuhr apparently thought that to withdraw from some areas of public life (the state's coercive power) is to withdraw from all areas. Carter has argued that "Tertullian believed that there is nothing inconsistent with the lordship of Christ about being well-educated, articulate, creative, industrious, and committed to public service . . . Niebuhr's categories simply have no room for someone with the views of the historical Tertullian."[34] It is possible to be non-coercive, or to operate outside of the paradigm of Christendom, and still have a robust cultural contribution. But Niebuhr had no motif for that.

For example, rather than rant against culture, the partial withdrawal from public life led the Quakers to innovate in broad areas of culture, from pacifism, to reform in prisons, to international organizations for peace. Niebuhr did not recognize that a posture toward "culture" (and Niebuhr meant "wider society" in this case) will be complex:

> Some elements of culture the church categorically rejects (pornography, tyranny, cultic idolatry). Other dimensions are acceptable within clear limits (economic production, commerce, the graphic arts, paying of taxes for peacetime civil government). To still other dimensions of culture Christian faith gives a new motivation and coherence (agriculture, family life, literacy, conflict resolution, empowerment). Still others it strips of their claims to possess autonomous truth and value, and uses them as vehicles of communication (philosophy, language, Old Testament ritual, music). Still other forms of culture are created by the Christian churches (hospitals, service of the poor, generalized education).[35]

For Anabaptists like John Howard Yoder, the enduring problem does not involve a paradox of Christians and wider society, or Christ and culture, as

33. Carter, *Rethinking Christ and Culture*, 92.
34. Ibid., 62.
35. Yoder, "How H. Richard Niebuhr Reasoned," 54–55.

Niebuhr put it. The kingdom of God is found on heaven and earth. So there is continuity between this world and the next; or as Parler put it,[36] between creation and redemption. In fact, Parler answers the enduring problem with a return to the Trinity. Chalcedon, for instance, recognized Jesus as a political human. To pit Jesus Christ against creation (culture) is to have an errant view of the Trinity and of the role of the church in the world. Jesus is at the nexus of creation and redemption. The question is not whether this world (again, labeled by some as "culture") has any connection to the kingdom of God, but whether we will respond in obedience in this life, and make God our King.[37]

SOME MAJORITY-WORLD ANSWERS TO THE ENDURING PROBLEM

Outside of Christendom, the church has had a minority voice, and has dealt with the enduring problem in a different way. For example, in China, there was never a "Christ-above-culture" paradigm of Christendom—the church was always a minority voice. Interestingly, Matteo Ricci, an Italian missionary to China in the sixteenth century, developed a Niebuhrian-sounding taxonomy of "Christianity complying Buddhism, Christianity supplementing Buddhism, and Christianity surpassing Buddhism." Twentieth-century scholars Zixing, Wu, Chao, and Zia relied more on the forces of globalization to answer the enduring problem.[38] "As we have torn down the 'bamboo screens' of isolation and come into contact with the wider world and learned more about contemporary theological trends outside of China, many students are opening their eyes and beginning to take an interest in social issues such as world peace, justice, the integrity of creation, etc."[39]

SUMMARY: TWO KINGDOM V. THE HOLISTIC APPROACH

The myriad of responses to the question of the Christian's role in culture indicate how enduring this problem really is. We must have a robust

---

36. Parler, *Things Hold Together.*

37. Ibid., 102.

38. Zemin, "Christ and Culture in China," 51–53.

39. Ibid., 65.

theology of culture to be effective World Changers. And our "theology of everything" (for that is what it will entail) must be context-specific. Our faith is malfunctioning when it is too coercive or too insular.[40] Moses and Jesus both withdrew from society, but returned to transform it. Christianity, as well, must "ascend" and return with transformational purpose.[41] If we ascend too long, without returning, we become idle. If we return with exploitive force and coercion, our faith also malfunctions.[42]

> As a prophetic religion, Christian faith will be an active faith, engaged in the world in a noncoercive way—offering blessing to our endeavors, effective comfort in our failures, moral guidance in a complex world, and a framework of meaning for our lives and our activities.[43]

In fact, to avoid our role in social action, economics, politics, material culture, etc., is to abdicate the first command to fill and subdue the world. So the enduring problem must employ a high view of culture.

Table 6 summarizes theorists who have tried to solve the enduring problem of the Christian's role in the world. The most basic division between the theorists is those who emphasize our existence between two worlds at odds with each other (i.e., a fleshly, cultural one, and a spiritual one ruled by God) and those who fundamentally understand our *kosmos* and all of cultural life to be under the rule of God. The latter view is more holistic.

---

40. Volf, *A Public Faith.*

41. Ibid., 7.

42. Ibid., 9.

43. Ibid., 54.

Table 6: Summary of Theorists who dealt with Christ and culture

Heaven against Earth; two kingdom emphasis	Theorists or prominent figures	Contribution to theology of culture
	Donatists, Gnostics	*Contemptus mundi*
	Augustine	City of God, City of man
	Thomas a Kempis	*Contemptus mundi*
	Tolstoy	*Contemptus mundi*
	Niebuhr	Prescriptive pluralism, with a neo-orthodox hermeneutic
	Collin Greene	Apostolic, Pluralist
Heaven and earth; holistic kingdom emphasis	Calvin, Schaeffer	Free from church and state, under God
	Yoder	Trinitarian, pacifism, Creation-Redemption continuum
	Crouch	We are culturative beings
	Tennent	Christ is our redemption & meaning in this world and the next
	Kuyper, Van Til, J. Barber, J. Frame	Sphere sovereignty
	Volf	Human Flourishing

The division between these theoretical approaches—an emphasis on heaven against earth (two kingdoms) and a holistic heaven-and-earth emphasis—is profound. An emphasis on two competing kingdoms will cause us to see pleasure, even sexuality within marriage, as ungodly. It will cause us to feel ambivalent about our employment, since the only truly legitimate occupations would be church work and missions (and maybe professors at Christian universities). We will emphasize evangelism over social action, since heaven "matters more" than earth. The Christian response to politics would either be withdrawal (if Satan is the prince of the world) or Christendom. Figure 12 shows the rather sinister ramifications of the heaven-against-earth emphasis.

Figure 12: Ramifications of the "heaven vs. earth" view of culture

In contrast, a holistic kingdom view emphasis would find no dichotomy between secular and sacred. It would empower us to envision almost any type of employment as service unto God. Work, engagement in culture, would be one of many ways to glorify God. It would cause us to enjoy eating, friends, recreation, sexuality, etc., as long as it does not become idolatrous. It would lead us into the political realm so that we could love God and neighbor. Figure 13 summarizes the outflow of the "heaven and earth" view of culture.

Figure 13: Ramifications of the heaven and earth view of culture

REFLECTION AND REVIEW QUESTIONS

1. How do you reconcile being "heavenly minded" while still enjoying so many things on Earth? Does it make you feel guilty or ambivalent to enjoy the things of the world?

2. What is the difference between the heaven-against-earth kingdom and heaven-and-earth kingdom emphasis, and which approach enables Christians to be World Changers?

3. What is the "enduring problem" and what sorts of responses to the enduring problem would enable Christians to be World Changers?

PART III: God's thoughts about culture

CHAPTER 9

God's plan for culture

CHAPTERS 1–8 ARGUE THAT Christians cannot consistently hold to a low view of culture, or they would be assenting to the faulty logic below:

1. God's first command to humans was cultural activity in Genesis 1:28 and 2:15, and

2. Culture is "this-worldly" or bad; therefore:

3. God commanded sin.

Christians would recognize that the conclusion 3 is erroneous; but they may not recognize that the problem in the logic actually lies in premise number 2. In contrast to premise number 2, we must recognize that if God commanded cultural activity, and all of God's commands are good (Ps 119:39), then involvement in this-worldly pursuits are right and just. This explains why Jesus, Paul, and the early church were concerned with the extent of our involvement in world.

Granted, God's plan is for humankind to be cultural *under his sovereignty*. So all our systems—production, socializing, religion, etc., must be in obedience to him. This project of bringing all our cultural spheres under God's reign has been referred to as "sphere sovereignty."

Notice how before the fall, God had already put these spheres of culture into place:

• Production systems: God gave them seed-bearing crops (Gen 2:8–9).

• Ecological relationships: "have dominion over everything" (Gen 1:26).

• Reproduction and social organization: "be fruitful and multiply"; "Man shall leave his father and mother" (Gen 1:22, 2:24).

- Social regulation: "They were naked and unashamed" (Gen 2:25, 3:7).

- Religion: They communed with God (implied in Gen 3:8).

- Exploration and language: Adam gave names to creation (Gen 2:19–20).

- Aesthetics: Adam wrote a song about the beauty of his wife (Gen 2:23).

In fact, throughout the Bible, we see a high value placed on many spheres of culture. The Torah is cultural, with its laws on usury, marriage, and trading with just weights. It values marriage and sex, friends, work and use of the land, justice and political power, expression, leadership—to name a few areas of cultural activity. And Jesus' inaugural address in Luke 4:19–22, based on Isaiah 61, shows his concern for the matters of this world: the poor, the blind, the outcast and politically oppressed.

Hence a problem arises with Niebuhr's claim (see chapter 8) that at times Christians have held to the "Christ-against-culture" motif. If we define culture as "the acceptable practices, beliefs, and actions shared by members of a society," how can Christ be against culture? Is Christ actually against language? Is Christ against all our acceptable practices, beliefs, and actions? Not by any means. He is *for* the peoples of all ethnic cultures, yet he requires all our spheres of culture to be brought under his lordship. So our theology of culture must move from Niebuhr's ambiguous "Christ-and-culture" taxonomy to Christ's view of specific cultural activities. In this chapter, we will examine Christ and political systems, Christ and economics, Christ and social systems, and so on. These are the systems which are common to all cultures. The more we understand these cultural universals in biblical perspective, the better we understand our role as Christians in this world.

WHAT ELEMENTS ARE FOUND IN ALL CULTURES?

We are all image bearers. While there are drastic differences that arise, often along ethnolinguistic (cultural) lines, we have many similarities that go beyond our shared physiology as the human species. A theory of culture, and especially a *theology* of culture requires that we develop some "theory of humankind"—a framework for describing the aspects of human culture that are universal, and which manifest, albeit in different forms, in every human society. Anthropologists have noted that the better we understand universals, the better we understand human nature,[1] which is a central question for systematic theology.

The list of similarities is so long (leading to the conventional wisdom that "people are people") that it could never be comprehensive. Instead, if we want to talk about universals, we need a systematic way to talk about general tendencies among the world's societies. For example, we could boil down all of humanity with two broadly defined characteristics: love and rebellion. We all feel responsibilities and affections, and have cultural ways to express these. We also all exhibit selfishness and pride, and these flaws are expressed culturally. Nichols attempted to systematize some universals of humanity—what he called "solidarity with Adam."[2] His list included worship of a creator, rebellion against the creator, moral values and abuse of those laws, rational communication and its perverse use, creativity and its misuse, societal organization and fragmentation.

Nichols's universals fit into a category that may be called "individual universals,"[3] since they are part of being a "normal" human being. Other universals found in every individual include the expression of certain emotions like happiness and surprise through facial expressions. There are structural universals in the human psyche, like the tendency to polarize good/bad, male/female, hot/cold. And there are linguistic universals: all languages have pronouns, for instance.

There also seem to be cultural universals, though, throughout most of the twentieth century, anthropologists who were committed to extreme relativism sought to disprove the notion of such universals. The acceptance of cultural universals would be a move away from postmodernism, and from particularism. If cultures are to be studied in and of themselves, as if they are monads, why even look for universalities? Additionally, in terms of research methods, it is impractical to speak of universals since we do not yet possess the capability to gather data on all the ethnolinguistic groups to *prove* that such universals exist.

For example, Margaret Mead argued that Samoan sexuality during adolescence subverted the notion of universal taboos related to sexuality. But Freeman has shown that Mead's research methods and analysis were flawed; Samoans have strong sexual taboos, which were operating even at

1. Boas, "Anthropology," 109.
2. Nichols, "Towards a Theology of Gospel and Culture," 76–78.
3. Brown, *Human Universals*, 39.

the time of Mead's fieldwork.[4] Similarly, Whorf's argument that Hopi concepts of time were so radically different from Western notions seemed to subvert the notion of a universal concept of past, present, and future. But hundreds of pages of Hopi discourse provided by linguist Ekkehart Malotki actually provide more support of a universally held concept of time.[5]

By the twenty-first century, anthropologists have moved away from extreme relativism and the rejection of universals. Our ability to communicate across cultures successfully reveals some of this universality. And anthropologists, who cross cultures in a professional capacity, tacitly rely on these cultural universals.[6] Therefore, many introductory anthropology textbooks are organized around universal systems. Anthropologists systematically describe cultural *systems* that persistently manifest themselves in every culture. The presence of these systems may be because God has made us with these needs. It may not be going too far to say that these universals are what it means to bear his image. Remember that God is sovereign over each of these areas, and his word has much to say about each area. There is a strong connection between these cultural universals and what theologians have called "common grace" or general revelation. The two concepts are not coterminous, but each assumes the other. That is, if God is sovereign over all the earth, then every human society will be sustained by his grace, which is common to all humankind.

Certainly, it would be impossible to prove that a certain cultural feature existed in *every* culture, since there are around 15,000 ethnolinguistic groups. Plus, the boundaries between cultures are not clearly demarcated, and cultures are constantly in a state of flux. However, cross-cultural experts have complied a short list of "cultural universals." These would be the starting point for developing a theoretical framework for describing and comparing cultures. Anthropologist George Murdock's "Common denominator of Cultures" suggested the following universals:

> Age-grading, athletic sports, bodily adornment, calendar, cleanliness training, community organization, cooking, cooperative labor, dream interpretation, education, eschatology, ethics, ethnobotany, etiquette, faith healing, family, feasting, fire making, folklore, food taboos, funeral rites, games, gestures, gift giving, government, greetings, hair styles, hospitality housing, hygiene, incest taboos, inheritance rules, joking, kin-groups, kinship

4. Freeman, *Margaret Mead and Samoa.*

5. Brown, *Human Universals,* 27–32.

6. Ibid., 1–2.

nomenclature, language, law, luck superstitions, magic, marriage, mealtimes, medicine, modesty concerning natural functions, mourning, music, mythology, numerals, obstetrics, penal sanctions, personal names, populations policy, postnatal care, pregnancy usages, property rights, propitiation of supernatural beings, puberty customs, religious ritual, residence rules, sexual restrictions, soul concepts, status differentiation, surgery, tool making, trade, visiting, weaning and weather control.[7]

While this list certainly provides us with ample starting points for understanding universal features of humanity, the brevity does indicate how truly divergent the world's cultures are![8]

The shortcoming of Murdock's list is that it is not systematized; it gives the impression that culture is made up of a practically random compilation of practices. However, we can make sense out of human relationships and behavior. Systems theory, a popular theoretical framework in the twentieth century, led to a more systematic view of culture. Miller recognized systems within societies for kinship, education, economy, political religious association, health, and recreation.[9] Anthropologist Leslie White recognized that culture is made of *competing* systems: Every society has several "vectors" or blocs, such as the technological, social, and ideological systems.[10] Christian anthropologists often utilize these "cultural systems" as a way of studying culture;[11] but each scholar tends to categorize the systems a bit differently, sometimes further atomizing a certain system, or conflating several.[12] In general, though, we speak of cultures as consisting of at least the following systems:

1. Political system (leadership, power)

2. Economic system (exchange, markets)

3. Religious system (worldview, identity)

7. Murdock, "The Common Denominator of Cultures," 124; cf. Kraft, *Christianity in Culture*, 87.

8. Some of Murdock's "universals" are fairly undisputed; others are more controversial.

9. Miller, *Living Systems*.

10. White, *The Concept of Cultural Systems*.

11. Grunlan and Mayers, *Cultural Anthropology*; Howell and Paris, *Introducing Cultural Anthropology*; Kraft, *Anthropology for Christian Witness*.

12. Note that not all anthropologists prefer systems theory as a way of organizing cultural data. Other theoretical frameworks would include, for instance, worldview.

4. Material system (technological, arts, handicrafts)

5. Social system (kinship, rules, ethics)

While these systems are universals, they cannot show up except in actual cultural forms. In fact, since we cannot point to abstract universals—only to specific cultural forms—we may erroneously conclude that cultural specifics exist, but the universal forms do not. "Just as water cannot be transported except in containers, so universal functions cannot be performed except through cultural forms."[13] But the water is no less real than its container; and these universals are no less real than the cultural manifestations of them.

These cultural systems are also all ways of proclaiming the gospel—either responsibly or not. How we organize our economic, political, health, and educational systems shows what we believe about the character of God. Loving God with all our heart, mind, and strength involves loving him through our social, economic structures, through our arts, through our language, and our synergistic cultural efforts.

Further, submitting to God in all of these cultural spheres (art, morals, ideas, social relationships) is what we mean by the kingdom of God. Our culturative norms in each of these areas encompass what it means to be in the image of God. As Abraham Kuyper has famously said,

> No single piece of our mental world is to be hermetically sealed off
> from the rest, and there is not a square inch in the whole domain
> of our human existence over which Christ, who is sovereign over
> all, does not cry "Mine."[14]

The proclamation of the kingdom of God involves showing how each of these universals must align with godly principles. To successfully proclaim godly systems of power, or godly economic systems, we must know how to recognize and evaluate these systems within cultures. After we have done diligent study of those systems—and have observed how each of these systems are interconnected, we will find ourselves fluent in those spheres of culture. That fluency will allow us to proclaim the lordship of Christ in culturally appropriate ways. So proclamation of the gospel is more than translating a message about the removal of guilt of sin—it is bringing each of these spheres of culture under the lordship of Christ. To do this, we need

13. Kraft, *Christianity in Culture*, 98.

14. Kuyper, "Sphere Sovereignty," 488.

to work out not only a general theology of culture in general (chapters 3–7), but a theology of each sphere of culture (see Figure 14).

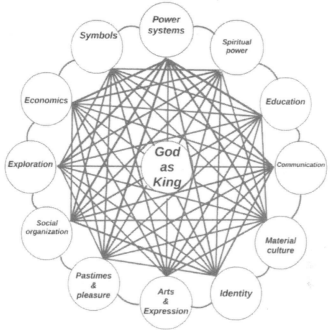

Figure 14: Theology of specific spheres of culture

Christ and political systems

A theology of political systems would start with the recognition that God intends for every society to employ methods for coercing and persuading people, and for resolving conflict. But a theology for the twenty-first century would need to recognize that there is a plurality of ways embedded in cultural norms for carrying out these divinely ordered purposes. Each society has systems for coercion, persuasion, and resolving conflict, including: family, judicial systems, local and national governments, and increasingly, transnational treaties and organizations like the UN Security Council.

Westerners may assume (erroneously) that political systems must involve modern systemic power structures, democracies, wealthy monarchs, or totalitarian dictators. Limiting politics to these "global" entities causes Westerners to miss the political system found at the family level, and within more traditional (or so-called primitive) cultures. For instance, tribal peoples do not hold elections, and their territory may be relatively small; but they do have a culturally acceptable way to wield power, persuade people, and resolve conflict. So when we form a theology of political systems, we must look beyond just the state-level governmental institutions, and look at power and conflict in general.[15]

Because the notion of this separation of church and state is so prevalent in Western cultures, evangelicals may find it strange to integrate theology and political cultural life. However, Christians have a long tradition of working out theologies of politics. Pope Gelasius I (fifth century) envisioned "two swords" or powers, both ruling under the sovereignty of God. This cooperation became known as caesaropapism, and was the hallmark of Christendom through the Medieval period. Aquinas and Calvin both theorized that God created us for political life as much as for every other cultural sphere, but that sin degraded this experience. "Citizenship in earthly political communities is thus as much a part of the revelation of God and of our identity as God's image bearer as are marriage, family, friendship, discipleship and shepherding."[16] The Bible gives a complex answer to the Christian response to political life, as it does for all spheres of cultural life. Jesus indicated that earthly powers are granted only as much power as God grants them (John 19:11). Romans 13:1–7 legitimates worldly governments; Acts 4:19 gives the other side of the coin: "Whether it is right in the sight of God to listen to you rather than to God, you must judge" (NIV). Calvin's view was that the state should not serve the church (as under Christendom) nor does it necessarily serve Satan (as exclusionists would argue) but the state must be brought under the sovereignty of God.[17] Since the first century, Christians have puzzled over whether the state's coercive power is legitimate. Should we go to war for our state? In fact, any religious system that has a claim on transcendent authority challenges earthly rule of law.[18]

A political system involves how power is distributed. When we study power within a culture, we look at coercive and supported power. In formal nation-states, the government has a monopoly on coercive power through

---

15. Anderson et al., *International Studies*, 11.

16. Skillen and McCarthy, eds., *Political Order and the Plural Structure of Society*, 37.

17. Van Til, *The Calvinistic Concept of Culture*, 95.

18. D. A. Carson, *Christ and Culture Revisited*, 200.

the use of the military and police. Traditional societies may have less coercive power; power is instead supported through consensus.[19]

Not all Christians support the use of coercive power. Anabaptists argue that we must put down the sword (coercive power) but still carry the plough (engage in work). The pacifist reading of Romans 13 is not a legitimization of governmental authority, but a restraining of it. Since governments inevitably take away individual rights, creativity, and property, Romans 13 is mitigating this tendency by placing governments below God. For John Howard Yoder, Lamech's boast in Genesis 4:24 is typical of governments—they will grab power and coerce their subjects; so God must limit it. In this interpretive tradition, the *lex talionis* (an eye for an eye) was a limitation of governmental coercion, not an endorsement of it.[20]

But note that government has many other functions besides coercion or violence. So a dismissal of political culture on the grounds of coercive power is to throw the baby out with the bathwater. Governments organize economic life, keep our appetites in check, and coordinate international policy.[21] Again, we see the integration of culture here (as in chapter 3). We can no more withdraw from political life than we can from language, production, or social organization.

A theology of political power also involves examining how societies lend legitimacy to power structures. Is the leader legitimate because of his bloodline, wealth, education, a supernatural calling, or because he was elected? Every culture seems to have norms for leadership that include how a leader is selected, what his duties are, his length of tenure, ways to censure him, and how the next leader will be selected.

The political system is also about maintaining alliances. Modern nation-states do this through treaties; traditional cultures maintain alliances by sharing life together, e.g., through intermarriage and the exchange of goods.

To summarize, a theology of culture in this century must recognize the plurality of ways that cultures organize their political lives. While we may defend our own cultural political life, we must avoid the temptation to idolize the hallmarks of Western governance, as it relates to individual choice (sometimes at the expense of the welfare of others). But to be involved in

---

19. Kurtz, *Political Anthropology.*

20. Parler, *Things Hold Together.*

21. Skillen and McCarthy, eds., *Political Order and the Plural Structure of Society.*

political life certainly includes bringing just structures that enable people to enjoy and glorify God.

Christ and economic systems

People in all societies produce goods (crops, handicrafts, livestock, and even people). They often exchange these goods to create alliances. And all cultures have norms for marking people's status based on the wealth they accumulate. As with the political sphere, Westerners may not recognize the economic system in nonindustrial societies, because Westerners equate economics with the accumulation of wealth as a necessary pathway for achieving happiness. Some societies in the world do not conceive of economics in this way.

In many traditional cultures, the accumulation of wealth brings about suspicion and disdain. Some will say the wealthy accumulated their riches through sorcery; many others will see the wealthy as greedy. In fate-oriented cultures, wealth is often conceived of as a reward for the few who deserve it, perhaps because they previously lived an honorable life. So it does not "go without saying" that everyone's goal, no matter the culture, is to accumulate wealth. Attitudes about wealth are changing because of globalization; nonetheless, these views are culturally patterned, and vary from culture to culture.

Before European contact, many tribal peoples needed no currency at all, but regularly exchanged gifts like betel nut, cassava, and fruits. And on more important occasions they exchanged pigs, cattle, or even gave women away in marriage. While there is some pragmatic value to trading in tribal societies—an inland village may have more almonds and chestnuts whereas a coastal village may have more coconuts and bananas—trade is largely about maintaining alliances. Tribal peoples often exchange yams for yams, coconuts for coconuts, and even brides for brides. The point in an exchange-based economy, in contrast to a market economy, is not to accumulate wealth or to meet a material needs. Exchange is about establishing relationships.[22] So even where there is no market system, or cash economy, there is still an economic system. While exchange is the predominant economic system in Melanesia, some cultures also used a sort of currency for trade and status. Before European contact, peoples in Papua New Guinea used cowrie shells as currency. Nowadays, the world's societies are hybrid-

22. Mauss, *The Gift.*

izing a cash economy with previously held cultural norms of exchange. Both of these economies are ways of ensuring prosperity and security.

As we work out a theology of culture, it is important to see how the economic system reflects underlying values. What does it show about the role of the individual within the context of the larger community? Is a person just "labor" to produce wealth? Is the person a commodity to be traded? Are relationships valued above the actual commodities being traded? In other words, is trade symbolic, or pragmatic?

World Changers must make themselves aware of the economic subsystems for a number of reasons. First of all, we need to know how to fulfill our role in society. Are we the rich in this culture? How do the rich behave in appropriate ways? How is generosity defined? Also, we want to see how economics are tied to other areas of life. How is economic activity a social activity? How does the generation of goods and services reflect the worldview of people?

Is any certain economic system more biblical than another? In other words, can we arrive at a theology of economics? The economic system is a means for managing people into productivity, or cultural behavior. That is, economic productivity is a measure of how well we are carrying out the cultural mandate to subdue the earth.[23] The church has a vital role to play in the production and distribution of wealth; especially as we testify that godliness is the goal and prosperity is a sign of godliness.[24] A theology of economics is about getting people to make something of the world, despite the fall.

Since the time of John Calvin, Protestants have based their theology of economics on biblical ideals of free markets—economies that are not heavily guided by governments—in passages about work and private property.[25] Work, Asmus and Grudem argue, is the biblical model for productivity (Prov 6:6–10; 2 Thess 3:10; 1 Tim 4:1–5; Col 3:23–24).[26] Rundle and Steffen argue that work was a "central part of [Paul's] mission strategy" since "spreading the gospel for free added credibility to his message and served as

---

23. J. Barber, *The Road from Eden*, 255; Kotter, "How Economic Profits Relate to the Creation Mandate."

24. Volf, "The measure of the church."

25. J. Barber, *The Road from Eden*, 255

26. Asmus and Grudem, *The Poverty of Nations.*

a model for his converts to follow" (Acts 18:1–3; 20:34–35; 1 Cor 4:11–13; 1 Thess 2:9; 2 Thess 3:8).[27]

Asmus and Grudem argue that free markets in liberal governments (ones that allow many personal freedoms) employ the political-economic ideology that best allows people to carry out the cultural mandate. Communism, governmental planning, slavery, were all imperfect ways of coercing people to fill the earth and subdue (make use of) it. Free markets encourage moral behavior, whereas markets that are heavily controlled by governments encourage bribery, corrupt courts, thievery, and extracting wealth from rightful owners.[28]

When the economy is productive, however, the sinfulness of human structures becomes apparent. People cannot serve two masters (Matt 6:24) and they often choose money. Whereas Jesus calls for sacrifice (Luke 9:57–62) and justice, capitalistic economics myopically focuses only on production, advertising, and consumption, which often leads to debt. It is this weakness of capitalism—especially its unashamed emphasis on (over-) consumption, that evangelicals find concerning. However, neither capitalism nor money are the root of all evil; the love of money (or self) is (1 Tim 6:10).

There are other models, besides capitalistic markets, which could potentially allow for economic production and justice. But models like redistribution never *create* anything. And, productivity—making something of the world (whether goods or services) is the only way that any nation has ever come out of poverty.[29] Ecclesiastes 2:24–25 (NIV) says that "a person can do nothing better than to eat and drink and find satisfaction in their own toil." And Colossians 3:23 (ESV) says "Work heartily, as for the Lord, and not for men." God commanded humankind in the cultural mandate to use its skill. Exodus 36:1 (ESV) says the Lord put skills and intelligence into various workers, to "work in accordance with all that the LORD has commanded." When Israel came into the promised land God did not promise them perennial donations of riches from other nations, but hills filled with iron and copper (which they would have to dig and refine) and fields of vines and fig trees (which they would have to tend and harvest each year). God's blessing of prosperity would come by productive work

---

27. Rundle and Steffen, *Great Commission Companies*, 43.

28. Asmus and Grudem, *The Poverty of Nations*, 193.

29. Chewning, ed., *Biblical Principles and Economics*; Novak, *The Spirit of Democratic Capitalism*.

(Deut 8:7–10)."[30] Proverbs 6:9–11, 14:34, and 28:19 all indicate that work is necessary for generating wealth—which is, after all, what a good economic system sets out to do.

Another essential element of a biblically based economic system is private property. While the Israelites divided land according to the tribe, Asmus and Grudem have argued that individual private property was the biblical model. Leviticus 25:10 (ESV) says "each of you shall return to his property and each of you shall return to his clan." The eighth commandment, the injunction against stealing (Ex 20:15) presupposes private property. Asmus and Grudem also cite laws about private property in Exodus 21:28–36, 22:1–15; Deuteronomy 19:14, 22:1–4, 23:24–25; and Proverbs 22:28, 23:10. Asmus and Grudem quote Sirico,[31]

> Private property demonstrates the interpenetration between our physical bodies and our capacity for transcendence. We engage nature with labor that our reason plans and directs—and produce something that did not previously exist. Not just another beaver dam exactly the same as the ones beavers have been building for millennia, but a Chartres cathedral, a Mona Lisa, or an electric light bulb, a smallpox vaccine, a revolution in agriculture that lifts millions of people out of dire poverty.[32]

In summary, Asmus and Grudem have argued that the free market is a God-given process for carrying out the cultural mandate:

> The free market is a wonderful, God-given process in human societies through which the goods and services that are produced by the society (supply) continually adjust to exactly match the goods and services that are wanted by the society (demand) at each period of time, and through which the society assigns a measurable value to each good and service at each period of time, entirely through the free choices of every individual person in the society rather than through government control.[33]

The ramifications for evangelicals in this century would be to embrace market activity rather than apologize for it—but we must be aware of the temptations of greed and consumerism. Calvin's economics focused on the shared possessions (Acts 2:42) but individual responsibility and work.

30. Asmus and Grudem, "The only way for poor to escape from poverty."

31. Sirico, *Defending the Free Market.*

32. Asmus and Grudem, *The Poverty of Nations*, 191.

33. Grudem, *Politics According to the Bible*, 276.

Calvin argued that both agriculture (nonindustrial work) and production are godly; what is ungodly is haughtiness and pride.[34]

In summary, "Christ observes not only how we pray, but how we hold the spade."[35] This enthusiasm for work is a long-standing trend within Protestantism. In fact, a stained glass window in a church down the street from my home includes icons of biblical figures, but at the very bottom, it has an oil derrick and a man plowing his field with his tractor. It fits in the church's theology of culture that their modern way of worshipping God is to use their local resources to prosper and help others.

Christ and religious systems

Though some nation-states are officially atheistic, every society has a religious system, which is integrated with the other systems. World Changers have long sought to bring these systems under the Lordship of Christ. Some have argued that religion is not merely a *part* of culture.[36] Humans are religious beings, created to experience the covenant relationship with God, and culture serves that purpose. So culture is a part of religion, and not the other way around. When Van Til makes this distinction, he introduces the concepts of *cultus* and *culture*. *Cultus*, what we normally mean by the religious life, is one way of living out our relationship with God. *Cultus* involves prayer, sacrifice, obedience. Culture, or everything else in life that is not directly related to *cultus*, is no less an act of worship—no less religious—than *cultus*. We are in error if we think of religion as a *part* of culture, as if it were ancillary or even unnecessary. To define religion as a phenomenon, albeit a universal phenomenon, which we could take or leave, the way we may see the cinema or football as a *part* of culture. Humans can no more separate themselves from religion than they can from nutrition or excretion. Nonetheless, as we proceed in our theology of culture, I plan to use the term religion to refer specifically to what Van Til meant by *cultus*: the outward religious life.

Religion seems to have existed for all time in all places, though it varies so greatly from culture to culture that it is nearly impossible to define. Tribal peoples use magic to generate fortune; others fear spirits in sacred waters or forests. Some Hindus are polytheists, others are pantheists.

34. Van Til, *The Calvinistic Concept of Culture*, 102–106.
35. Ibid., 146–147.
36. Van Til, *The Calvinistic Concept of Culture*.

Formal Buddhism is atheistic, and Buddhists seek to attain enlightenment through meditation. Is there any unifying theme here that allows us to establish definitely that religion is a culturally universal system? Corduan has suggested that religion is "a system of beliefs and practices that by means of its cultus directs a person toward transcendence and thus, provides meaning and coherence to a person's life."[37] By transcendence, Corduan means people are looking for eternal meaning beyond themselves and even beyond their society. They may not believe in God or gods, but their religious system allows them to construct metaphysical explanations for suffering, and the purpose of life. And by *cultus*, Corduan means that religion involves publicly practiced rituals, in contrast to an individual's own sense of "spirituality," which would not be religion, per se.

A shortcoming of Corduan's attempt at a universal description of religion is that it focuses on the search for transcendence to the neglect of the this-worldly nature of religion. Many behaviors that we consider to be religious (magic, prayer, sorcery, divination, witchcraft, amulets, sacrifice, taboos, washings, and rituals) are not as much about *transcendence* as they are about securing fortune in this life, and the redirection of misfortune towards one's enemies. Tribal peoples use magic to make their gardens grow, heal sicknesses, and to encircle their enemies. Polytheists likewise complete rituals to ensure longer life, better crop yields, and healthy pregnancies. Monotheists do not typically follow these practices, but pray and worship, in part to ensure health, happiness, direction, safety, and "traveling mercies." While the search for transcendence is an important part of religion, a definition of religion must include "salvation" in this life: health, guidance, peace (at least among allies), and heirs.

A theology of *cultus*, then, requires bringing all the outward rites and rituals under Christ's lordship, as well as the invisible aspects like the nature of truth, the purpose of life, and the concept of the afterlife.

Christ and technological systems

Much of what we observe when we become acquainted with the world's cultures is the material culture: the arts, crafts, technology, clothing, instruments, tools, etc. Materials and cultural artifacts vary from place to place, but is certainly a universal that societies modify the materials around them in contextual-specific ways. For example, tribal societies typically specialize

37. Corduan, *Neighboring Faiths*, 28.

in fishing, hunting, weaving baskets, and constructing homes out of "bush materials." Peasant societies specialize in production activities like farming specific cash crops (e.g., coffee or rice) or manufacturing. Material culture in urban societies is extremely complex and diversified.

The technique of using our natural resources is referred to as technology. So technology is not specifically limited to the automated and mechanized marvels of the twentieth and twenty-first centuries. Stone adzes and weaving techniques are also technologies which are culture-specific.

Cross-cultural novices and travel guides usually limit their descriptions of societies to the material culture. They report on the most visible elements like clothing styles, music, sports, and food. To achieve a more in-depth understanding of cultures, it is important to note how material culture affects (and reflects) the more subtle religious, economic, political, and social systems. How do housing materials or arts and crafts relate to the culturally patterned attitudes about time, hospitality, status, and role? Often, material culture is the "data" which can be used to plot a particular culture within a cross-cultural theoretical framework.

What is God's plan for our material culture and our technology? This sphere of culture is probably the arena where humans unleash their creativity the best. While it would be strange to think of God as having technology or material culture, it is clear that our God loves to create. Note that Jesus was a *tekton* (carpenter)—he used his contextually specific materials to create things that made sense for his cultural logic.[38] And creating is what we do with the materials around us. God's plan is for us to use our material culture and technology to bless him and others—not to harm. Our iGods (as Fuller professor Craig Detweiler has called them) are responsible not only for evils like the proliferation of pornography, but also for transforming how we disseminate the gospel. The globalization of modern technology has undoubtedly fomented consumerism among the least privileged peoples, but has also brought these people educational opportunities they never could have obtained in previous decades.[39]

The term *technology* seems so mechanical or "instrumental" that we get the impression that it is morally neutral.[40] In reality, though, technology has a corrupting and redeeming power[41] and a theology of culture requires

38. Detweiler, *iGods*, 222.

39. Ibid., 201–2.

40. Kallenberg, *God and Gadgets*, 106.

41. Dyer, *From the Garden to the City*.

us to determine how to use our material culture in ways that redeem. Consider Kallenberg's example of a simple hammer:

> Even a hammer is not morally neutral. Sure, it can be used to build a house or cave in someone's skull. But setting aside these actual uses, the hammer is not in and of itself neutral. We only have hammers because humans need to construct shelter. Constructing shelter is morally good because it meets a genuine human need. (Thus Habitat for Humanity is a morally good program.)[42]

And Christians have a long tradition of using material culture and creative nature to bless others.

> Christianity is both the source of modern technology and the source of our inability to make a moral sense of our technological capabilities . . . [because] historically, Christian theology never fully grasped the implications of this ability, thus eventually leaving humans with tremendous creative power but no clear understanding of how those powers should be used. [But] a transformed Christianity—one that fully comes to grips with the creative capacities it has unleashed—is the only understanding of the world and the place of humans in the world that can allow us to make moral, and ultimately spiritual, sense of our technological capabilities.[43]

Since material culture is integrated with all other aspects of culture (politics, economics, expressive culture, etc.), our evangelical approach will inevitably have an effect on each of these areas.

Christ and social systems

Anthropologists have especially focused on the universal social aspect of culture. What is God's plan for our social relationships? It seems that God has designed social relationships as the way in which we learn, love, serve, lead, and forgive. The social systems are one of the primary ways we see God's attributes reflected in humanity.

Anthropologists have noticed that our social relationships are the mechanism by which culture is transmitted. Since culture is learned, rather than biologically determined, societies must transmit values and norms for

---

42. Kallenberg, *God and Gadgets*, 107.

43. Jardine, *The Making and Unmaking of Technological Society*, 9.

proper behavior to subsequent generations. In other words, societies need a way to socialize their members.[44] Wallace theorized that the social subsystem is primarily about generating similarity and organizing differences.[45] Societies generate similarities (i.e., cultural norms) by developing rules to delineate certain people as kin, affines, allies, or exchange partners. They organize differences by developing rules for how people of different statuses, genders, ethnicities, etc., must act when they are together in a group.

In the mid-twentieth century, the study of culture was dominated by social anthropology—especially descriptions of kinship systems. British social anthropologists developed comprehensive taxonomies for kinship. Anthropology became loaded with terms like affine, cosanguine, neolocal, and bilateral descent. We used genograms to trace kinship relations like mother's father's sister's son, or father's mother's brother's daughter. Cognitive anthropologists wanted to discover how people from various cultures kept all this information about kinship straight in their own minds, and how they transmitted this information. Social anthropologists wanted to discover if there were universals for kinship. For a time, "formal" anthropologists believed there were only six kinship systems that described all of the cultures: Hawaiian, Sudanese, Eskimo, Iroquois, Crow, and Omaha. "Particularlists" adamantly disagreed with the notion that the world's cultures can be boiled down to six "universal" systems, and said that each kinship system must be studied and described on its own terms.

But kinship is only one of many aspects of the social system in a culture. This system also includes ways of controlling people's behavior. Cultures use the social system to transmit norms such as sexuality, inheritance, and gender roles. The methods of educating young people are part of the social system, since cultures use education to train children in ethics, values, and social etiquette. Below are a number of patterns that fall under the sphere of social systems:

- education, transmission of wisdom
- gender roles and equality
- age roles
- rites of passage
- groups, organizations, race

44. Anderson et al., *International Studies*, 110.
45. Wallace, *Culture and Personality*.

- socioeconomic mobility

- ascribed and earned status

- social control/discipline and coping/comforting

- obligations and rights

- ethics

- defense

- marriage

- bride wealth

- allegiances and loyalties

- duties to the in-group and out-group

A robust theology of culture requires us to bring each of these social relationships under Christ's lordship, and essentially involves exegeting 1 Peter 2:17 according to each cultural situation: "Show proper respect to everyone, love the family of believers, fear God, honor the emperor" (NIV).

Evangelicals have thought through some of these social relationships more than others, and our focus has been on two social units: 1) the smallest social unit: the nuclear family; and 2) the church.

The family

Evangelicals have spent more of their time thinking though the theology of the family than any other cultural subsystem. If you look at the shelves in a Christian bookstore you'll be hard-pressed to find a section on Christ and politics or Christ and recreation. But there are entire sections on social relationships: what does it mean to be a Christian husband or wife; what does it mean to be a Christian parent or child? In fact, the theology of the family is the defining program for evangelicalism in the twentieth century, especially as evangelicals have noted the ways in which the dominant Western culture is undermining marriage, marital purity, the role of father and mother.

The family is also often the primary locus of social control. A dominant role of social systems is keeping people in line. Individuals, left to their own devices, would steal, cheat, lie, and behave violently. Societies have organized themselves in ways to effectively keep this sinful nature in check. This pressure to obey the rules begins with the parents, as they discipline their own children. Other social institutions that keep people in line (courts, police, local and national governments) are modeled after the parental role.

The church

God's plan for the social organization of Israel was spelled out throughout the Pentateuch, as God laid out status and role, clan divisions, the use of land, and described numerous family obligations, as well as obligations to foreigners. In the New Testament, the church is the new social unit. A theology of social systems requires understanding the role of each believer's place within the body of Christ (Rom 12).

Christ and expressive culture: aesthetics, beauty, and pleasure

Every society has means for enjoying the beauty of creation through expressive culture such as visual arts, dance, storytelling, and music. God has created us with this universal characteristic. As I argued in the introduction of this book, if we are going to glorify God, we must do so through culture—we have no other way to enjoy him!

The role that Christians should play in expressive culture has come under intense debate. Is the answer for Christians to boycott the film industry the way that Southern Baptists voted to boycott Disney?[46] Should Christians create their own parallel romance novels and film production companies, in response to secular companies? Should the paintings on our church walls be limited to Thomas Kinkaid's works? Is it even right for us to try to express the beauty of God—who is high above creation—through art and sculpture? Can Christians dance? Should our church buildings be grandiose or plain? How should Christians dress? All of these questions are related to a theology of expressive culture—of how we view the role of culture and how we form our own identities.

The ambivalence toward the visual arts persists in Protestant churches, which tend to be drab in comparison to the tradition of embracing expressive culture in the Roman Catholic and Orthodox churches. Reformed churches have typically been fairly iconoclastic, forbidding portrayals of Jesus in sculpture or paintings.

46. CNN, "Southern Baptists Boycott Disney."

John Barber's monumental study of Christian involvement in culture has revealed that Christians have always embraced expressive culture (sarcophagi, wall paintings, architecture, songs)—for its didactic, apocalyptic and symbolic functions.[47] In fact, they repurposed expressive culture: Whereas secular societies have used the arts to idolize leaders or humans, Christians use the arts to put humans and leaders in their place, with God on the throne. And Jesus himself used the expressive arts. An article in the evangelical magazine *Christian Observer* in 1827 argued that the incarnation is an example of divine sanctioning of expressive culture: "It is not only innocent, but laudable, to consecrate the powers of taste and fancy to his glory, by himself condescending to use the language of poetry, and the most splendid and impressive imagery."[48]

Beauty

John Calvin argued that Christians must focus on the beauty of holiness rather than the holiness of beauty, lest we exchange the creation for the creator. And yet, Calvin introduced the psalter and congregational singing to church life.[49] Evangelicals typically recognize hymn-singing as a legitimate form of artistic expression, as long as the words are recognizable.[50] Even Handel's Messiah was controversial in the late eighteenth century because, despite its didactic function, evangelicals opposed the "theatricality of public performances."[51]

Not all Protestants have held a philistine attitude toward expressive culture. In fact, there is a long tradition within Protestantism that encourages expressive culture. Abraham Kuyper argued for a moderated involvement in the arts.[52] He reasoned that beauty is anything that glorifies God, but ugliness within creation also teaches us a lesson. Beauty is scriptural, but acting as if it is the highest ideal is to neglect other important attributes of God. Even physical beauty was a value in Scripture: Sarah was very beautiful (Gen 12:11); Job's second set of daughters were more beautiful than the first (Job 42:15); Absalom and Moses were described as attractive

47. J. Barber, *The Road from Eden.*
48. Rosman, *Evangelicals and Culture*, 144.
49. Van Til, *The Calvinistic Concept of Culture*, 110–111.
50. Rosman, *Evangelicals and Culture*, 98.
51. Ibid., 104.
52. Kuyper, *Wisdom & Wonder.*

(Exod 6:2; Heb 11:23). Kuyper developed a threefold taxonomy of beauty, to resolve the extremist tendencies of hedonism on the one hand or asceticism on the other. These were Kuyper's three beauties:

- Eden beauty—creation before humankind's cultural activity
- Current beauty—the beauty of the world, as God's creation, albeit in its fallen state
- Paradise beauty—our eternal experience of beauty in heaven

Kuyper's three beauties allow us to appreciate beauty in its various forms on earth without making it into an idol by conflating it with the eternal beauty we will enjoy in heaven.

Film

Johnston's theology of film traces postures toward expressive culture that range from avoidance to dialogue to accommodation.[53] Nowadays, many Christians lean somewhere between dialogue and accommodation. Instead of arguing "We should get more Christians in Hollywood and fix the problem" they are asking "How can we use the most popular films to engage people in dialogue about God?" Christ figures (whether intentional or subconscious) abound in popular films, and are excellent ways to use expressive culture to engage in theological topics.[54] Most impactful films touch on ethical dilemmas, which are also open doors for discussing the Christian worldview.

While Hollywood (and now Bollywood and many other foreign film industries) provides a platform for us to engage our neighbors in theological discussions, there is a distressing side of film in modern cultures which cannot be redeemed simply through dialogue. Gratuitous violence and sexuality are hardly adequate platforms for instigating theological discussions.

Popular culture

A similar discussion is happening among Christians about their role in other areas of popular culture (in the West, anyway). Musical themes regularly

---

53. Johnston, *Reel Spirituality*.
54. Malone, *Movie Christs and Antichrists*.

contain a search for redemption.[55] Why else would the psalm say "sing to the LORD a new song" (Ps 96:1, NIV) unless God wants us to utilize the expressive arts? The role of theology in Western music can be traced from Bach[56] all the way to modern hip hop.[57] Other thinkers have examined how theologizing is done in comic strips like *Peanuts*,[58] and television shows like *The Simpsons*[59] and *Seinfeld*.[60] It should not be surprising that Christian thinkers are considering the theological implications of virtually every aspect of popular culture, since a theology of culture, after all, eventually develops into a robust theology of everything.

As with any facet of contextualization, World Changers must begin by studying expressive culture in its context—to understand the media in and of itself. After we have understood how people express themselves within a cultural context, we can make evaluations based on biblical criteria, and seek to be change agents. But in an effort to find the underlying message of every work of art, every dance movement, and every piece of music, evangelicals are misapplying the art form. By insisting on the didactic usefulness of all art, we are left choosing between 1) finding propositional truths in every creative expression in our culture, or 2) giving up any attempt to make the art useful. But we have a third option: we can appreciate art without expecting it to be directly useful as an evangelistic tool.

Christ and identity

Universally, societies have patterned norms for managing identity. What is the role of the individual in decision-making? What is the status of the in-group vs. the out-group? For example, many vernacular demonymns mean something like "the people," implying that ethnic outsiders are less than human. Given that we organize our lives around so many identities (ethnic, socioeconomic, gender, regional), what is God's plan for our identity?

Evangelicals have brought this issue to the fore as they meditate especially on our new identity in Christ (2 Cor 5:17; Gal 2:20; 1 Pet 2:9; Rom 12:2; Col 3:3). Jesus challenged the culturally patterned notions of identity

55. S. Turner, *Hungry for Heaven.*
56. Stapert, "Bach as Theologian."
57. Sorett, "Believe Me, This Pimp Game is Very Religious."
58. Short, *The Gospel According to Peanuts.*
59. Pinsky, *The Gospel According to the Simpsons.*
60. Hibbs, *Shows about Nothing.*

in his context. In a shift that may seem peculiar to those outside of Christ, the emphasis on our new identity in Christ is the diminishing of ourselves, and the prominence of Christ.

Christ and symbols: myth and ritual

Most of our cultural information (values, norms, expectations) is transmitted subtly through myth and symbols, rather than through a list of propositions. For instance, mothers tell their young children the frightening stories of Little Red Riding Hood and Hansel and Gretel to imply the danger of strangers. Homer's epics *Iliad* and *Odyssey* were far more effective at fostering a sense of Greek nationalism than if Homer had simply chanted "Greece is the best." The sculpture of four soldiers raising the US flag at Iwo Jima is more powerful than a plaque that reads "Our soldiers are brave." Universally, cultures harness the affective quality of symbols and myth to say what words alone could not.

One of the most visible symbolic components within society are rites of passage. These rites make up a colorful and creative part of cultural life, as societies celebrate birthing, puberty, marriage, and death. Cultures include an endless variety of other rituals, from circumcision, to birthdays, to the falling of the umbilical cord, appearance of the first tooth, first shaving, etc. These rituals appear at transitions in life, when a person changes identity and role in society. For example, puberty rituals happen when a young person is neither child nor adult. Likewise, two single people change their status and role in society at the time of the marriage ceremony. Some anthropologists have theorized that these periods, when people's identities are in transition, are the most vulnerable times in life. This vulnerability causes great anxiety for people; they see these transitions as spiritually charged events, where misfortune is most likely to happen. Therefore, anthropologists theorize that societies have innovated these rites of passage to relieve anxiety and ensure safety.[61]

Interestingly, rites of passage are tied to another cultural universal that is loaded with symbolic meaning: myth. Cognitive anthropologists theorize that the primal myths in societies contain elements of dominant rituals in the culture. As parents tell the myths to their children, they reinforce the ritualistic practices. But there is a chicken-and-egg enigma here: Maybe the rituals came first, and the myths emerged over time as a way of legitimizing

---

61. V. Turner, *The Ritual Process*; van Gennep, *The Rites of Passage*.

the rituals. Either way, myth and ritual work together to symbolically transmit underlying values, and to foster a sense of identity.

Cultures also all seem to be organized around dominant metaphors (viz. Victor Turner), or key symbols[62]—what James Fernandez (1986) called the culture's tropes. These tropes or dominant metaphors can be oft repeated maxims like "if at first you don't succeed, try, try again;" or they can be more tangible, like the automobile, or Mt. Fuji. Anthropologist Victor Turner theorized that cultures have dominant metaphors which "condense" a variety of values in a culture in a symbolic way.[63] For instance, the Mukula Tree is an important cultural symbol for the Ndembu in Zimbabwe, symbolizing bloodline and specifically matrilineal descent. The Irish pub may symbolize the values of socializing, entrepreneurship, and relaxation. For US-Americans, the automobile symbolizes our values of individualism, production, freedom, status, and consumption. Jindra has suggested that the court system is a "central focus" (viz. Melville Herskovits) for USA culture, while the *quinceañera* would be an apt metaphor for Latin American culture.[64]

God created us to be affected by symbols and ritual. We see ritual tied to narratives in Scripture in a number of instances. The story of the exodus is tied to the Passover ritual (Exod 12); the story of Jacob wrestling with God is tied to a taboo about eating the hip joint (Gen 32:32); the story of Abraham's call from God is tied to the ritual of circumcision (Gen 17). The communion ritual is tied to Jesus' last meal with his disciples (Matt 26:17–30). And for Christians, the cross symbolizes sacrifice, victory over Satan, an empty tomb. World Changers capitalize on the affective power of symbols and use them to empower people to glorify God and enjoy him.

Christ and communication

Communication through language is often pointed to as the ability that separates humans from the animal kingdom—or even a fundamental attribute of being in the image of God. In fact, all of our cultural activity is an act of communication, in one form or another.[65] We communicate

---

62. Ortner, "On Key Symbols."

63. V. Turner, *The Forest of Symbols.*

64. Jindra, "Culture Matters."

65. Hall, *The Silent Language,* 186.

through words, but also use gestures, color, gaze, touch, smells, and many other nonverbal means—including silence—to communicate.

We use communication for much more than transmitting messages from speaker to receiver. Communication is used to maintain power differentials and mark sociocultural status. We communicate to delineate in-groups and out-groups. We also use language to upgrade "face." That is, when we feel shame (or have lost face) we communicate in culturally patterned ways to regain our status. And when we ask something of others, we are threatening their face, because we are taking away their autonomy.[66] So we soften our language to prevent them from losing too much face. These are just some examples of the multiple uses of language. A theology of communication takes into account the numerous actions that are performed as we communicate. We need to be aware of God's plan for our use of language in the following areas:

- Clarifying and obfuscating
- Leveling the playing field (identifying with others), creating power distance, building rapport
- Requesting and accepting or denying, commanding, demurring
- Apologizing, fighting, thanking
- Cursing and blessing, praising, congratulating, judging
- Promising and making oaths, deceiving
- Facework: giving honor, building up self, showing humility
- Directness, commanding, formality, tact

A theology of communication requires us to ask what God's plan is for our use of verbal and nonverbal communication. Justice is a good starting point for understanding language use. For example, speakers of American Standard English often marginalize speakers of nonstandard English such as Black American English (BAE) or English learners. We employ our own shibboleths for "prejudicial listening." For example, villains in movies commonly have Eastern European or Russian accents (and note that villains in Russian films have American accents); but we use French loan words like *a propos* or *bete noir* to sound sophisticated. God's plan for communication is certainly more inclusive than our national cultures are.

66. Hu, "The Chinese Concept of 'Face.'"; Mao, "Beyond politeness theory."

A theology of communication also involves a large degree of cultural pluralism. A monocultural observer, for instance, may recoil to see two men holding hands, or reclining beside each other on a mat; but the symbolism is so culturally embedded that to suggest such nonverbal communication is "wrong" would be ill-informed. This can be extended to how we decode messages like women wearing short hair, or head coverings. And it would be equally ill-informed to collocate shouting or dancing or spinning around in church with piety, while decoding more stoic postures in church as impious. All of these behaviors are culturally encoded behaviors and only make sense in the space where they are situated. But all need to be under the lordship of Christ, in a way that makes sense in their context.

Christ and wellness systems

One of the foundational pursuits in any society is to ensure wellness and ward off misfortune. Wellness includes harmony, happiness, health, and in many societies, the accumulation of wealth. Misfortune involves disharmony, death and dying, natural disasters and famine, and the loss of wealth.

Western cultural systems for wellness include a complicated interplay of medicines developed through clinical trials, technology, science, and a vast market system. For example, scientists develop insecticides and hybrid seeds, engineers develop the combines to plant and harvest those crops, civil engineers and rural planners design irrigation systems to bring water to the crops, and a complex market system delivers the harvest to our stores. The 97 percent of Westerners who work outside of the agricultural industry earn money in myriads of other complex market activities to have enough money to purchase those crops to stay healthy. A similar complex system allows us to stay fit and receive advanced medical care.

Tribal and peasant societies, in stark contrast, typically attempt to generate wellness through divination, magic, or sorcery. Shamans guard the secrets of their herbal remedies. Clairvoyants and diviners determine the cause of sickness and death—usually witchcraft or the breaking of a taboo. Sorcerers use amulets or chants to ward off blight, insects, drought, and even thieves. Magicians summon the rain, and later usher in the dry season. Families protect totems which they believe to be spiritually charged with the ability to provide bountiful harvests (or to cause sickness).

People from any theological background may agree that God's plan for our wellness and fortune-generating systems is that we depend on him

(Matt 6:33; Phil 4:6), and also that we use our good fortune to bless others (Deut 16:17; Prov 3:27). While wellness and good fortune are blessings, we must avoid the temptation to make wellness our ultimate goal—our idol. However, there is significant disagreement about what depending on God actually entails. Can we depend on God and still take modern medicines? Is a shaman depending on God for his blessing in the herbal remedies? Can a diviner or clairvoyant use the Bible and prayer as he determines the cause of a sickness or disaster? A theology of culture must interface with these cultural issues.[67]

Christ and exploration

Evangelicals have had a love-hate relationship with formal education over the past three centuries. On the one hand, they have emulated Paul in 1 Corinthians 2:2, who "only knew Christ and him crucified."[68] If the Holy Spirit will "guide you into all the truth" (John 16:13, NIV), why study the world's wisdom? If Scripture is sufficient for knowledge, why read books which puff up knowledge rather than love? (1 Cor 8:1). On the other hand, many notable intellectuals have come from the evangelical tradition, and have made contributions in math, the sciences, philosophy, and so on.

The anti-intellectualism of early twentieth-century evangelicalism was a later development—certainly not grounded in Calvinism or Methodism. As early as John Calvin, Protestants recognized no dichotomy between science and faith, but between two ways of doing science: science with faith, or science opposing theology.[69] Calvin argued that exploration was a divine imperative:

> If it has pleased the Lord that we should be assisted in physics, logic, mathematics, and other arts and sciences, by the labour and ministry of the impious, let us make use of them; lest, if we neglect to use the blessings therein freely offered to us by God, we suffer just punishment for our negligence.[70]

Harrison records how numerous Christian thinkers experienced it as their work of worship to explore the universe. Kepler, the famous astronomer

---

67. Nehrbass, "Dealing with Disaster."

68. Rosman, *Evangelicals and Culture*, 9.

69. Van Til, *The Calvinistic Concept of Culture*, 126.

70. Calvin, *Institutes*, II, 2, 16.

and contemporary of Galileo, said "I had the intention of being a theologian. For a long time I was restless, but now see how God is, by my endeavors, also glorified in astronomy."[71] Einstein had a similar attitude.[72] These thinkers believed that since humans are made in God's image, we are most joyous when we discover and interact with the laws of nature that the Creator set in motion.[73]

Evangelicals see God as the author of both "books": science and theology. "God sees no conflict between his two lovely volumes."[74] Christians have long recognized the continuity between Christ, through whom all things were made, and the created world (Col 1:15–16). As Noll put it,

> There simply is nothing humanly possible to study about the created realm that, *in principle*, leads us away from Jesus Christ. To be sure, humans may misunderstand knowledge gained by studying the world, put it to evil uses, transform it into an idol, or otherwise abuse it. But these shortcomings do not alter the fact that in the biblical view, the world was brought into existence by Jesus Christ.[75]

Since their inception, the curricula of evangelical universities has contained classics, math, physics, chemistry, astronomy, history, geography, philosophy, etc.[76] A theology of exploration requires Christians to work out God's view of our pursuit of God's truth in relationship to these disciplines. Our role in the world requires the study of bioethics, stewardship of the environment, and economic and social justice. In fact, evangelicals can experience the study and exploration of God's creation as an act of worship. This realization led a number of Christian colleges in the twentieth century to shift from the Bible institute model to Christian university system.

Christ and recreation: pleasure and leisure

There is a long-standing suspicion of the pursuit of pleasure within evangelicalism. Historically, evangelical societies have been task-oriented and

71. Harrison, *God's Many-Splendored Image*, 150.

72. Ibid., 154.

73. Ibid. 152.

74. Johnson, *The World According to God*, 120.

75. Noll, *Jesus Christ and the Life of the Mind*, 25.

76. Rosman, *Evangelicals and Culture*, 158.

geared toward a precise reckoning of time (discussed in chapter 10). This mixture has caused us to place a high value on "making the most of every opportunity" (Eph 5:16, NIV) at the expense of leisure and recreation. We still engage in leisurely activities, but feel guilty for doing so, because we have not adequately understood a theology of pleasure. As evangelicals, we typically emphasize the priority of proclamation over everything else, so pleasure and leisure are pushed aside and neglected. But a theology of culture requires us to work out our theology of eating and fasting, of pastimes, sexuality, recreation, and exercise, etc., since these activities make up our cultural lives.

Evangelicals have worked out three approaches toward these "less important" worldly pursuits: 1) Struggle through worldly pleasures as a necessary evil; 2) use worldly pleasures as a time of refreshing so we can get back to the more important work; or 3) turn every worldly pursuit into an opportunity for sharing the gospel. After examining these postures toward recreation and pleasure, I will argue that there is a fourth approach: enjoy pleasure for all its worth, as an end in and of itself, without making it an idol.

Pleasure as a necessary evil

Is it okay for Christians to spend time relaxing on the beach, when there are so many lost souls walking by? Is it okay to go on vacation while the world is suffering? Nineteenth-century preacher John Venn argued, "God has pronounced a curse upon the earth, and upon the man who looks to it for happiness, and foolish is he who thinks to evade that sentence."[77] An article in *Christian Observer* warned that God would protect Christians in the course of Christian duty, but not during their pastimes. "You may suffer mere amusement, but not court it."[78] Rosman argues, "No evangelical would have assumed that Simeon was giving sanction to theatre-going when he said that God has given them all things to richly enjoy [1 Tim 6:17b]. The text 'Whatsoever you do, do all to the glory of God' was used to show that many activities were illegitimate since they could not be done to God's glory."[79]

77. Rosman, *Evangelicals and Culture*, 40.

78. Ibid., 87.

79. Ibid., 43.

In every decade, we seem to have created new litmus tests to determine which leisurely pursuits are godly and which are not. In the nineteenth century, it was common to condemn spas, novels, horse races, hunting, playing cards, dancing, and the theater. Such activities were especially forbidden for clergy.[80] Rosman points out that while evangelicals had their cultural shibboleths, laity and clergy still sought to live the comfortable middle-class lives of wider society.

In my experience as a pastor, this killjoy attitude does not cause evangelicals to pursue pleasure any less than their peers do (humans seem to be designed to pursue pleasure and recreation); but it does cause them to feel guilty for doing so.

Make the most of every opportunity

Another approach in evangelicalism has been not to condemn pleasure and recreation outright, but to redeem these by turning activities like golf into evangelism platforms, or a date at the restaurant into a chance to evangelize the waitress. As with all aspects of culture, the question is how we can glorify God through our pleasure, sports, exercise, and leisure. Does our golfing and restaurant-going show others that Christ is great? Compare Tim Tebow's signature victory dance (where he points to God) to Kelley Washington's (from the Ravens) "squirrel dance."

Recreation as a time to recharge

Wilberforce put forth a theology of pleasure and pastimes that resounds with evangelicals today: Recreation is to refresh us so we can return with renewed vigor for "the more serious occupations of life."[81] It would be erroneous to reductively characterize historical evangelicals as killjoys. The same John Venn recognized the need for a theology of pleasure. When he preached on 1 Corinthians 3:21–23, he said "The world is yours to enjoy it with moderation, thankful for the convenience it affords you while a pilgrim and a stranger in it."[82] Calvin said,

---

80. Ibid., 50–54.

81. Ibid., 87.

82. Ibid., 42.

> Let us discard, therefore, that inhuman philosophy which, allowing no use of the creatures but what is absolutely necessary, not only malignantly deprives us of the lawful enjoyment of the divine beneficence, but which cannot be embraced till it has despoiled man of all his senses, and reduced him to a senseless block.[83]

Pleasure as an ends, not just a means

To view recreation and relaxation as a necessary evil, or a way to pass the time until our next chance to evangelize, is to miss out on all that God planned for pastimes and pleasure. As soon as play has an ulterior motive, it ceases to be play.[84] Plus, to maintain such a view is to be not entirely honest with ourselves. We cannot escape pleasure because it is integrated with the rest of our cultural lives. First of all, many of our recreations also have a political and social side to them. For example, I go camping to be with friends, or to solidify the bonds of my nuclear family; but I camp in a way that fits my socioeconomic class. I cannot summit Mt. Everest because (among other reasons) it is too costly; but I can afford new camping gear and sometimes drive our newish SUV out of state on family trips. I have a co-worker who rides a bicycle to work not just for recreation but to make a political statement about carbon emissions. My brother takes his son shooting in the desert for fun, but also in part to exercise his political right to bear arms. And there is a religious aspect to our recreation—sometimes you may hike in the woods to be with God. So our pastimes and pleasures are as complex and interconnected to all our cultural lives as every other aspect of life. It is myopic to emphasize the evangelistic side of pastimes at the expense of recognizing the political, social, economic, and symbolic aspects of recreation.

Theologian Ben Witherington put it this way: "turning away from play as if it were frivolous, as if it were something adults should leave behind, is itself a sign of immaturity. . . . Is it really a mature move to turn your back on good things that can bring you joy? . . . Just because something is neither rest nor work nor worship doesn't make it a waste of time."[85]

83. Calvin, *Institutes*, III, 10, 3.

84. Witherington, *The Rest of Life*, 52.

85. Ibid., 42–43.

SUMMARY

When we are enjoying the various spheres of culture, without idolizing them, we are functioning the way God intended us to as his image-bearers. We are to feast, but not be gluttonous. We are called to use politics and economics to bring about justice, but should not see humans as merely materials, labor, or means for power. The kingdom of God involves all spheres of culture, from pastimes, to politics, to language and education. Since the fall, we have corrupted each of these spheres; and it is the job of World Changers to engage and transform these spheres of cultural activity so people can enjoy and glorify God.

REFLECTION AND REVIEW QUESTIONS

1. In which of the subsystems described in this chapter have Christians been the most effective in engaging their world? Where have they been the least effective?

2. In what ways are human cultures similar, wherever they are found? Why do they have these similarities?

3. In what way is the kingdom of God tied to our understanding of cultural subsystems?

CHAPTER 10

God's plan for cultural variables

BEFORE I MOVED WITH my wife and children to the South Pacific for a ten-year translation project, I told one of my professors of intercultural studies that it was a goal of mine to discover whether people all over the world were more or less the same—or if they were quite different. "What is your hypothesis?" she asked. I responded, "I think that because we are in the image of God, people all over are pretty much the same." "I think you'll find out they're actually quite different" she rightly predicted. Tourists and other short-term sojourners tend to deny the differences, and naively assume there is a long list of commonalities.[1] A visitor from the US may visit a church in Haiti and report back to her home church, "People are people, wherever you go. They have a similar faith, they care for their families just like we do. We have so much in common!" Maybe so; but it would take several years of regular interaction with people in another society to test whether your hosts are quite similar to you. Anthropologists (and especially particularists), on the other hand, have a tendency to focus on the overwhelming differences between cultures—to the neglect of the commonalities.[2] So the answer to the question, "Are we more different or the same" is "yes." There are more commonalities than cross-cultural experts tend to remember, and there are far greater differences than cross-cultural novices are aware of. After several years of living in a tribal setting, I discovered how truly different people can be, based on their cultural background.

To attain the level of cross-cultural literacy necessary for becoming World Changers, we must recognize the profound ways in which the cultures differ—even at the deepest levels of values and worldview. In this

1. Bennett, "Towards Ethnorelativism."
2. Ferraro, *The Cultural Dimension of International Business*, 36.

chapter, we will examine thirteen "value orientations" that have emerged in cross-cultural theory as salient differences between cultures. A theology of culture requires us to see how God's approach to culture reflects or perhaps confronts those value orientations. Last, we'll consider some other ways to describe cultures on their own terms, rather than fitting them into these dyadic categories that were typical of cross-cultural studies in the twentieth century.

DYADIC CATEGORIES

By this point, we have noted substantial commonalities—or universals— between cultures. These universals can be systematized into a theoretical framework, including the political, economic, religious, material, and social systems found in any culture (chapter 9). There are also significant variations among cultures that can also be put into a theoretical frame- work for describing those differences. Cross-cultural theorists have come up with a number of ways of describing the differences between cultures. Usually these comparisons are based on dyadic (two-element) categories of value orientations.

Early "value orientation" theories polarized certain values like compe- tition vs. cooperation,[3] shame vs. guilt,[4] or short-term vs. long-term plan- ning.[5] The data seem to suggest that many dominant *national* cultures will lean heavily toward one end of the spectrum rather than maintain the polar opposites simultaneously. For instance, a culture will not be both hierarchal and egalitarian, or competitive and cooperative—though some cultures are far more polarized than others. The USA has the most individualistic culture on the planet; Australia has the most egalitarian national culture. Argentina is right in the center between individualism and power distance, and between egalitarianism and hierarchy.[6]

So these value orientations are tendencies or generalizations; they are not descriptive of everyone in a given society. As Hofstede collected his data, he worked mostly with professionals in the host cultures.[7] Subse- quent theorists have noticed that there is a significant amount of variation

3. Mead, ed., *Cooperation and Competition among Primitive Peoples.*

4. Piers and Singer, *Shame and Guilt.*

5. Hofstede et al., *Cultures and Organizations.*

6. The Hofstede Center, https://geert-hofstede.com/countries.html.

7. Hofstede, *Culture's Consequence.*

within the societies that Hofstede studied. For example, a study of women, children, or ethnic minorities in some societies would return different results for variables like being/doing, or individualism/collectivism.[8] And we are seeing variation to a much greater degree in highly heterogeneous ("melting pot" or "salad bowl") cultures in this era of globalization. Also, while the "culture difference" theory of Hofstede (and others) uses a model with polar opposites, no culture is *entirely* polarized. Cultures lean (sometimes heavily) one direction while maintaining some tendency toward the value on the other pole. For example, members of culture X may promote a strong "in-group" mentality and may exhibit very hospitable behavior toward insiders, and yet be far less hospitable toward strangers. So it is difficult to plot Culture Xers on a continuum either as "spontaneous hospitality" or "planned hospitality" since the orientation changes depending on the context. Or they may be very expressive of emotions to insiders, and very stoic toward outsiders. So it is not that people of Culture X are incapable of hospitality and are always stoic; their orientation to both values depends on the social context.

Theorists such as Lingenfelter and Mayers employed a sixfold model of dyadic value orientations, including time vs. event orientation, task vs. person orientation, dichotomistic vs. holistic thinking, status vs. achievement, concealment or exposure of vulnerability, and crisis vs. non-crisis orientation.[9] Still others have introduced the ideas of polychronic or monochronic time reckoning.[10] Geert Hofstede's dyadic categories included the idea of "masculine or feminine" cultures, which described the degree of aggression and competition in a culture.[11] Other theorists have renamed this category "tough vs. tender."[12] Quite recently, Hofstede's researchers introduced a pragmatism scale, rating some cultures as resistant toward change while others embrace it.

Even though the theoretical orientation of dividing ethnic or national cultures into dyadic categories is increasingly contested, it is important for World Changers to be aware of the canonical cultural variables that are discussed in the field of intercultural studies. And these variables allow us to think through God's plan for cultures in light of their vast differences. Theorists have put so much effort into understanding these value orientations

8. See Tanno, "Ethical Implications of the Ethnic 'Text.'"

9. Lingenfelter and Mayers. *Ministering Cross-Culturally.*

10. Hall and Hall, *Understanding Cultural Differences.*

11. Hofstede, *Culture's Consequences.*

12. Hoppe, "An Interview with Geert Hofstede."

because, quite often, cross-cultural misunderstandings and conflicts are related to a clash of these cultural variables mentioned below.[13]

WHAT ARE GOD'S THOUGHTS ABOUT CULTURAL VARIABLES?

To work out a theology of cultural variables, I worked with a team of about thirty graduate students whose hermeneutics are informed by their variegated international backgrounds. I discovered that when we try to work out God's approach to these cultural variables, it becomes obvious that God is not nearly as polarized as we have made cultures out to be. God is both flexible and ordered; Scripture approves of long-term planning and faith; godliness is lived out through relationships and through accomplishing tasks. God embodies the spectrum of many of these cultural continua, and perhaps that is precisely why we see such a variety of cultures.

Below is a synthesis of the dyadic categories of value orientations that have emerged as salient among cross-cultural theorists. These canonical labels are meant to mitigate, not exacerbate, cross-cultural misunderstanding. If we did not develop a canonical set of value orientations based on cross-cultural research and theory, we would be left with much more dangerous "folk" bifurcations. For instance, you may hear people refer to certain national cultures as "backwards," "smart," or "dishonest," with the unmarked pairs "civilized," "unintelligent," and "honest" referring to their own national culture. But these dyads never developed out of actual cross-cultural research projects, so they are of little use when it comes to working out an understanding of the cross-cultural process. There are many other potentially "neutral" dyads that have not become part of canonical cross-cultural theory. Or there may be a difference between consumption-oriented cultures and conservation-oriented cultures. Obvious bifurcations like "vegetarian versus omnivore" may also be statistically significant distinctions, but they have not become part of typical cross-cultural theory. Note that in some parts of the world, cultural differences are described with other binary categories: coastal versus highland; Christian versus non-Christian; or Hutu versus Tutsi. So the desire to categorize cultures in an effort to understand them is widespread, and is as much an art as a science.

As you read the descriptions, think of your society at large (not just your own preferences), and mark the extent to which your ethnic culture

13. Lingenfelter, *Agents of Transformation*; Storti, *The Art of Crossing Cultures*.

aligns with each of these descriptions. Note that here I do not conceptualize of these orientations as polarized; it is possible to construe yourself as high on both scales—or low on both scales. But the value of this theoretical approach is that many people do construe themselves as leaning towards one value over its opposite, and trends do emerge within a society which reveal a "modal personality" within a given society. Also, consider biblical data on these value orientations, and try to plot a kingdom view of these dyadic categories.

1. A Kingdom construal of the individual and society

We must begin with the way cultures cause people to construe the individual in the context of the wider society. This variable is often referred to as the individual-collectivist value orientation, and it repeatedly surfaces as the most salient cultural variable. In fact, this fundamental variable actually serves as a base for many of the other value orientations.[14] As the basis for many other interactions, this value orientation is responsible for misunderstandings in cross-cultural interactions. Societies that are oriented toward individualism emphasize "I" and personal autonomy; collectivist cultures emphasize "we," and the interests of the group.

From an early age, Westerners begin deciding for themselves where they will study, who they will court and marry, where they will live, and what job they will have. It is so ingrained in us to make these decisions for ourselves that we think it is unfair when we hear that traditional couples in a place like India have arranged marriages. If it is our individual decisions that guarantee our happiness, we wonder, *How can they be happy if they don't get to do what they want?*

Mois lives in a tribal setting in the South Pacific, which is highly collectivist. When he became a member of the national parliament, the tribe informed him that he would need to give some of the young men in the tribe low-level government jobs. The tribe decided which of the young men (all with second- to sixth-grade educations) would secure these jobs and would move to the capital city. This select group included a young man named John, who became the third assistant to the minister of health. Every two weeks, John sent back his paycheck to the tribal leaders. If he kept some of the money for himself, because life in the capital city was expensive, the tribe chastised him, "We secured this job for you. So the wages are ours." This approach toward securing employment and the use

14. Triandis, "Collectivism vs. Individualism."

of wages is practically unfathomable to individualists like us in the USA. But it is a reality around the world for people in collectivist societies. Even if people in collectivist societies are aware of their own interests, they are more motivated by fear of ostracism from the group. The group is the social safety net in collectivist societies, so the group's wishes must take priority.

The individual/collective orientation also permeates how societies handle money and belongings. A Westerner who travels to a collectivist society will be regularly disoriented when his associates in the host country expect to ride in his vehicle, regardless of where he happens to be going. He will be dismayed when they "borrow" his umbrella and don't return it, or collect shellfish on what he considers to be his "private beachfront." While people in collectivist societies may recognize that certain goods (especially land) belong to a certain family line, they assume (and remember that culture is largely assumed) that resources are available for the group's benefit. When my wife and I lived in a tribal setting, our friends and neighbors referred to the truck I had purchased as "our truck." If I agreed to take a pregnant woman to the hospital, no fewer than a dozen family members would crowd in the bed of the truck "to help." In collectivist societies, travel is done in groups, sickness is a group affair, and problems are solved as a group.

The individualist/collectivist value orientation even affects whether people view discourse as "owned" by an individual or a group. In collectivist societies, conflicts are public. Conversations, news, and jokes are told in large groups. When I was working on my doctoral dissertation, I designed a research project that involved interviewing dozens of Pacific Islanders in private. I was quite out of touch with reality to think that I would indeed be conducting interviews one-on-one with people in a highly collectivist society! Whenever I arranged a "private" interview, the group consisted of the interviewee and at least half a dozen relatives who were there to "help."

I mentioned earlier that these value orientations are tendencies—so no society is purely individualistic or purely collectivist. East Asia is often given the blanket label of "collectivist." However, Chang's study of the impact of Confucius' *Analects* on East Asian society reveals a high value on the individual. Confucius' values of *li* (propriety) and *jen* (human-heartedness) require the individual to be humble, honest, and transparent.[15] So China and (even more so) Japan may score highly on collectivism while also receiving a high score on individualism.

---

15. Chang, "Language and Words."

When I teach on the individualist/collectivist dyad, I often ask my audience to determine whether Christianity endorses collectivism or individualism. It's a trick question, since the Bible endorses both. Because of Scripture's multidimensional approach to the individual and the community, the responses I hear from my audiences are also usually multidimensional. Some argue adamantly that Christianity uniquely has given us the idea of the individual (with his own soul and accountability to God). Remember that the parables of the Lost Sheep, Coin, and Prodigal Son in Luke 15 show the value God places on individual souls. Others argue that the Industrial Revolution has compelled us to idolize the individual, whereas pre-Industrial biblical worldview emphasized the community. Shelley has argued that the Roman Catholic church saw the individualism of democratic revolutions (such as the French and American Revolutions) as dangerous because they were based on the glorification of man.[16] Of course, the Scripture teaches that we should look neither to self nor to the community for fulfillment or purpose; rather, we look to God (Isa 43:7; Matt 6:33).[17] Parler has pointed out that in Paul's epistles, the vision was neither collectivism nor individualism, but interdependence.[18]

People from individualistic cultures would be quick to point to Scriptures where God judges the individual—as Jesus often did (Mark 2:5, Matt 8:10, Luke 15, 23:32–43). Those from collectivist cultures would easily pick out the times when God judged entire societies like Egypt (Num 33:4) or Israel (Judges 2:14) and how Jesus judged the religious leaders collectively (Matt 23). Moreau et al. have found passages where the individual comes into focus in terms of conversion (Acts 17:27, Rom 12:1–2), personal leading (1 Cor 7:24), spiritual gifts (1 Cor 12:7), matters of conscience (Rom 14:5, Gal 6:4–5), and giving of finances (1 Cor 16:2).[19] But the authors have also traced a theme of collectivism in terms of conversion (John 4:53, Acts 16:31–34), giving (Acts 10:2), and spiritual gifts (Rom 12:4–5).[20]

So we see that God is oriented toward both individualism and collectivism. But it is quite certain that Scripture is counter to the modern individualist tendency for people to make decisions that only benefit themselves and their immediate families. Scripture may admonish individuals to make decisions, but always for the sake of the community.

---

16. Shelley, *Church History in Plain Language*, 354.

17. Houdmann, "Individualism vs. Collectivism."

18. Parler, *Things Hold Together*, 221.

19. Moreau et al., *Effective Intercultural Communication*.

20. Ibid, 161–162.

For example, individuals in the early church were free to do what they wanted with their own property (Acts 5:3–4), but they were admonished to make personal decisions that benefited the extended church family (Acts 2:44–45, 6; Phil 2:4). The Trinity, an eternal collective individual, never models self-serving—always submission and sacrifice (John 4:34).

We are in a world where we will continually struggle over these two conflicting value orientations. The individualist/collectivist value orientation subtly influences virtually everything we do cross-culturally, and will be central to our efforts to be World Changers. Mark on Table 7 the tendency toward individualism and collectivism in your ethnic culture and mark a kingdom posture toward the two value orientations.

Table 7: Developing a theology of individualism and collectivism

Individualism	Collectivism
<ul><li>You decide for yourself who you'll marry, where you'll live, what job you'll have</li><li>Salary is for yourself and your dependents</li><li>Success is a sign of your own hard work</li><li>Fear dependency on others</li><li>Personal rights are asserted</li><li>Winning personal records is valued</li><li>Possessions are your own; borrowing is discouraged</li><li>You label your belongings</li><li>Travel in your own car</li><li>Conversations can be closed; negotiations are done in private</li><li>Luke 15, 19:15; 1 Thess. 4:11</li></ul>	<ul><li>You look to the group for direction in who you'll marry, where you'll work and study, what job you'll have</li><li>Salary is for extended family and the group</li><li>Success is because the group helped you</li><li>Fear ostracism from the group</li><li>Harmony is preferred</li><li>Standing out can be shameful</li><li>Possessions belong to the group</li><li>Borrow without a specified return date</li><li>Travel in large groups; shameful to leave someone alone</li><li>Conversations are inclusive, decisions are made in public</li><li>John 11:50; Acts 2:44–45, 4:32–35; 2 Rom 12:16; 1 Pet 3:8</li></ul>
Your ethnic culture:	
Individualist Collectivist	Low ˙ ˙ ˙ ˙ ˙ ˙ High Low ˙ ˙ ˙ ˙ ˙ ˙ High
A Kingdom view of the individual and society:	
Individualist Collectivist	Low ˙ ˙ ˙ ˙ ˙ ˙ High Low ˙ ˙ ˙ ˙ ˙ ˙ High

2. A Kingdom view of being and doing

How long does a wedding ideally last? If the ceremony lasted much longer than an hour in the US, people would be irritated, though we expect the reception to last into the evening. In some societies, events like weddings, puberty rituals and funerals can last days, weeks, or even months. Westerners enjoy socializing, but generally think that the point of getting together is to accomplish a task. At a wedding, once the vows are exchanged, the cake has been cut, and the standard dances have been danced—that is, once all the tasks are done—it is time to go home. For Westerners, the task at a funeral is the sermon and internment; in "being" cultures, the purpose for gathering is to mourn and show solidarity. This takes much longer than an hour or two.

To put it another way, *doing* cultures are outcome oriented, and *being* cultures are more other oriented. If a funeral rite lasts two weeks in a *being* culture, people may show up on the first day or much later. They may stay a day or a week. There will certainly be tasks to accomplish, like cooking and giving speeches, but the majority of the time is spent socializing rather than accomplishing tasks.

This bifurcation becomes painfully manifest when people try to work together cross-culturally. People from "doing cultures" cling to deadlines and measure success in terms of productivity or meeting goals. People from being-oriented cultures are much more willing to adjust goals and deadlines when doing so will strengthen relationships. So "doers" end up seeing "be-ers" as unproductive, because they don't display what Max Weber called the "Protestant ethic."[21] The "be-ers," on the other hand, see "doers" as unfriendly since they put tasks ahead of people.

I especially noted this "outcome vs. other" tension when I worked on fundraisers in the South Pacific. We sold tickets to showings of movies; other times we sold plates of rice and meat. On occasion, we held soccer matches and sold tickets to the event. Each time, I noticed that the fundraisers themselves cost more than the amount raised, so I saw these events as failures, and called them fundlosers. The people in the host country, however, seemed quite pleased with the events, since they served to spread awareness about the church's cause. These "fundlosers" also increased the status of the church, and allowed for socializing or "being." From the host culture's perspective, these were not a loss!

21. Weber, *Die protestantische Ethik und der "Geist" des Kapitalismus.*

The doing-being dyad is related to the collectivist/individualist domain (mentioned in the previous section).[22] Collectivist societies (Kim refers to these as interdependents) tend to emphasize "being" whereas individualist societies (to whom Kim refers as independents) tend to emphasize "doing." A large exception to this would be many East Asian societies (Especially in China, Korea, and Japan) which are highly collectivist yet also emphasize production and deadlines.

There are biblical examples of both "being" and "doing," so it would be erroneous to insist that task-oriented cultures are more biblical, or that event-oriented cultures are more biblical. Proverbs 13:4 and 14:23 emphasize task completion. On the other hand, the characteristics of love in 1 Corinthians 13:4–8 are more about character and relationship than accomplishing a task. But Scripture is not right in the center on this value orientation. Did God prefer the sacrifice, or the relationship that it represented? He far prefers the connection with his people over their acts of praying, sacrificing, and following the law (Isa 1:11; Amos 5:21)—and yet, it is through these acts of piety and sacrifice that we cultivate our relationship with him.

Mark in Table 8 your culture and a Kingdom posture toward the values of being and doing.

Table 8: Developing a theology of being and doing

Being	Doing
• Event-oriented	• Task-oriented
• Work can wait	• Productivity
• Events start when people come and end when they leave	• Deadlines
	• Achieve a goal; accomplish a task
• 1 Cor 13:4–8; Isa 1:11; Amos 5:21	• Prov 13:4, 14:23
Your ethnic culture:	
Being	Low ˮ ˮ ˮ ˮ ˮ ˮ High
Doing	Low ˮ ˮ ˮ ˮ ˮ ˮ High
A Kingdom view of the Being and Doing:	
Being	Low ˮ ˮ ˮ ˮ ˮ ˮ High
Doing	Low ˮ ˮ ˮ ˮ ˮ ˮ High

22. Kim, "Culture-Based Conversational Constraints Theory," 106.

3. A Kingdom view of time reckoning

Our understanding of the individualist/collectivist and being/doing dyads helps us to understand two divergent patterns for reckoning time. In industrialized societies, the clock regulates daily life, both causing stress as we feel rushed, and alleviating stress as we organize and budget our time. On the other hand, people from less industrialized societies resist the pressure of the clock, or rarely think about the time.[23] I heard Melanesians call this phenomenon "black man time"; I have heard Africans call it "African time," Thai call it "Thai time," and Mexicans call it "Mexican time." Despite the multiple ecocentric names, the same phenomenon exists across the continents: many people around the world find that they are not nearly as guided by the clock as Westerners are.

The notion that "time is money" is so ingrained in Westerners, the differences in reckoning of time (ROT) cause regular cross-cultural incidents, as we all expect cultural sameness. American travelers to Africa, Latin America, or Oceania may show up at a dinner party or church service five minutes before the hour at which the event begins. One Indonesian was confused when the Western businessman arrived on time, because "only servants show up on time."

The monochromic/polychronic or sequential/synchronic orientation causes serious culture clashes when deadlines are involved.[24] While industrialized nations have their share of procrastinators, these societies tend to be driven by deadlines. We have five- or ten-year goals, and then plan which deadlines must be met at the end of the month and the end of the year to eventually reach those goals. On the other hand, people from tribal and peasant societies do not seem to feel the same pressure of deadlines. For them, time is not money. Saving time is not a motivating factor. These societies are called polychronic (literally "multi-time") since the one resource they have in abundance is time. Some call this freedom from deadlines the "*mañana* [Spanish for "tomorrow"] mentality"—put off until tomorrow what doesn't have to be done today.

This value orientation has been deeply misunderstood by Westerners. I have heard numerous expatriates refer to people from tribal and peasant societies as lazy. "They don't set goals." "Their food just grows on trees, so they don't have to work." "They don't seem to want anything in life; they

23. Hall and Hall, *Understanding Cultural Differences.*
24. Hampden-Turner and Trompenaars, *Riding Waves of Culture.*

just live for today." If you have lived in a peasant or tribal setting, you've observed that the locals are usually anything but lazy. These are the billion people who carry their forty-five–pound water jugs several miles each day to do the laundry by hand. They are the men and women who till the ground and drive rickshaws in India or work in clothing factories in Bangladesh. However, it is notable that polychronics are not consumed with the passion that Westerners have for their personal careers, education, exercise, entertainment, and self-image. The rat race is possible because of deadlines.

Some may think *But isn't that why those societies are not developing? Because they don't set goals and meet deadlines?* We must remember that driven-ness and goal-setting are advantageous to Westerners, but are not particularly useful in tribal and peasant societies. Westerners see the fruit of their planning and goal-setting as they earn, save, achieve, and retire with enough money to pay the bills. Much of the world's population does not operate under this model. Many people from tribal and peasant societies have little incentive to join the rat race, climb the ladder, save, and retire. In some regions, multitudes are truly trapped in their socioeconomic class with no hope for "improvement." Oppressive governments and fate-oriented worldviews hold them back. Others, such as Pacific Islanders, feel no need to join the rat race since they can farm enough food for themselves, build their own structures out of local materials, and will always have extended family as a safety net. To Westerners, this is interpreted as laziness; to the islanders, it is paradise.

Is God polychronic or monochronic? Does the Christian worldview encourage goal-setting and deadlines, or flexibility? Is punctuality a biblical virtue? It would be very difficult to argue a theology of biblical punctuality, unless Ecclesiastes 3:1 is exegeted improperly: "For everything there is a season, and a time for every matter under heaven" (ESV). It is equally difficult to find biblical support for a loose reckoning of time. There are, however, themes of what Richards and O'Brien call "*chronos* vs. *kairos*" time in Scripture.[25] It is not that the Greek word *chronos* is always meant to be precise time reckoning and *kairos* loose. Instead, Richards and O'Brien build a case for both loose and precise time reckoning in Scripture, under these respectively named paradigms. For instance, the magi found the precise time (*chronos*) that the star appeared (Matt 2:7). But Galatians 4:4, Ephesians 5:15–16, Mark 1:15, and Matthew 24:36 use a much more loose

---

25. Richards and O'Brien, *Misreading Scripture with Western Eyes.*

reckoning of time, such as the "end of the age/time" or the "time/day of the Lord".[26]

A biblical theology of time requires thinking through goal-setting and how we treat people who do not meet our own cultural standards of punctuality. Goal-setting can be biblical, but is sinful when it is attached to the pride of human accomplishments. Deadlines are useful, but a greater biblical virtue is putting others first (Phil 2:3–11).

Mark in Table 9 your perception of your own ethnic culture and a kingdom posture toward the reckoning of time.

Table 9: Developing a theology of time reckoning

Monochronic	Polychronic	
• Sequential	• Synchronic	
• Precise reckoning of time	• Loose reckoning of time (Gal 4:4; Eph 5:15–16; Matt 24:36)	
• A time for every thing (Eccl 3:1)	• Synchronic (many tasks—may not finish them all)	
• Perform tasks sequentially (until finished)	• Show up an hour after the meeting time—or even later	
• Be punctual	• Deadlines are negotiable	
• Deadlines are important	• People are more important than time (Phil 2:3–11)	
Your ethnic culture:		
Monochronic	Low ˝ ˝ ˝ ˝ ˝ ˝ High	
Polychronic	Low ˝ ˝ ˝ ˝ ˝ ˝ High	
A kingdom view of time reckoning:		
Monochronic	Low ˝ ˝ ˝ ˝ ˝ ˝ High	
Polychronic	Low ˝ ˝ ˝ ˝ ˝ ˝ High	

4. A kingdom view of order and flexibility

Try to recall attending a meeting where the chairman followed Robert's Rules of Order. The rules specify what can be said, by whom, in which order, and the proper way to disagree. These rules come out of a cultural

26. Ibid., 142, 164.

time and place where society was even more ordered than American society is today. Imagine you showed up to a restaurant where you were meeting a friend for lunch, and he came with a printed agenda for what you would discuss, and in which order! I have a friend from mainland China who clings to order and agendas, even at lunch meetings. This is partly idiosyncratic, but his cultural background has taught him to value order over ambiguity.

Some cultures predispose people to rely on rules to order their daily life. Such cultures not only have *patterns* for how to dress, what to eat, or when to pray (patterns are found in every culture)—but they have sanctions to enforce those patterns. The roles between men and women are clearly defined, as well as the roles for religious leaders, laypeople, the elderly, and the young. Other cultures are more "loose," tolerating a great deal of variety. Flexible cultures certainly have statuses, roles, mores, but there is room for innovation and individuality. Another way to put it would be that flexible cultures are more tolerant of a wider range of behaviors than ordered cultures are.

Societies in the Middle East are some of the most ordered. The endemic penchant for order manifests itself in the highly prescriptive laws found in ancient Judaism and in Islam. In the times of the Old Testament, the Israelites' culture was highly ordered. The first five books of the Old Testament contain 613 orders for daily routines, diet, clothing, status, role, and morality. Only priests could offer sacrifices; holidays were to be kept uniformly by everyone; people who broke the taboos were "unclean" or severely punished. The man who was caught gathering sticks on the Sabbath was stoned to death (Num 15:32). As if the laws of the Torah were not enough to bring order to the lives of Israelites in antiquity, the Pharisees and ancient rabbis added thousands of laws to the Torah, which were published in the Mishnah and subsequently in the Talmud.

Islamic countries that implement Sharia law are also highly ordered. Going against the norm (e.g., converting to Christianity or confronting the government) is a capital offense. And as Islam was exported to Indonesia centuries ago, it brought along the "ordered" value orientation of the Middle East. Indonesia has recently been in the process of converting its legal code from the Dutch system that it inherited under colonialism to a "tighter" system which details penalties for insulting the president, practicing black magic, committing adultery, and even for women who wear jeans.[27] As Is-

27. Otto, "Indonesia Weighs Curbs on Sex, Magic."

lam and Judaism took root in more flexible or "loose" societies, the reliance on order faded significantly. Differences in expression were tolerated. Similarly, when Christianity has taken root in more ordered cultures, it takes on legalism; in more flexible cultures, it emphasizes freedom.

This value orientation is also undoubtedly tied to the individualism-collectivism spectrum. Since collectivist societies value conformity, they are fairly homogeneous; they require orthodoxy and orthopraxis for the sake of the group's cohesiveness. Individualistic societies do not require people to conform to the same extent, since the cohesiveness of the group is not essential for the survival of the society. Nowadays, we would refer to flexible cultures as "tolerant" or "diverse." Ordered societies pressure for people to conform.

People from flexible societies characterize ordered cultures as prudish or totalitarian. People from ordered cultures see flexible cultures as licentious. Both the Old Testament and New Testament emphasized an orderliness and obedience of God's principles. But the law was never an end in and of itself. It was valued, but not idolized.

Mark in Table 10 where your own ethnic culture falls on the flexible and order continuum, and how that compares to a kingdom view of order and flexibility.

Table 10: Developing a theology of order and flexibility

Ordered	Flexible
• Many rules governing daily life (Levitical law, Sharia law) with strict penalties such as death • Ambiguity causes anxiety • Tight control of environment (Torah) • Behaviors are prescribed for different roles and statuses • Less tolerant of differences	• Fewer laws governing daily life; less strict penalties • Ambiguity does not cause anxiety • Grace • Loose—roles are less prescribed • More tolerant of differences
Your ethnic culture:	
Tight Loose	Low ¨ ¨ ¨ ¨ ¨ ¨ ¨ High Low ¨ ¨ ¨ ¨ ¨ ¨ ¨ High
A Kingdom view of the flexibility and order:	
Tight Loose	Low ¨ ¨ ¨ ¨ ¨ ¨ ¨ High Low ¨ ¨ ¨ ¨ ¨ ¨ ¨ High

5. A Kingdom view of risk and vulnerability

The flexible/ordered value orientation is related to the degree to which people are comfortable with risk. People in risk-taking cultures are willing to find themselves in vulnerable positions where they may draw attention to themselves or even fail. They consider the reward of innovation to be worth the risk of failure, so these cultures tend to encourage change (labeling it as progress). Societies which avoid risk have expressions like "saving face"; the *status quo* is valued over change. Another way to describe this value orientation is "uncertainty avoidance." Risk-taking cultures have a low uncertainty avoidance; risk-averting cultures prefer to avoid uncertainty.

Japan rates as one of the world's most uncertainty-avoiding nations.[28] On the whole, Japanese save for the future; they will often stay with a known employer rather than take the risk of accepting a higher paying job at an unknown company. A recent study suggests that poorer nations (namely Ethiopia, Nicaragua, and Vietnam) cultivate a value of risk-taking, whereas wealthier nations (specifically Germany and Japan) foster risk avoidance.[29]

When I pastored a small church in rural Indiana, I found myself in a subculture that avoids risk. The congregation was well past retirement age—most had lived through the Great Depression of the 1930s. I wanted to implement changes to the worship style, the style of dress, the building itself—and even some changes to worldview. The lovely congregation continually resisted my innovations. I became frustrated, but remembered that this was a cultural reality: My subculture of twenty-somethings from Southern California taught me to take risks, whereas their retirement-age midwestern culture taught them to value the *status quo*. It was not that I or they were stupid or had bad ideas—we came with different cultural values.

Other theorists have honed in on how this bifurcation between being vulnerable or nonvulnerable affect displays of emotion. Hampden-Turner and Trompenaars referred to a bifurcation between "neutral vs. emotional."[30] It may seem strange to keep track of whether cultures are open to showing emotion or not, but this difference actually is the source of serious cross-cultural misunderstandings. In many non-European cultures, showing anger is one of the most socially unacceptable behaviors. I have

28. http://geert-hofstede.com/japan.html.

29. Vieider and Schneider, "People in Poorer Countries Show Higher Tolerance for Risk."

30. Hampden-Turner and Trompenaars, *Riding Waves of Culture*.

seen church leaders publically disciplined for showing anger, while sexual misconduct was swept under the rug. In Asia and the Pacific, a common criticism of Westerners is that they try to use anger to advance their agenda. While this may be an effective way of dealing with conflict in the West, it is counterproductive in stoic or non-vulnerable cultures.

The same cultural penchant for remaining stoic is true with displaying affection or exuberance. Westerners naively hug host culture nationals, thinking they are "showing God's love" but come across as awkward or flirtatious. And Westerners misinterpret churches in more stoic cultures: they may erroneously think that because they are not clapping their hands, singing loudly, or being otherwise visually affected by the worship service that they are not truly worshipping. It is important, before passing judgment or behaving strangely cross-culturally, to understand the value of non-vulnerability.

In Table 11, mark your ethnic culture's preference toward vulnerability or non-vulnerability, and that of Scripture. Does your ethnic culture encourage taking risk, and being vulnerable with emotion? How about a kingdom view of vulnerability and the avoidance of uncertainty? A willingness to take risk may be associated with biblical commands to have faith. But the Bible also condones planning ahead.

Table 11: Developing a theology of risk and vulnerability

Risk aversion	Risk taking
• Worried about failure	• New inventions; innovation
• Loyalty to company and church	• You can quit your job, change your denomination
• Save money for the future	
• Status quo	• Invest in stock market
• Save face rather than be vulnerable	• Willing to be vulnerable
• Avoid uncertainty	• Willing to live with uncertainty
• Stoic, non-emotional	• Expressive of emotion
Your ethnic culture:	
Risk averse Vulnerable	Low `" " " " " "` High Low `" " " " " "` High
A kingdom view of the vulnerability and risk:	
Risk averse Vulnerable	Low `" " " " " "` High Low `" " " " " "` High

6. A Kingdom view of planning for the future

The notion of taking risk is also related to cultural variations about planning for the future. Lingenfelter and Mayers referred to this as the crisis or non-crisis value orientation.[31] Lingenfelter noticed that the Yap Islanders in Micronesia did very little to prepare for hurricanes, even though they experienced devastating storms year after year. The Yapese have a more non-crisis orientation than Westerners do—they are not easily motivated by unseen threats about economic or natural disasters. Long-term–oriented cultures are highly motivated by such threats.

World Changers need to gauge where the host culture falls on the short- vs. long-term orientation, because this value will determine their approach toward the negotiation and persuasion. If you work within a culture with a long-term orientation (e.g., Japan) you will need to address the long-term benefits. If the culture is short-term oriented, you'll need to articulate the immediate benefits.

US-Americans, on the whole, are schizophrenic about this value orientation. We refuse to save for tomorrow, demanding instant gratification. On the other hand, we retrofit our buildings to be earthquake safe, we wear our seat belts and helmets, and even endure colonoscopies in order to mitigate disaster.

Evangelicals also tend to be ambivalent about planning for the future. Pastors, for example, can opt out of social security in part because planning for the future goes against Jesus' teachings about worry in the Sermon on the Mount (Matt 6:34).

Mark on Table 12 where your culture falls on the spectrum of short-term and long-term orientations, and how this compares to a kingdom view of short-/long-term planning.

---

31. Lingenfelter and Mayers, *Ministering Cross-Culturally.*

Table 12: Developing a theology of crisis orientations

Short term	Long term
• Don't expect anything bad to happen • Live for today • Spend like there's no tomorrow • Non-crisis orientation • Prov 19:11; Matt 6:33; Jas 4:13–15	• Plan for a crisis • Save for the future • Enforce building codes • Crisis orientation • Prov 6:6–8, 16:3, 21:5, 24:27; Luke 14:28
Your ethnic culture:	
Short term Long term	Low " " " " " " " High Low " " " " " " " High
A kingdom view of the planning for the future:	
Short term Long term	Low " " " " " " " High Low " " " " " " " High

7. A kingdom view of fate and personal efficacy

Cultural values about planning for the future are related to views of fate. Tanna, the island on which my wife and I lived for a decade, is right in the hurricane track of the South Pacific. Every year, a dozen or more hurricanes form in the Pacific; several of them make landfall and wreak havoc. In 2004, Cyclone Ivy devastated the nation's islands, flattening most of the huts, felling coconut trees (which are vital to the food supply), and destroying roads and other infrastructure. It is the sort of devastation you hope to never witness again, but which logic (and past experience) tells you will happen in a regular cycle long into the future.

Interestingly, the local cultural logic did not tell the islanders that hurricanes must necessarily strike the islands according to a regular pattern long into the future. According to the local logical system, bad things happen when people break taboos, cause social disharmony, or deliberately practice black magic. A hurricane would not strike the island unless evil people deliberately willed it to do so. Under this system of logic, the more I encouraged people to prepare for the next hurricane, the more suspicious people became of me. The only people who issued warnings about impending disasters are sorcerers and diviners who threaten people to further their own agenda. If the Internet indicated a forming cyclone, I tried to be altruistic by encouraging people to strengthen their huts, gather some foods, and stay inside. Instead of coming across as helpful, I came across as dangerous. "Don't say there will be a hurricane; there can't be one this year. We just need to remain positive and believe the best."

There are other "logics" that guide how people in other cultures plan (or don't plan) for the future. In the caste system of India, the notion of karma causes people to accept misfortune, rather than mitigate it and attempt to change their fortunes. Karma is a mechanistic force which we might liken unto "fate" in the Western world. Hampden-Turner and Trompenaars referred to these polar tendencies in culture as internal vs. external control.[32] Internal control cultures value personal efficacy, while external control cultures accept God's will, or fate, as a dominant force in shaping the future.

Many people in Muslim cultures conceive of their futures as guided by a more personal, rather than mechanistic, force. The will of Allah (God) is responsible for fortune and misfortune that befalls people; it cannot be changed, and would be sinful to attempt to do so—that would be fighting against God. Note that many Christians, especially in the Reformed tradition, also consider it to be either sinful or futile to fight against the will of God. Gamaliel, a first-century Jew, articulated this same attitude about the futility of trying to negate God's will in Acts 5:39.

On the other hand, many Westerners adamantly advocate for personal efficacy. We have adages about planning for the future, controlling your own destiny, and achieving your dreams. We also expect bad things to happen like earthquakes and fires, so we plan ahead on macro scales, by fitting entire cities with storm drains, passing exhaustive building codes, and enforcing safety measures through governmental oversight. Because we expect cultural sameness, we see people from Hindu, Muslim, or tribal backgrounds as irresponsible or lazy when they seem to be reticent to plan for the worst contingency. We shake our heads in confusion when we hear reports about high-rise buildings in less developed countries that were never built to code. It is not that Muslim, Hindu, and tribal cultures are incapable of building buildings to code, or that they are lazy or illogical. It is more accurate to understand these cultures on their own terms: They recognize powerful personal or impersonal forces which explain the misfortune that befalls them.

32. Hampden-Turner and Trompenaars, *Riding Waves of Culture.*

Which cultures are closer to the biblical standard—the ones which emphasize fate, or personal efficacy? Both tendencies are in Scripture. Solomon told us to "look to the ant" who plans ahead for winter (Prov 6:6). On the other hand, James 4:1–15 is the best proof text for the assertion that plans are futile since everything that happens is directed by God: "Now listen, you who say, 'Today or tomorrow we will go to this or that city, spend a year there, carry on business and make money.' Why, you do not even know what will happen tomorrow. What is your life? You are a mist that appears for a little while and then vanishes. Instead, you ought to say, 'If it is the Lord's will, we will live and do this or that'" (NIV).

Since disaster and sickness are a regular reality in life, it is important to work out a theology of fate and personal efficacy. Mark in Table 13 your ethnic culture's view, and that of the Scripture.

Table 13: Developing a theology of fate and personal efficacy

Fate	Personal efficacy
• "*Inshalla*" (if it is God's will) • Karma • Accept your station in life • Talking about possible negative events in the future will bring about something negative • External control • Jas 4:1–15	• You are responsible for solving your own problems • Prov 6:6 • God helps those who help themselves • Have a contingency plan; prepare for crises • Internal control
Your ethnic culture:	
Fate Personal efficacy	Low ˮ ˮ ˮ ˮ ˮ ˮ High Low ˮ ˮ ˮ ˮ ˮ ˮ High
A kingdom view of the fate and personal efficacy:	
Fate Personal efficacy	Low ˮ ˮ ˮ ˮ ˮ ˮ High Low ˮ ˮ ˮ ˮ ˮ ˮ High

8. A kingdom view of logic

These notions about fate and efficacy are related to cultural orientations regarding logic and causation. Human beings have a number of ways of gathering knowledge: experience, intuition, rote learning, etc. Cultures tend to emphasize one approach toward reasoning over the other. A theology of culture requires understanding cultural logics, and God's plan for how we reason.

Since the Enlightenment, Europeans have had a strong preference for the scientific method. We break down the object of study into parts; we label everything, categorize, make hypotheses, and design experiments. We reason that the world is full of dichotomies. In fact, this chapter is a perfect example of dichotomistic thinking—we have polarized certain value orientations, labeled them, and then collected data from around the world to see how the theory fits.

Many cultural logics, on the other hand, are more holistic: They can tolerate a great deal of ambiguity or contradictions, as long as the "big picture" makes sense. While we were living in the island nation of Vanuatu, my wife and I witnessed a woman suffering from an ectopic pregnancy. She was rushed to the capital city for surgery, and eventually recovered. While she was in the hospital, her daughter contracted meningitis and died two days later in the hospital. Several months later, the woman's husband died of a heart attack. To dichotomistic thinkers like me and my wife, these three events were unrelated. We cannot reason how an ectopic pregnancy, meningitis, and heart attack are related. The islanders, however, thought more holistically. Through their culturally patterned logic, the three events were clearly related. "She obviously has sexual sin in her life, which is why she is being punished with these maladies" people explained to us. Westerners are seriously disturbed by the notion that God (or Mother Nature, however the cosmic punisher could be described) would cause a woman to have an ectopic pregnancy and lose her daughter and husband. This is one poignant example of how the deductive/inductive value orientation can create a sharp divide when people work cross-culturally.

Does the Bible promote inductive or deductive reasoning? An honest survey of Scripture will turn up a strong bent towards holistic, inductive reasoning. For example, a dichotomistic thinker would need to find *the single reason* that Jacob's flock prospered when they drank near the white poplar branch, while Laban's flock became speckled and scrawny while watering near the stripped poplar branch. Holistic thinkers, on the other hand, keep their options open: it could have been magic, it could have been a coincidence, it could have been God's blessing *despite* or *because* of Jacob's trickery (Gen 30:25–31:16). But dichotomists do not like ambiguous reasoning; they want to know a predictable cause and effect.

Consider another example which is more of a metanarrative in the OT: The prophets repeatedly warned that Israel would go into exile, and would experience sickness and famine, due to disobedience. The Assyrian conquest of Israel and the exile of Judah into Babylon were not *just* because foreign powers gathered enough soldiers to overcome Israel; there were more inductive, holistic (big picture) reasons for the defeat like God's punishment for idolatry. Further, we see Jesus making his points with parables—ambiguous stories—not with syllogisms. However, the Bible uses plenty of dichotomistic thinking, beginning with Adam categorizing the animals and giving each a name in Genesis 2:19–20. Also, Jesus employed high-level logic when he forced the religious leaders to make a logical "either P or Q" choice in Matthew 22:44–46 and Mark 11:29–33.

In this era of globalization, people from holistic cultures will need to become familiar with deductive/dichotomistic logic in order to function in higher education. And dichotomistic thinkers will need to hone their inductive skills to be able to relate to people from those cultural backgrounds.

On Table 14, mark your own ethnic cultural orientation toward inductive or deductive reasoning, and that of the Old and New Testament.

Table 14: Developing a theology of logic and inductive reasoning

Deductive	Inductive
• Experiment based	• Experience based
• Dichotomistic	• Holistic
• Scientific method	• Anecdote, conventional wisdom
• Break things down into categories	• See the big picture
• Syllogisms, logic	• Emotion, harmony
• Truthfulness is fundamental	• Tradition is fundamental
• Propositions (arguments)	• Narrative (stories)
• Precision is essential	• Ambiguity and contradiction is fine
Your ethnic culture:	
Inductive	Low " " " " " " High
Deductive	Low " " " " " " High
A kingdom view of the logic:	
Inductive	Low " " " " " " High
Deductive	Low " " " " " " High

9. A Kingdom view of hospitality

Cross-cultural theorists have noted that hospitality is a paramount value throughout the world. It is a recurring theme in biblical literature, as well as sacred literature in other cultures. While hospitality takes on many shapes (usually involving food and lodging), there seems to be an overarching dyad which distinguishes two patterns for hospitality. Sarah Lanier, in an attempt to use neutral language, called these two approaches "planned" and "spontaneous" hospitality.[33]

Westerners value hospitality, but can be quite disoriented when the need for offering hospitality is thrust upon them without warning. Even when there is sufficient warning, many US-Americans, Aussies, Kiwis, and Western Europeans prefer to meet in restaurants rather than at home. We say that houseguests are like fish—they stink after a few days. This is drastically different from the hospitality norms in much of Africa, the Pacific, the Middle East, and Asia. It is unthinkable to have a guest stay in a hotel. The host can stretch the food in the home to accommodate everyone.

The distinction between planned and spontaneous hospitality may seem incidental to a Westerner, where hospitality itself is rather incidental. However, hospitality is so important in many other parts of the world that it is essential for cross-cultural workers to understand this basic value orientation. It can be very disorienting for an African or Asian international student to find himself in dorm life in the US, where hospitality is infrequent and measured. He may see US-Americans as cold, and US-American society as lonely. On the flip side, US-American travelers can be quite disoriented by the norms for hospitality in other parts of the world. At times when they want their privacy and peace and quiet, they are expected to play the part of either guest or host.

Bible scholars have long noted that hospitality is a prominent value in Scripture. Does the Bible advocate planned or spontaneous hospitality? We would be hard-pressed to find biblical support for hospitality which is measured, infrequent, or buffered by hotels and restaurants. The man who refused to wake up his household in the middle of the night to feed his neighbor's guests was hardly the hero of Jesus' parable. Some verses which support spontaneous and nearly unlimited hospitality include: Genesis 19, Isaiah 58:7, Hebrews 13:2, 1 Peter 4:9, Matthew 25:34–46, Romans 12:13, Leviticus 19:33–34, Titus 1:8, Luke 14:12–14, Mark 9:41. We must

---

33. Lanier, *Foreign to Familiar.*

recognize, though, that in each of these biblical cases, the norms for hospitality were certainly learned, assumed, patterned, complex, and integrated. That is, they were culturally contextualized.

You may come from a part of the world where hospitality is more spontaneous and frequent, or where cultural norms require hospitality to be planned and buffered. In Table 15, mark your cultural patterns for hospitality below, and those of the Old and New Testament.

Table 15: Developing a theology of hospitality

Planned hospitality	Spontaneous hospitality
<ul><li>Meet in restaurants</li><li>Meet infrequently</li><li>Guests stay in a hotel</li></ul>	<ul><li>Meet at home</li><li>Meet often</li><li>You'd be ashamed to have someone stay in a hotel—they must stay in your home</li><li>Bring a gift</li><li>Lev 19:33–34; Isa 58:7; Heb 13:2; 1 Pet 4:9; Matt 25:34–46; Mark 9:41; Luke 14:12–14; Rom 12:13; Titus 1:8</li></ul>
Your ethnic culture:	
Planned Spontaneous	Low ¨ ¨ ¨ ¨ ¨ ¨ High Low ¨ ¨ ¨ ¨ ¨ ¨ High
A kingdom view of hospitality:	
Planned Spontaneous	Low ¨ ¨ ¨ ¨ ¨ ¨ High Low ¨ ¨ ¨ ¨ ¨ ¨ High

10. A kingdom view of hierarchy and equality

Every culture seems to differentiate status and roles depending on gender, age, wealth, bloodline, ethnicity, or any number of other criteria.[34] Some cultures, though, have far more stratification or "social inequality" than others. Hofstede found that collectivist societies are more likely to be hierarchal, whereas individualists tend towards egalitarianism.[35] A major

---

34. Howell and Paris, *Introducing Cultural Anthropology*, 66.

35. Ting-Toomey, "The Matrix of Face," 75.

exception to this correlation would be tribal peoples in Melanesia, who are egalitarian and collectivist.

K. P. Yohannan tells the story of a high-caste Hindu who fainted at a train station in India's summer heat. A railway employee filled up a cup and gave it to the man, but he refused to drink from it. "He would rather die than accept water in the cup of someone from another caste." Then another person noticed that the sick man had left his own cup on the seat, so he filled it with water and gave it to the sick man, "who immediately accepted the water with gratitude."[36] The Brahmin held (somewhat subconsciously) to his deeply ingrained value of hierarchy even to the point of death.

What are God's plans for hierarchy or equality? Those from egalitarian cultures probably find biblical support for egalitarianism, and those from hierarchal cultures see more power distance in the Bible. That's because the Bible has more than one power system in place.[37] God regularly sent prophets to upend the balance of power. Paul told the churches, "Our desire is not that others might be relieved while you are hard pressed, but that there might be equality" (2 Cor 8:13, NIV). Jesus stooped down to wash his disciples feet (John 13) and he warned the disciples not to "lord it over" people like the Gentiles (Matt 20:24–26). Jesus seemed to be no respecter of the social inequality perpetuated by the priests, Pharisees, scribes, soldiers, and proconsuls.

On the other hand, Leviticus 19:32 indicates special respect for the elderly. The early church organized itself with a tier of servant leaders called apostles, overseers, deacons, and deaconesses (1 Cor 12:28, Phil 1:1). Also, Peter and Paul said the authority of the king was from God (1 Pet 2:17).

World changing will inevitably involve challenging our own (as well as others') views of social power. Mark below your ethnic cultural orientation toward power distance, as well as a kingdom view of hierarchy and equality.

---

36. Yohannan, *Revolution in World Missions*, 154.
37. Moreau, et al., *Effective Intercultural Communication*, 169.

Table 16: Developing a theology of hierarchy and equality

Hierarchy	Equality
• Rules	• Consensus
• Titles	• Power diffused to many people
• Don't question authority	• Delegation of authority
• Military structure—top-down	• Informal social relations
• Privileges come with power	• Minimum deference for superiors
• Castes, classes	• Superior can be questioned
• 1 Cor 12:28; Phil 1:1; 1 Pet 2:17	• Less respect for old age
	• Mechanism to redress grievances
	• John 13; 2 Cor 8:13; Matt 20:24–26
Your ethnic culture:	
Hierarchy	Low ¨ ¨ ¨ ¨ ¨ ¨ High
Equality	Low ¨ ¨ ¨ ¨ ¨ ¨ High
A kingdom view of power difference:	
Hierarchy	Low ¨ ¨ ¨ ¨ ¨ ¨ High
Equality	Low ¨ ¨ ¨ ¨ ¨ ¨ High

11. A kingdom view of meritocracy

In some hierarchal cultures, privileges like status, wealth, and power are ascribed rather than achieved. There is very little opportunity for upward mobility, since you are born into your status. Egalitarian cultures emphasize upward mobility—earning your way.

Should leadership be passed along bloodlines, or should the most qualified leader be elected by popular vote? Are elderly automatically more qualified to speak and make decisions, or should all opinions be weighed? Should everyone have the right to go to a university, or is higher education a privilege reserved for certain ethnicities—or perhaps only for males? Some cultures are more likely to ascribe power, wealth, and privilege to a limited group, depending on heredity (as in the British royalty), gender (as in Iran), or ethnicity (as in the Southern US under Jim Crow laws). Other cultures lean more toward a meritocracy, where power, wealth, and privileges are earned. In meritocracies, all people theoretically have the chance to become wealthy or to rule, depending on the choices they make.

God set up the original system of ascription. Abraham and his children had a special privilege to occupy the promised land; the priestly line was traced through the tribe of Levi all the way to Jesus; and the kingly line in the Southern Kingdom was established through the single dynasty of King David, all the way to Zedekiah (and eventually to Jesus). The Northern Kingdom included twenty monarchs from nine dynasties.[38] On the other hand, there are numerous stories where the rich are brought low, and nobodies rise to prominence. In the end, God respects neither merit nor the sorts of statuses that human cultures ascribe to people (Rom 2:11; Jas 2:1–13); God directs the world through his own wisdom and grace, employing aspects of both merit and ascription.

In Table 17, mark your ethnic cultural orientation toward merit, and that of the Old and New Testament.

Table 17: Developing a theology of merit

Ascribed	Achieved
• One ethnicity is more privileged than another • Old people are wiser than younger • Royalty is in the blood	• Rags to riches stories • Democracy
Your ethnic culture:	
Ascribed	Low ˮ ˮ ˮ ˮ ˮ ˮ High
Achieved	Low ˮ ˮ ˮ ˮ ˮ ˮ High
A kingdom view of merit:	
Ascribed	Low ˮ ˮ ˮ ˮ ˮ ˮ High
Achieved	Low ˮ ˮ ˮ ˮ ˮ ˮ High

12. A kingdom view of toughness and tenderness

Some societies are more aggressive than others. They have larger militaries and competitive markets (think of China and the USA). Geert Hofstede referred to this cultural value orientation of aggression as "masculine"—not because he saw these cultures as "more manly" but because

---

38. Geisler, *A Popular Survey of the Old Testament*, 136.

he associated aggression with masculinity. The term is obviously outdated now, but the dyadic category still fits. Some of the world's cultures are "tough" and others are tenderer. It may be surprising to discover that Latin American countries score fairly low on Hofstede's "masculine" index. That's because despite their penchant for *machismo* (male aggression), Latin Americans also value ideals that Hofstede saw as "tender" such as family cohesiveness and collaboration.

During the Old Testament era, Israel experienced "tough" values. Jesus, on the other hand, has been history's epitome of tender ideals such as self-sacrifice and dignity of all. Consider how Jesus showed compassion for the unclean woman in Luke 13.[39] In Table 18, mark your ethnic culture's preference toward aggressiveness and cooperation; and mark how a kingdom approach may challenge your own cultural attitudes about gender roles.

Table 18: Developing a theology of tenderness and toughness

Tough	Tender
• Militarized	• Small military
• Competitive	• Collaborative
• Higher wages for men; men get a sense of value from work	• Women's rights
• Joshua, Judges	• Luke 13:10–17
Your ethnic culture:	
Tough Tender	Low ¨ ¨ ¨ ¨ ¨ ¨ High Low ¨ ¨ ¨ ¨ ¨ ¨ High
A kingdom view of tenderness and toughness:	
Tough Tender	Low ¨ ¨ ¨ ¨ ¨ ¨ High Low ¨ ¨ ¨ ¨ ¨ ¨ High

13. A kingdom view of conflict resolution

Theorists have noted that there are drastic cultural variations in how we solve conflict. Much of what World Changers address involves an

---

39. Moreau et al., *Effective Intercultural Communication*, 187–189.

amount of conflict, so we need to work out a biblical approach to this value orientation.

Salacuse's conflict resolution theory involves a two-dimensional model which compares dyadic value dimensions across two axes. On one axis is the uncooperative vs. cooperative value orientation; and on the other axis is the assertive vs. unassertive value orientation. So a culture which is oriented toward cooperation and assertion is considered "collaborative." One which is oriented toward assertiveness and noncooperation is "competitive." A culture which is neither assertive nor cooperative is "avoiding" and one that values cooperation but non-assertiveness is "accommodating." Right in the center of all of these tendencies is compromise.[40] Of course, these cultural preferences for resolving conflict can cause misunderstanding across cultures, as one communicator may be expecting collaboration, while the other interlocutor may prefer avoidance or competition.

The limitation of these models of cross-cultural negotiation and conflict resolution is that they are often based on US business practices. A stronger model would be one that is based on the accumulation of cross-cultural data—how do other cultures actually solve conflict? Hammer's model utilizes two long-recognized cross-cultural value orientations: individualism/collectivism and vulnerable/non-vulnerability.[41] So the preferred conflict resolution strategy for cultures that are oriented toward directness and vulnerability (emotional expressiveness) is "engagement." Cultures which value emotional restraint and indirectness are accommodating. Ones which prefer directness and emotional restraint use discussion as the preferred conflict resolution strategy. And cultures which are emotionally expressive but use an indirect communication style have a "dynamic" conflict resolution strategy, engaging in hyperbole and metaphors, or using third-party mediators.[42]

Does the Bible prescribe competitive or cooperative methods for dealing with conflict? Missions professor Duane Elmer suggests that "the Bible supports several means of handling conflict in addition to those used in Western cultures."[43] Rather than wishing people would handle conflict

---

40. Salacuse, "Teaching International Business Negotiation," 194.

41. Hammer, "The Intercultural Conflict Style Inventory."

42. Jackson, *Introducing Language and Intercultural Communication*, 261–62.

43. Elmer, *Cross-Cultural Conflict*, 46.

more like we do we need to understand how people are valued and respected within their cultural orientations.[44]

In Table 19, mark your ethnic culture's preference for conflict resolution, and that of Scripture.

Table 19: Developing a theology of negotiation

Competitive	Cooperative
• Winners and losers • Democracy	• Consensus
Your ethnic culture:	
Competitive Cooperative	Low " " " " " " High Low " " " " " " High
a kingdom view of negotiation	
Competitive Cooperative	Low " " " " " " High Low " " " " " " High

HOW CAN WE DESCRIBE CULTURAL DIFFERENCES WITHOUT INSISTING ON REDUCTIVE DYADS?

The "value orientation" approach above has come into disfavor among many cross-cultural theorists for forcing cultures into categories that have been pre-determined by outsiders. Why not just study cultures for what they are, rather than require them to be placed on a continuum? The problem is that abandoning all labels, theory, and cross-cultural analysis makes the discipline of cross-cultural studies impotent. There must be some theoretical framework for understanding Culture and cultures.

An alternative would be to exegete dominant cultural metaphors (discussed briefly in chapter 9). The advantages to metaphors is that they are located within a culture, and are culture-specific, as opposed to the "value orientations" approach, which imposes an external framework on cultures. Metaphors can allow us to look at specific unique contributions from societies, like running for the Tarahumara, or perhaps business and industry for Chinese.

44. Ibid., 53.

Gannon and Rajnandini suggest that another advantage of metaphors is that they are multifaceted (three to six dimensions), probabilistic not applied to every individual.[45] One example that Gannon and Rajnandini give is Japan's wet gardens. The gardens represent tranquility, temperance, animism, in-group, proper procedure, and harmony. Another metaphor suggested by the authors is Thailand's beloved king, representing censorship, paternalism, military strength, saving face, the middle way. Gannon and Rajnandini consider football to be an excellent metaphor for US-American culture: we huddle together in small groups to perform a certain task. This approach to cultural differences neatly covers some salient aspects of culture like individualism, aggression, consumerism, entertainment, and competition.

Perhaps another fitting metaphor for the USA would be the automobile, representing independence, consumption, power, ingenuity. Most US-Americans would not be offended to hear an anthropologist assert that cars are status symbols.

So the value of metaphors is that they tend to foster a positive reaction from people, whereas labeling "value orientations" can lead to negativity. And Christians would not find it offensive to say that the cross is a "dominant metaphor" in Christianity, as it represents simultaneously suffering and redemption. Quite the opposite—metaphors and symbols help foster cultural identity.

CONCLUSION: USING VALUE ORIENTATION THEORY TO BECOME WORLD CHANGERS

It should be clear by this point that developing a theology of culture is not just about describing other cultures, though that is the best starting point. But it requires moving from describing to cataloging those cultural differences and generating theories to explain 1) how those differences arose; and 2) how to engage other cultures in light of those differences.[46] A theology of culture incorporates a kingdom view of these commonalities, and informs us of our role in today's world.

Suppose, for example, that you worked cross-culturally with Japanese folks. You might note that as you participated in events, and asked cultural informants for help interpreting those events, a recurring theme

---

45. Gannon and Pillai, *Understanding Global Cultures.*

46. Ferraro, *The Cultural Dimension of International Business*, 9, 19.

was loyalty. Employees spoke of loyalty to their company, even when a competing firm offered a higher salary. You note that employees and family members are reluctant to speak their own opinion when an older or higher ranking person is in the room. You hear recurring discourse about tradition, ancestors, and "the way things have always been done." As you interview young people, it seems that they look to their extended family for guidance when they make decisions about where to live and whom they marry. At this point, you just have data. Now you need to make sense of it.

Then you would look at the contributions of cross-cultural experts who have cataloged cultural differences and have generated theories to explain those differences. As you studied this theoretical framework, you would note themes of collectivism versus individualism, long-term versus short-term orientation, and high risk avoidance versus low risk avoidance. This cross-cultural theory helps you make sense of your own data from Japanese culture as you note that Japanese people seem to be more collectivist than US-Americans; they have a long-term orientation, and are more likely to avoid risk.

Once you have catalogued the differences between Japanese culture and your own, you could work out a kingdom view of these cultural variations. Then you could develop a plan for crossing the cultural boundary and redeeming cultural spheres in line with God's kingdom. Cross-cultural workers have suggested, for instance, that American managers should make the following adjustments when working in Japan:

- Look to the oldest member of the group as the decisionmaker;

- Explain how the change you want to implement will reinforce group cohesion, since it is born out of long-standing practices and values;

- Rather than pitching your idea as innovative and ground-breaking, demonstrate the ways in which your plan is free from risk;

- Do not single out workers for praise or rebuke; speak to the whole group; and

- Use an indirect communication style rather than being blunt.

Your data and knowledge of cross-cultural theory have enabled you to describe underlying values, and ultimately to develop a biblical and practical approach for crossing cultures. Figure 15 below summarizes the way that cross-cultural studies moves from observing data, to cataloging differences, to developing theories that explain those differences, and finally to practical steps for crossing cultures effectively. And that leads us to the discussion in the last part of this book, on competencies for cross-cultural impact.

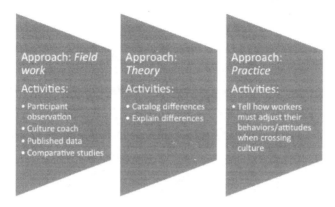

Figure 15: How to study another culture

REFLECTION AND REVIEW QUESTIONS

1. Are humans throughout the world more similar or different? What evidence would you use to support your answer?

2. How do you account for the differences between the world's cultures?

3. Which cultural value orientations would be the most disorienting for you to adjust to, in a cross-cultural setting?

4. Are there certain cultural value orientations that seem more biblically based than others? Which ones?

PART IV: Competencies for cross-cultural impact

CHAPTER 11

Becoming world changers

I BEGAN THIS BOOK by arguing that globalization matters to everyone because the only way to buy, sell, manage, compete, and communicate in the world of the twenty-first century is to be cross-culturally literate. And it matters even more to Christians because the only way to make a difference in the world of competing ideas, and to truly carry out God's command to love neighbor as yourself, is to be cross-culturally literate.

Christians are increasingly working cross-culturally under the umbrella of various types of organizations, from multinational corporations (MNCs), to humanitarian, aid, and development organizations, to educational institutions, to representatives of their own government or foreign government advisors. "We must master the cultural environment by means of purposeful preparation as well as sustained learning throughout our overseas assignment."[1] The past fifty years of cross-cultural studies has shown us that success at home does not ensure success cross-culturally—hence the need for cross-cultural training. It would be unimaginable to attempt to manage an organization, sell, or produce products in your home culture without understanding negotiation, communication, and marketing within that cultural context; so why not train those who work cross culturally to learn the culture there?[2] This chapter covers the competencies necessary for Christians to be World Changers, and suggests how Christians can engage the world of cultures and Culture in the twenty-first century.

1. Ferraro, *The Cultural Dimension of International Business*, 8
2. Ricks, *Big Business Blunders.*

WHAT COMPETENCIES DO TWENTY-FIRST-CENTURY CHRISTIANS NEED TO BE READY FOR CROSS-CULTURAL WORK?

Experts in intercultural studies have carried out numerous research projects to understand the perspectives, competencies, and knowledge sets that are necessary to make an impact cross-culturally. Workers need to have traits like empathy, flexibility, openness, and curiosity.[3] They need a good dose of cultural pluralism (chapter 7) to combat tacit ethnocentrism. They need cultural orientation and preparation for dealing with cultural differences that they will encounter. More recent approaches also show that cross-cultural workers must understand dynamics of identity management, agency, and hegemony.

MNCs, mission organizations, and governments that send people cross-culturally develop criteria for selecting the candidates that are most likely to be effective. These predictive instruments are usually based on sound research that shows correlations between personality traits and successful work in a cross-cultural environment. The Cross Cultural Adaptability Inventory (CCAI) is a basic list of traits that predict the readiness of candidates to work cross-culturally.[4] The inventory includes traits like emotional resilience (more recently called Emotional Intelligence, or EQ), perceptual acuity, autonomy, and flexibility.[5] Elmer provides a more comprehensive list of competencies, based on a literature survey of precedent research studies that predict cross cultural effectiveness.[6] These competencies include:

1. Tolerance

2. Sensitivity

3. Security

4. Flexibility

5. Enterprising

---

3. Byram, *Teaching and Assessing Intercultural Communicative Competence*; Hammer and Gudykunst, "Dimensions of Intercultural Effectiveness."

4. Kelley and Meyers, *CCAI: Cross Cultural Adaptability Inventory Manual.*

5. Ferraro, *The Cultural Dimension of International Business*, 180.

6. Elmer, M., *The Intercultural Competency Scale,* in Steffen and McKinney, *Encountering Missionary Life and Work*, 89.

6. Approachable

7. Receptivity

8. Positive

9. Forthright

10. Social openness

11. Respectful

12. Flexibility

13. Persevering

14. Perceptivity

15. Venturesome

16. Social confidence

The US Foreign Service published a list of thirteen similar qualifications. Minor differences in the list include judgment, planning, and communication skills.[7] Actually, as we compile lists of qualifications for working cross-culturally, the traits that are deemed necessary continues to mount and become practically daunting. It seems World Changers need to be Jacks-of-all-trades—true Renaissance men (and women)—who are well rounded and flexible, yet organized and dependable.

Chen and Starosta condense the competencies to the affective, behavioral, and cognitive domains.[8] In other words, cross-cultural workers need the knowledge skills and attitudes to work effectively. It is not enough to know the right way to behave in another culture; the cross-cultural worker must be transformed—to develop the attitudes that make him or her successful in the new culture. Livermore's model of Cultural Intelligence (CQ) uses a similar taxonomy: knowledge, strategy, drive (or motivation), and behavior (adaptation).[9]

The lists above indicate that succeeding at being a World Changer is really about interpersonal abilities. "You can adjust to the country, and to the community, and even to the job, and still not be able to get along with

7. US State Department, "US Foreign Service Officer Qualifications."
8. Chen and Starosta, "Intercultural Communication Competence."
9. Livermore, *Cultural Intelligence.*

the locals. And if you cannot get along with the locals, you will never be successful in an overseas assignment."[10]

But can these "necessary competencies" actually be taught? Or are we all limited by our personalities—suggesting that those who are innately approachable, respectful, and venturesome will succeed cross-culturally, while those who are less flexible and less tolerant should probably stay at home? Those who tend to label these qualifications as "traits" suggest that they are innate—ingrained. Those who label them as "competencies" suggest they can be taught. CCT is based on the conviction that many of these qualities can be taught, or at least honed.

These competencies (or personality traits) are measured by the domain of Cultural Intelligence (CQ) called motivational CQ. Those with high motivational CQ are interested in other cultures; they are undaunted when people laugh at their language mistakes; they see cross-cultural work as an adventure rather than a necessary evil. And it turns out that they are also the ones who are most likely to be effective in cross-cultural work. For example, Ng et al. noted that of 305 real estate agents, ones with high motivational CQ made more sales cross-culturally; leaders with high motivational CQ were more innovative and perform better in general.[11] Because there is a strong correlation between Motivational CQ and job performance (plus job satisfaction), organizations select workers with high motivational CQ for cross-cultural work.

The brilliance of CQ is that it moves us beyond the adaptation, assimilation, or acculturation models that plot the sojourner somewhere between "withdrawal" and "going native." In the twenty-first century, it is increasingly inappropriate to imagine that cross-cultural workers would "give up" some of their first culture in order to assimilate. Instead, a high CQ means that we retain all of Americanness (or Asianness, etc.) that allows us to function so seamlessly within our home culture; yet we also gain the competencies, attitudes, and interpretive skills that allow us to move seamlessly in a host culture. In the business world, CQ is important for negotiating deals, keeping expatriate managers overseas, and effectively training leadership in the host country. But ultimately, being competent in cross-cultural interactions is important so we can love the Other better.[12]

10. Storti, *The Art of Crossing Cultures*, 22.

11. Ng et al., "Cultural Intelligence."

12. Livermore, *Cultural Intelligence*, 15.

Since isolation is out of the question, the only viable solution to our cultural incompetence is to increase our cross-cultural literacy. A couple of decades ago, E. D. Hirsch introduced the idea of cultural literacy: the figures of speech, historical events and trivia Americans must know to understand and talk about their own culture.[13] We could extend this idea to cross-cultural literacy: the corpus of information we need to have successful interactions people from other cultures.

In the corporate world, cross-cultural literacy is necessary for the bottom line. People who are competent in their host culture stay longer and work more effectively. That decreases the chances of attrition, which is costly to a company. From a Christian standpoint, we would embrace the possibility that cross-cultural competence will increase profitability; but the goal is set significantly higher. Livermore's application of cultural intelligence has "loving the other" as the end goal.[14] In other words, to truly apply the greatest commandment, (to love God and neighbor, in Matthew 22:37) we need to understand our neighbor.

HOW AN EVANGELICAL THEOLOGY OF CULTURE FOSTERS WORLD CHANGERS

I have argued throughout this book that a comprehensive theology of culture is essential for being a World Changer in the twenty-first century. Below I have applied the numerous theoretical concepts I explored in the previous ten chapters in this book.

1. Research your world: keep abreast of what's going on. A good resource is *How to Be a World Class Christian*.[15] Be aware of how pernicious global trends like border disputes, colonialism, and hyper-nationalism affect the cross-cultural process in your area (chapter 1).

2. Know your biblical responsibility in the global marketplace. Think about your role in relation to the sojourner in your mist. Understand how you can leverage the forces of globalization for your own calling. Implement a plan for cultural diversity in your sphere of influence (chapter 1).

13. Hirsch, *Cultural Literacy*.
14. Livermore, *Cultural Intelligence*.
15. Borthwick and Warren, *How to Be a World-Class Christian*.

3. Understand how images of Westerners in today's world affect the strategies of cross-cultural work. Work out your own theology of "God's blessing" on your own nation (chapter 2).

4. Understand that cultural patterns meet basic needs. Some are random—they just come to be as the result of diffusion. But see humankind as culturative. Being in the image of God means we love to create, express, and rule. Look for how this nature comes out in variouscross-cultural contexts (chapter 3).

5. Understand the integrated nature of culture. Always look for how religion is political, or how social organization is also an economic activity, or how language is not only symbolic but social and expressive (chapter 3).

6. Understand that ethnicity is a fuzzy category rather than bounded. Cultural norms are contested and changing, rather than static. This realization keeps us from essentializing and from making ethnic attributions (chapter 4).

7. Maintain a view of cultural pluralism. This should help reconcile God's culturative nature with the reality that none of the world's cultures—not at any time in history—is endorsed uniquely by God (chapter 5).

8. Study particular cultures on their own terms, rather than fit them into etic categories. But use cross-cultural theory to advance your understanding of other cultures (chapter 6).

9. Be committed to cultural pluralism on the one hand, and to a biblical evaluation of culture on the other. Look for ways that the cross-cultural context can improve you (chapter 6).

10. Understand that we glorify God through work and worship. Scripture's answer to the enduring problem is not withdrawal from cultural life, which is impossible anyway. God's plan was for us to be cultural. Instead, the answer is to enjoy culture without idolizing it (chapter 7).

11. View the kingdom of God and culture as partners rather than enemies. Rather than pitting this world against the kingdom of God, see how your cultural life falls squarely under God's sovereignty (chapter 7).

12. Recognize spheres of culture. Lend legitimacy to those spheres as God-ordained activities. Ask "How can God's plan for this sphere of culture be realized in your own specific society?" (chapter 8).

13. Become aware of evangelical attitudes and contributions to the various spheres of culture (chapter 8).

14. Study the Scripture and cross-cultural theory enough to 1) understand cultural variations and 2) feel confident that your cross-cultural approach is biblical (chapter 9).

15. Develop an approach to cultural accommodation that values the home culture while also emphasizing effectiveness in the host culture. This will not be an adjustment model, which is more like "putting up with another culture." Nor will it be accommodation—which is like relinquishing the self (chapter 10).

REFLECTION AND REVIEW QUESTIONS

1. How do you keep yourself educated on global trends in culture? How do you stay aware of how you can be praying for the world?

2. Which competencies do you think you need to develop to be a World Changer?

3. What is the relationship between a theology of culture and changing the world?

Works Cited

Abrams, C. P. "The Origin of Race." http://bible-truth.org/race.htm.

Anderson, Sheldon, et al. *International Studies: An Interdisciplinary Approach to Global Issues*. Philadelphia: Westview, 2008.

Asmus, Barry, and Wayne Grudem. *The Poverty of Nations*. Wheaton, IL: Crossway, 2013.

——— "The only way for poor to escape from poverty." http://www.foxnews.com/opinion/2014/01/24/only-way-for-poor-to-escape-from-poverty/.

Banks, Robert. *God the Worker: Journeys into the Mind, Heart and Imagination of God*. Valley Forge, PA: Judson, 1994.

Barber, Benjamin R. "Jihad vs. McWorld." *Atlantic Monthly*, March, 1992, 53–65.

Barber, John. *The Road from Eden: Studies in Christianity and Culture*. Palo Alto, CA: Academia, 2008.

Barna Group. "How America's Faith has Changed Since 9-11." http://www.barna.org/barna-update/article/5-barna-update/63-how-americas-faith-has-changed-since-9-11.

Barreto, Eric D. *Ethnic Negotiations*. Tübingen: Mohr Siebeck, 2010.

Barrett, Richard A. "The Paradoxical Anthropology of Leslie White." *American Anthropologist*, 91 no. 1 (1989) 986–99.

BBC World Service. "Global Views of United States Improve While Other Countries Decline." http://www.worldpublicopinion.org/pipa/pipa/pdf/apr10/BBCViews_Apr 10_rpt.pdf.

Bennett, Milton J. "Towards a Developmental Model of Intercultural Sensitivity." In *Education for the Intercultural Experience*, edited by RM Paige, 21–71. Yarmouth, MA: Intercultural, 1993.

——— "Towards Ethnorelativism: A Developmental Model of Intercultural Sensitivity." In *Cross-Cultural Orientation: New Conceptualizations and Applications*, edited by R. M. Paige, 27–70. New York: University Press of America, 1986.

Berger, Peter, and Thomas Luckmann. *The Social Construction of Reality*. Harmondsworth: Pelican, 1967.

Berry, J. W. "Conceptual Approaches to Acculturation." In *Acculturation: Advances in Theory, Measurement, and Applied Research*, edited by K. Chun et. al., 17–37. Washington, DC: American Psychological Association, 2003.

Boas, Franz. "Anthropology." *Encyclopedia of the Social Sciences*, edited by Edwin R. A., 72–111. New York: Macmillan, 1930.

Borthwick, Paul, and Rick Warren. *How to Be a World-Class Christian: Becoming Part of God's Global Kingdom.* Rev. ed. Downers Grove, IL: InterVarsity, 2009.

Bradshaw, Bruce. *Change Across Cultures: A Narrative Approach to Social Transformation.* Grand Rapids: Baker Academic, 2002.

Brierley, P. "Missionary Attrition: The ReMAP Research Project." In *Too Valuable to Lose: Exploring the Causes and Cures of Missionary Attrition,* edited by William D. Taylor, 85–103. Pasadena: William Carey Library, 1997.

Brown, Donald. *Human Universals.* Philadelphia: Temple University Press, 1991.

Bruggemann, Walter. *Genesis.* Atlanta, GA: John Knox, 1982.

Byram, M. *Teaching and Assessing Intercultural Communicative Competence.* Clevedon, UK: Multilingual Matters, 1997.

Calvin, John. *Institutes of the Christian Religion.* Philadelphia: Westminster, 1950.

Campbell, Cynthia. *A Multitude of Blessings: A Christian Approach to Religious Diversity.* Louisville: Westminster John Knox, 2006.

Carroll, John B., ed. *Language, Thought and Reality: Selected Writings of Benjamin Lee Whorf.* Cambridge, MA: MIT Press, 1964.

Carson, Ben. *America the Beautiful: Rediscovering What Made This Nation Great.* Grand Rapids: Zondervan, 2012.

Carson, D. A. *Christ and Culture Revisited.* Grand Rapids: Eerdmans, 2008.

Carter, Craig. *Rethinking Christ and Culture: A Post-Christendom Perspective.* Grand Rapids: Brazos, 2007.

Casey, Anthony. "How Shall They Hear? The Interface of Urbanization and Orality in North American Ethnic Church Planting." PhD diss., Southern Baptist Theological Seminary, 2013.

Chang, H.-C. "Language and Words: Communication in the Analects of Confucius." In *The Global Intercultural Communication Reader,* edited by M. Asante et. al., 95–109. New York: Routledge, 2008.

Chapman, Mark D. "The Social Doctrine of the Trinity: Some Problems." *Anglican Theological Review,* 83 no. 2 (2001) 239–54.

Chen, G.-M., and W. Starosta. "Intercultural Communication Competence." In *The Global Intercultural Communication Reader,* edited by M. Asante, Y. Miike, and J. Yin, 215–37. New York: Routledge, 2008.

Chewning, R. C., ed. *Biblical Principles and Economics: The Foundations.* Colorado Springs: NavPress, 1989.

Chukueku, A. "Partnership in Mission: Means of Tackling Emerging Challenges in African Missions of the Twenty-First Century." *Ogbomoso Journal of Theology,* 15 no. 2 (2010) 111–24.

CNN. "Southern Baptists Boycott Disney." http://www.cnn.com/US/9706/18/baptists.disney/.

Conn, Harvie M. *Eternal Word and Changing Worlds: Theology, Anthropology, and Mission in Trialogue.* Grand Rapids: Zondervan, 1984.

Corduan, Winfried. *Neighboring Faiths: A Christian Introduction to World Religions.* 2nd ed. Downers Grove: InterVarsity, 2012.

Cortez, Marc. *Theological Anthropology: A Guide for the Perplexed.* New York: T & T Clark, 2010.

Cosgrove, Mark P. *Foundations of Christian Thought: Faith, Learning and the Christian Worldview.* Grand Rapids: Kregel, 2006.

Crouch, Andy. *Culture Making: Recovering Our Creative Calling.* Downers Grove: InterVarsity, 2008.

Cunningham, Loren. *The Book that Transforms Nations: The Power of the Bible to Change any Country.* Seattle: YWAM, 2007.

Dawkins, Richard. *The Selfish Gene.* 2nd ed. London: Oxford University Press, 1990.

deClaisse-Walford, N. "God Came Down . . . and God Scattered." *Review and Expositor,* 103 (2006) 403–19.

Delany, M. *Principia of Ethnology: The Origin of Races and Color, with an Archaeological Compendium of Ethiopian and Egyptian Civilization, from Years of Careful Examination and Inquiry.* Philadelphia: Harper & Bros, 1880.

Detweiler, Craig. *iGods: How Technology Shapes Our Spiritual and Social Lives.* Grand Rapids: Brazos, 2013.

Diamond, Jared. *Guns, Germs and Steel: The Fates of Human Societies.* New York: W. W. Norton, 1999.

Durkheim, Emile, and Marcel Mauss. *Primitive Classification.* Chicago: University of Chicago Press, 1963.

Dyer, John. *From the Garden to the City: The Redeeming and Corrupting Power of Technology.* Grand Rapids: Kregel, 2011.

Eagleton, Terry. *The Idea of Culture.* Oxford: Wiley-Blackwell, 2000.

Elmer, Duane. *Cross-Cultural Conflict: Building Relationships for Effective Ministry.* Downers Grove, IL: InterVarsity, 1993.

Elmer, M. I. *The Intercultural Competency Scale: A Description of the Factors and the Total Score, Form E.* 1988.

Fernandez, James. *Persuasions and Performances: The Play of Tropes in Culture.* Bloomington, IN: Indiana University Press, 1986.

Ferraro, Gary. *The Cultural Dimension of International Business.* 6th ed. Boston: Prentice Hall, 2010.

Flett, Eric Gordon. *Persons, Powers and Pluralities: Toward a Trinitarian Theology of Culture.* Eugene, OR: Wipf & Stock, 2011.

Food And Agriculture Organization. "What the New Figures on Hunger Mean." http://www.fao.org/english/newsroom/news/2002/9703-en.html.

Freeman, Derek. *Margaret Mead and Samoa.* Cambridge, MA: Harvard University Press, 1983.

Freud, Sigmund. *Totem and Taboo* Translated by J. Strachey. New York: Norton & Co., 1950.

Friedman, Thomas. *The World is Flat: A Brief History of the Twenty-First Century.* New York: Farrar, Straus and Giroux, 2005.

Funderburg, Lise. "The Changing Face of America." *National Geographic.* http://ngm.nationalgeographic.com/2013/10/changing-faces/funderburg-text

Gannon, Martin J., and Rajnandini Pillai. *Understanding Global Cultures: Metaphorical Journeys Through 29 Nations, Clusters of Nations, Continents, and Diversity.* 4th ed. Thousand Oaks, CA: Sage, 2010.

Geertz, Clifford. *Local Knowledge.* New York: Basic, 1983.

Geisler, Norm. *A Popular Survey of the Old Testament.* Grand Rapids: Baker, 1977.

———. *Systematic Theology.* Vol. 1. Minneapolis: Bethany House, 2002.

George, Sam. "Diaspora: A Hidden Link to 'From Everywhere to Everywhere' Missiology." *Missiology,* 39 no. 1 (2011) 45–56.

Gingrich, Newt. *Rediscovering God in America: Reflections on the Role of Faith in Our Nation's History and Future*. Nashville: Integrity, 2006.

Gingrich, Newt, and Callista Gingrich. "A City upon a Hill: The spirit of American exceptionalism." 2011.

Gorringe, T. J. *Furthering Humanity: A Theology of Culture*. Burlington. VT: Ashgate, 2004.

Greenwald, Bruce, and Judd Kahn. *Globalization: The Irrational Fear that Someone in China Will Take Your Job*. Hoboken, NJ: John Wiley & Sons, 2009.

Grieco, E. M., et al. "The Foreign-Born Population in the United States: 2010: US Census Bureau." http://www.census.gov/prod/2012pubs/acs-19.pdf.

Grudem, Wayne. *Politics According to the Bible*. Grand Rapids: Zondervan, 2010.

———. *Systematic Theology*. Grand Rapids: Zondervan, 1995.

Grunlan, Stephen A., and Marvin Mayers. *Cultural Anthropology: A Christian Perspective*. Grand Rapids: Zondervan, 1988.

Hall, Edward T. *The Silent Language*. New York: Doubleday, 1959.

Hall, Edward T., and Mildred Reed Hall. *Understanding Cultural Differences: Germans, French and Americans*. Boston: Intercultural, 1990.

Hammer, M. R. "The Intercultural Conflict Style Inventory: A Conceptual Framework and Measure of Intercultural Conflict Resolution Approaches." *International Journal of Intercultural Relations* 29 (2005) 675–95.

Hammer, M. R., and W. B. Gudykunst. "Dimensions of Intercultural Effectiveness." *International Journal of Intercultural Relations* 2 (1978) 382–93.

Hampden-Turner, Charles, and Fons Trompenaars. *Riding Waves of Culture: Understanding Diversity in Global Business*. New York: McGraw-Hill, 1998.

Harris, Marvin. *The Rise of Anthropological Theory: A History of Theories of Culture*. New York: Thomas Y. Crowell, 1968.

Harris, P. R., et al. *Managing Cultural Differences: Global Leadership Strategies for the Twenty-First Century*. 6th ed. London: Elsevier, 2004.

Harrison, Nonna Verna. *God's Many-Splendored Image*. Grand Rapids: Baker Academic, 2010.

Hatch, E. *Theories of Man and Culture*. New York: Columbia University Press, 1976.

Hedges, C. *American Fascists: The Christian Right and War on America*. New York: Free Press, 2007.

Hegeman, David Bruce. *Plowing in Hope*. Moscow, ID: Canon, 2007.

Herppich, B. "Korean Diaspora and Christian Mission." *Missiology* 40 no. 3 (2012) 353–54.

Hibbs, Thomas S. *Shows about Nothing: Nihilism in Popular Culture from the Exorcist to Seinfeld*. Dallas: Spence, 1999.

Hiebert, Paul. *Transforming Worldviews*. Grand Rapids: Baker, 2008.

Hirsch, E. *Cultural Literacy: What Every American Needs to Know*. Vancouver: Vintage, 1988.

Hodgen, Margaret T. *Early Anthropology in the Sixteenth and Seventeenth Centuries*. Philadelphia: University of Pennsylvania Press, 1964.

Hoekema, Anthony A. *Created in God's Image*. Grand Rapids: Eerdmans, 1986.

Hofstede, Geert. *Culture's Consequences: Comparing Values, Behaviors, Institutions and Organizations Across Nations*. Beverly Hills, CA: Sage, 1980.

Hofstede, Geert, et al. *Cultures and Organizations: Software of the Mind*. New York: McGraw Hill, 2010.

Holliday, Adrian. "Small Cultures." In *Intercultural Communication Reader,* edited by Zhu Hua, 196–218. Routledge: New York, 2011.

Hoppe, M. "An Interview with Geert Hofstede." *Academy of Management* 18 no. 1 (2004) 75–79.

Houdmann, M. "Individualism vs. Collectivism: What Does the Bible Say?" http://www.gotquestions.org/individualism–vs–collectivism.html.

Howell, Brian, and Jenell Williams Paris. *Introducing Cultural Anthropology: A Christian Perspective.* Grand Rapids: Baker, 2010.

Hu, H. C. "The Chinese Concept of 'Face.'" *American Anthropologist* 46 (1944) 45–64.

Hughes, Philip E. *The Book of Revelation: A Commentary.* Downers Grove, IL: InterVarsity, 1990.

Huntington, Samuel P. *The Clash of Civilizations and the Remaking of World Order.* New York: Simon and Schuster, 2011.

———. "The West: Unique, not Universal." *Foreign Affairs* 75 no. 6 (1996) 28–46.

Jackson, Jane. *Introducing Language and Intercultural Communication.* New York: Routledge, 2014.

Jardine, Murray. *The Making and Unmaking of Technological Society: How Christianity Can Save Modernity from Itself.* Grand Rapids: Brazos, 2004.

Jenson, R. *Essays in Theology of Culture.* Grand Rapids: Eerdmans, 1995.

Jindra, M. "Culture Matters: Diversity in the United States and its Implications." In *This Side of Heaven: Race, Ethnicity and Christian faith,* edited by Robert Priest and A. Nieves, 63–81. New York: Oxford University Press, 2007.

Johnson, G. *The World According to God.* Downers Grove: InterVarsity, 2002.

Johnston, Robert K. *Reel Spirituality.* 2nd ed. Grand Rapids: Baker Academic, 2006.

Kallenberg, Brad. *God and Gadgets: Following Jesus in a Technological Age.* Eugene, OR: Cascade, 2011.

Keil, C. F. *Biblical Commentary on the Old Testament.* Grand Rapids: Eerdmans, 1983.

Kelley, C., and J. Meyers. *CCAI: Cross Cultural Adaptability Inventory Manual.* Minneapolis: National Computer Systems, 1995.

Kelly, W. "Applying a Critical Metatheoretical Approach to Intercultural Relations: The Case of US-Japanese Communication." In *The Global Intercultural Communication Reader,* edited by M. Asante et. al, 215–38. New York: Routledge, 2008.

Kim, M.-S. "Culture-Based Conversational Constraints Theory." In *Theorizing about Intercultural Communication,* edited by W. Gudykunst, 93–117. Thousand Oaks, CA: Sage, 2005.

Kline, Meredith G. *Kingdom Prologue: Genesis Foundations for a Covenantal Worldview.* South Hamilton, MA: M. G. Kline, 1993.

Kohls, L. Robert. *Survival Kit for Overseas Living.* 4th ed. Boston: Nicholas Brealey, 2001.

Köstenberger, Andreas, and Peter O'Brien. *Salvation to the Ends of the Earth: A Biblical Theology of Mission.* New Studies in Biblical Theology 11. Downers Grove, IL: InterVarsity, 2001.

Kotter, David. "How Economic Profits Relate to the Creation Mandate." http://www.sbts.edu/blogs/2014/05/06/how–economic–profits–relate–to–the–creation–mandate/.

Kraft, Charles. *Anthropology for Christian Witness.* Maryknoll, NY: Orbis, 1996.

———. *Christianity in Culture.* Maryknoll, NY: Orbis, 1981.

Kroeber, A. L. "The Superorganic." *American Anthropologist* 19 (1917) 163–213.

Kruse, Colin. *New Testament Models for Ministry: Jesus and Paul.* Nashville: Thomas Nelson, 1985.

Kurtz, D. V. *Political Anthropology: Power and Paradigms*. Boulder, CO: Westview, 2001.

Kuyper, Abraham. "Sphere Sovereignty." In *Abraham Kuyper, A Centennial Reader,* edited by J. D. Bratt, 461–90. Grand Rapids: Eerdmans, 1988.

———. *Wisdom & Wonder: Common Grace in Science & Art*. Grand Rapids: Christian's Library, 2011.

Lang, Gretchen. "Cross-Cultural Training—How Much Difference Does it Really Make?" *New York Times.* http://www.nytimes.com/2004/01/24/news/24iht-rcross_ed3_.html?pagewanted=all .

Lanier, Sarah. *Foreign to Familiar: A Guide to Understanding Hot—and Cold—Climate Cultures*. Hagerstown, MA: McDougal, 2000.

Lausanne Movement. "Lausanne Covenant." Paper presented at the International Congress on World Evangelization, Lausanne, Switzerland. http://www.lausanne.org/content/covenant/lausanne-covenant.

Lee, H. "Beyond Partnership, Towards Networking: A Korean Reflection on Partnership in the Web of God's Mission." *International Review of Mission* 91 no. 363 (2002) 577–82.

Leech, K. *The Social God*. Eugene, OR: Wipf and Stock, 2003.

Lewis, M. Paul, et. al., eds. "Ethnologue: Languages of the World: Browse by Language Family." http://www.ethnologue.com/browse/families.

Lingenfelter, Sherwood. *Agents of Transformation*. Grand Rapids: Baker, 1996.

———. *Transforming Culture*. 2nd ed. Grand Rapids: Baker, 1998.

Lingenfelter, Sherwood, and Marvin Mayers. *Ministering Cross-Culturally*. Grand Rapids: Baker, 1986.

Livermore, David. *Cultural Intelligence: Improving your CQ to Engage our Multicultural World*. Grand Rapids: Baker Academic, 2009.

Livingstone, David N. *Adam's Ancestors: Race, Religion and the Politics of Human Origins*. Baltimore: Johns Hopkins, 2008.

Long, Stephen. *Theology and Culture: A Guide to the Discussion*. Eugene, OR: Cascade, 2008.

Lumeah, N. "Curse on Ham's Descendants: Its Missiological Implications on Zairian Mbala Mennonite Brethren." PhD diss., Fuller Theological Seminary, 1988.

Malinowski, Bronislaw. *A Scientific Theory of Culture and Other Essays*. Vol. 9. Chapel Hill, NC: University of North Carolina Press, 1944.

Malone, Peter. *Movie Christs and Antichrists*. New York: Crossroad, 1990.

Mao, L. R. "Beyond politeness theory: 'Face' revisited and renewed." *Journal of Pragmatics* 21 (1994) 451–86.

Mauss, Marcel. *The Gift: The Form and Reason for Exchange in Archaic Societies*. New York: W. W. Norton, 1990.

Mead, Margaret. *Coming of Age in Samoa*. New York: William Morrow & Co., 1928.

———, ed. *Cooperation and Competition among Primitive Peoples*. New York: McGraw Hill, 1937.

Meier, J. "Nations or Gentiles." *Catholic Biblical Quarterly* 39 no. 1 (1977) 94–102.

Miller, James Grier. *Living Systems*. Niwot, CO: University Press of Colorado, 1994.

Moltmann, Jürgen. *The Trinity and the Kingdom of God*. London: SCM, 1981.

Monaghan, John, and Peter Just. *Social and Cultural Anthropology*. Oxford: Oxford University Press, 2000.

Moore, Jerry D. *Visions of Culture: An Introduction to Anthropological Theories and Theorists*. 2nd ed. Lanham, MD: AltaMira, 2004.

Moore, T. M. *Culture Matters: A Call for Consensus on Christian Culture Engagement.* Grand Rapids: Brazos, 2007.

Morales, P., and P. Eleazar. "How Can North American Mission Agencies Effectively Cooperate with and Encourage Two-Thirds World Mission Sending Agencies?" *Journal of Latin American theology* 8 no. 1 (2013) 15–34.

Moreau, Scott, et al. *Effective Intercultural Communication.* Grand Rapids: Baker Academic, 2014.

Morgan, Lewis H. *Ancient Society.* London: MacMillan & Company, 1877.

Morrison, Terri, et al. *Kiss, Bow, or Shake Hands: The Bestselling Guide to Doing Business in More than 60 Countries.* 2nd ed. Avon, MA: Adams Media, 2006.

Morton, Samuel George. *Crania Americana.* Philadelphia: Dobson, 1839.

Mounce, Robert. *The Book of Revelation.* Grand Rapids: Eerdmans, 1997.

Murdock, G. "The Common Denominator of Cultures." In *The Science of Man in the World Crisis,* edited by R. Linton, 123–42. New York: Columbia University Press, 1945.

Muthuraj, J. G. "The Meaning of Ethnos and Ethne and its Significance to the Study of the New Testament." *Bangalore Theological Forum* 29 no. 3–4 (1997) 3–36.

Naik, Gautam. "The Mother of all Languages." *Wall Street Journal.* http://online.wsj.com/news/articles/SB10001424052748704547604576262572791243528.

Nehrbass, Kenneth. *Christianity and Animism in Melanesia: Four Approaches to Gospel and Culture.* Pasadena, CA: William Carey Library, 2012.

———. "The Controversial Image of the US American in Missions." Paper presented at the Evangelical Missiological Society, Dallas, 2015.

———. "Dealing with Disaster: Critical Contextualization of Misfortune in an Animistic Setting." *Missiology* 39 no. 4 (2011) 459–71.

———. "Korean Missiology: A Survey of Dissertations and Theses from Western Institutions." *Reformed Theology and Mission* 2 (2012) 149–73.

Ng, K., et al. "Cultural Intelligence: A Review, Reflections, and Recommendations for Future Research." In *Conducting Multinational Research: Applying Organizational Psychology in the Workplace,* edited by A.M. Ryan, et al., 29–58. Washington, DC: American Psychological Association, 2012.

Nichols, Bruce J. "Towards a Theology of Gospel and Culture." In *Gospel and Culture,* edited by John Stott and R. Coote, 69–82. Pasadena, CA: William Carey Library, 1979.

Niebuhr, H. Richard. *Christ and Culture.* New York: Harper & Brothers, 1975.

Noll, M. *Jesus Christ and the Life of the Mind.* Grand Rapids: Eerdmans, 2011.

Novak, M. *The Spirit of Democratic Capitalism.* Lanham, MD: Madison, 1991.

Ortner, Sherry. "On Key Symbols." *American Anthropologist* 75 no. 5 (1973) 1338–46.

Ott, Craig. "Globalization and Contextualization: Reframing the Task of Contextualization in the Twenty-First Century." *Missiology* 43 no. 1 (2014) 43–58.

Otto, Ben. "Indonesia Weighs Curbs on Sex, Magic." *Wall Street Journal,* May 22, 2013. http://www.wsj.com/articles/SB10001424127887324010704578414273631917186

Packer, George. "How Susie Bayer's T-shirt Ended Up on Yusuf Mama's Back." *New York Times.* http://www.nytimes.com/2002/03/31/magazine/how-susie-bayer-s-t-shirt-ended-up-on-yusuf-mama-s-back.html.

Pagel, Mark. "Does Globalization Mean we will Become One Culture?" BBC. http://www.bbc.com/future/story/20120522-one-world-order.

Paris, J. "Race: Critical Thinking and Transformative Possibilities." In *This Side of Heaven: Race, Ethnicity and Christian Faith*, edited by Robert Priest and A. Nieves, 19–32. New York: Oxford University Press, 2007.

Parler, Branson. *Things Hold Together: John Howard Yoder's Trinitarian Theology of Culture*. Harrisonburg, VA: Herald, 2012.

Pearse, Meic. *Why the Rest Hates the West*. Downers Grove, IL: InterVarsity, 2004.

Piers, G., and M. Singer. *Shame and Guilt: A Psychoanalytic and a Cultural Study*. New York: W. W. Norton & Company, 1972.

Pinsky, Mark I. *The Gospel According to the Simpsons*. Louisville: Westminster John Knox, 2001.

Piper, John. "Treasuring Him." http://sermonjamtranscript.wordpress.com/tag/john–piper/.

Priest, Robert, and Alvaro L. Nieves, eds. *This Side of Heaven: Race, Ethnicity and Christian Faith*. New York: Oxford University Press, 2007.

Probyn-Rapsey, Fiona. *Made to Matter: White Fathers, Stolen Generations*. Sydney, Australia: Sydney University Press, 2013.

Putman, Robert D. "E Pluribus Unum: Diversity and community in the twenty-first century—The 2006 Johan Skytte Prize Lecture." *Scandinavian Political Studies* 30 no. 2 (2007) 137–74.

Rauchway, Eric. *Blessed Among Nations: How the World Made America*. New York: Hill and Wang, 2006.

Reeves, D. "Poverty and Inequality in a Global Economy." In *Introducing Global Issues*, edited by D. Neil. Snarr and Michael Snarr, 141–65. Boulder, CO: Lynne Riener, 2012.

Richards, E. Randolph, and Brandon J. O'Brien. *Misreading Scripture with Western Eyes: Removing Cultural Blinders to Better Understand the Bible*. Downers Grove, IL: InterVarsity, 2012.

Richardson, Don. *Eternity in their Hearts*. Ventura, CA: Regal, 1981.

Ricks, David A. *Big Business Blunders: Mistakes in Multi-National Marketing*. Homewood, IL: Dow Jones-Irwin, 1983.

Risner, James. "A Theological Justification for the Contribution of Culture to the Theological Task." PhD diss., Southern Baptist Theological Seminary, 2013.

Ritzer, George. *The McDonaldization of Society*. Thousand Oaks, CA: Pine Forge, 1993.

Roembke, Lianne. *Building Credible Multicultural Teams*. Pasadena, CA: William Carey Library, 2000.

Rogers, Everett M. *The Diffusion of Innovations*. New York: Free Press, 2003.

Rookmaaker, H. R. *Modern Art and the Death of a Culture*. Downers Grove, IL: InterVarsity, 1970.

Roosevelt, Theodore. "Letter to the President of the American Defense Society." Paper presented at the American Defense Society, New York, 1919.

Rosman, D. *Evangelicals and Culture*. 2nd ed. Eugene, OR: Pickwick, 2011.

Ross, A. "The Dispersion of the Nations in Genesis 11:1-9." *Bibliotheca Sacra* 138 (1981) 119–38.

Rowntree, Lester, et al. *Diversity Amid Globalization: World Regions, Environment, Development*. Upper Saddle River, NJ: Pearson, 2009.

Rudin, Arnold James. *The Baptizing of America: The Religious Right's Plans for the Rest of Us*. New York: Thunder's Mouth, 2006.

Rundle, Steve, and Tom Steffen. *Great Commission Companies: The Emerging Role of Business in Missions.* Grand Rapids: InterVarsity, 2013.

Rynkiewich, Michael. *Soul, Self and Society: A Postmodern Anthropology for Mission in a Postcolonial World.* Eugene, OR: Cascade, 2011.

Salacuse, Jeswald W. "Teaching International Business Negotiation: Reflections on Three Decades of Experience." *International Negotiation* 15 (2010) 187–228.

Scarborough, R. *Enough Is Enough: A Practical Guide to Political Action at the Local, State, and National Level.* Charleston, SC: Frontline, 2008.

Schaeffer, Francis. *How Should We Then Live?* Grand Rapids: Revell, 1976.

———. *Francis A. Schaeffer Trilogy: The Three Essential Books in One Volume.* Wheaton, IL: Crossway, 1990.

Shelley, Bruce. *Church History in Plain Language.* Nashville: Thomas Nelson, 2008.

Shin, H. "Language Use and English-Speaking Ability: 2000: US Census Bureau." October, 2003.

Short, Robert L. *The Gospel According to Peanuts.* Louisville: Westminster John Knox, 2000.

Silzer, Sheryl. *Biblical Multicultural Teams.* Pasadena, CA: William Carey International University Press, 2011.

Sirico, Robert. *Defending the Free Market: The Moral Case for a Free Economy.* Washington, DC: Regnery, 2012.

Skillen, James W., and Rockne McCarthy, eds. *Political Order and the Plural Structure of Society.* Atlanta: Emory University Press, 1991.

Slimbauch, Richard. "First, Do No Harm: Short-Term Missions at the Dawn of a New Millennium." *Evangelical Missions Quarterly* 36 no. 4 (2000) 428–41.

Smay, Diana, and George Armelagos. "Galileo Wept: A Critical Assessment of the Use of Race in Forensic Anthropology." *Transforming Anthropology* 9 no. 2 (2000) 19–30.

Snarr, Michael T. "Introducing Globalization and Global Issues." In *Introducing Global Issues,* edited by D. Neil. Snarr and Michael T. Snarr, 1–11. Boulder, CO: Lynne Rienner, 2012.

Sorett, Josef. "Believe Me, This Pimp Game is Very Religious: Toward a Religious History of Hip Hop." *Culture and Religion* 10 (2009) 11–22.

Stapert, Calvin. "Bach as Theologian: A Review Article." *Reformed Journal 37* (May, 1987) 19–27.

Starnes, Todd. *God Less America: Real Stories From the Front Lines of the Attack on Traditional Values.* Charleston, SC: Frontline, 2014.

Steffen, Tom. *Passing the Baton.* Rev. ed. Pasadena, CA: Center for Organization & Ministry, 1997.

Steffen, Tom, and Douglas L. McKinney. *Encountering Missionary Life and Work.* Grand Rapids: Baker, 2008.

Stevens, R. P. *The Other Six Days.* Grand Rapids: Eerdmans, 1999.

Stiglitz, Joseph E. *Globalization and its Discontents.* New York: W. W. Norton & Company, 2003.

Storey, John. *Cultural Theory and Popular Culture: An Introduction.* New York: Routledge, 2012.

Storti, Craig. *The Art of Crossing Cultures.* Boston: Intercultural, 2001.

Sweet, Leonard. *The Gospel According to Starbucks: Living with Passion.* Colorado Springs: WaterBook, 2007.

Tanner, Kathryn. *Theories of Culture: A New Agenda for Theology*. Minneapolis: Fortress, 1997.

Tanno, D. "Ethical Implications of the Ethnic 'Text' in Multicultural Communication Studies." In *The Global Intercultural Communication Reader*, edited by M. Asante et al., 27–36. New York: Routledge, 2008.

Taylor, William. "Introduction: Examining the Iceberg Called Attrition." In *Too Valuable to Lose: Exploring the Causes and Cures of Missionary Attrition*, edited by W. Taylor, 3–14. Pasadena, CA: William Carey Library, 1997.

Tennent, Timothy. *Invitation to World Missions: A Trinitarian Missiology for the Twenty-First Century*. Grand Rapids: Kregel, 2010.

The Hofstede Center. "Country Comparison." http://geert–hofstede.com/countries.html.

Tillich, Paul. *Theology of Culture*. New York: Oxford University Press, 1964.

Ting-Toomey, Stella. "The Matrix of Face: An Updated Face-Negotiation Theory." In *Theorizing about Intercultural Communication*, edited by W. Gudykunst, 71–92. Thousand Oaks, CA: Sage, 2005.

Tocqueville, Alexis de. *Democracy in America*. London: Saunders and Otley, 1840.

Trial, R. *Exegetical Summary of Acts*. Dallas: Summer Institute of Linguistics, 2003.

Triandis, H. C. "Collectivism vs. Individualism: A Reconceptualization of a Basic Concept in Cross-Cultural Psychology." In *Cross-Cultural Studies of Personality, Attitudes and Cognition*, edited by G. Berma and C. Bagley, 60–95. London: Macmillan, 1988.

Turner, Steve. *Hungry for Heaven: Rock and Roll and the Search for Redemption*. London: Virgin, 1988.

Turner, Victor. *The Forest of Symbols: Aspects of Ndembu Ritual*. Ithaca: Cornell University Press, 1967.

———. *The Ritual Process: Structure and Anti-Structure (Foundations of Human Behavior)*. Chicago: Aldine, 1969.

Tylor, Eward. *Primitive Culture: Researches into the Development of Mythology, Philosophy, Religion, Language, Art, and Custom*. Vol. 2. London: J. Murray, 1891.

United Nations Development Programme. *Human Development Report*. Oxford: Oxford University Press, 1999.

US State Department. "US Foreign Service Officer Qualifications—13 dimensions." http://careers.state.gov/uploads/7e/3b/7e3b2a09abdf83eb5afc24af5586c896/3.0.0_FSO_13_dimensions.pdf.

USCWM. "Who are the Unreached?" https://www.uscwm.org/the–call/the–unreached.

van Gennep, Arnold. *The Rites of Passage*. Chicago: University of Chicago Press, 1961.

Van Til, Henry R. *The Calvinistic Concept of Culture*. Grand Rapids: Baker Academic, 1959.

Verkuyl, J. "The Biblical Foundation for the Worldwide Mission Mandate." In *Perspectives on the World Christian Movement*, 4th ed., edited by Ralph Winters and Steven Hawthorne, 28–33. Pasadena, CA: William Carey Library, 2009.

Veseth, Mike. *Globaloney 2.0: The Crash of 2008 and the Future of Globalization*. New York: Rowman & Littlefield, 2010.

Vieider, F., and K. Schneider. "People in Poorer Countries Show Higher Tolerance for Risk." *Wissenschaftszentrum Berlin fur Sozialforschung*. http://www.wzb.eu/en/press-release/people-in-poorer-countries-show-higher-tolerance-for-risk.

Volf, Miroslav. *A Public Faith: How Followers of Christ Should Serve the Common Good*. Grand Rapids: Brazos, 2013.

————. "The measure of the church." Paper presented at the Evangelical Theological Society, San Diego, 2014.

Von Rad, Gerhard. *Genesis (Old Testament Library)*. Louisville: Westminster John Knox, 1973.

Wallace, Anthony. *Culture and Personality*. New York: Random House, 1961.

Walls, Andrew. *The Cross-Cultural Process in Christian History*. New York: T & T Clark, 2002.

Waltke, Bruce K. *Genesis: A Commentary*. Grand Rapids: Zondervan, 2001.

Wan, Enoch. "Diaspora Mission Strategy in the Context of the United Kingdom in the 21st Century." *Transformation* 28 no. 1 (2011) 3–13.

Ward, Colleen. "Thinking Outside the Berry Boxes: New Perspectives on Identity, Acculturation and Intercultural Relations." *International Journal of Intercultural Relations* 32 (2008) 105–14.

Warhurst, Alyson. *Corporate Social Responsibility and the Mining Industry*. Paper presented at the Euromines, Brussels, 1998.

Way, Baldwin M., and Matthew D. Lieberman. "Differences? Collectivism, Individualism and Genetic Markers of Social Sensitivity." *Social Cognitive and Affective Neuroscience* 5 no. 2 (2010) 201–11.

Weber, Max. *Die protestantische Ethik und der "Geist" des Kapitalismus'*. Tubingen: Verlag, 1905.

White, Leslie A. *The Concept of Cultural Systems: A Key to Understanding Tribes and Nations*. New York: Columbia University Press, 1975.

Whitten, Mark Weldon. *The Myth of Christian America: What You Need to Know about the Separation of Church and State*. Macon, GA: Smith and Helwys, 1999.

Wilkinson, Richard G., and Kate Pickett. *The Spirit Level: Why More Equal Societies Almost Always Do Better*. London: Allen Lane, 2009.

Witherington, Ben. *The Rest of Life*. Grand Rapids: Eerdmans, 2012.

Yoder, John Howard. "How H. Richard Niebuhr Reasoned: A Critique of *Christ and Culture*." In *Authentic Transformations: A New Vision of Christ and Vulture*, edited by G. Stassen and John Howard Yoder, 58-69. Nashville: Abingdon, 1959.

Yohannan, K. P. *Revolution in World Missions*. Carrolton: GFA Books, 2004.

Yunus, Muhammad. *Banker To The Poor: Micro-Lending and the Battle Against World Poverty*. Philidelphia: PublicAffairs, 2003.

Zemin, Chen. "Christ and Culture in China: A Sino-American Dialogue." *Chinese Theological Review* 9 no. 1 (1993) 47–68.